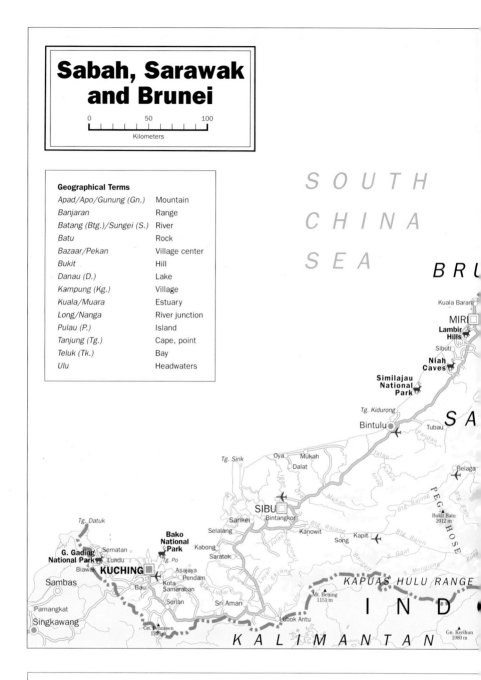

Sabah, Sarawak and Brunei

```
0          50          100
|__|__|__|__|__|__|__|__|__|
        Kilometers
```

Geographical Terms

Apad/Apo/Gunung (Gn.)	Mountain
Banjaran	Range
Batang (Btg.)/Sungei (S.)	River
Batu	Rock
Bazaar/Pekan	Village center
Bukit	Hill
Danau (D.)	Lake
Kampung (Kg.)	Village
Kuala/Muara	Estuary
Long/Nanga	River junction
Pulau (P.)	Island
Tanjung (Tg.)	Cape, point
Teluk (Tk.)	Bay
Ulu	Headwaters

SOUTH CHINA SEA

BRU

Kuala Baram
MIRI
Lambir Hills
Sibuti
Niah Caves
Similajau National Park
Tg. Kidurong
Bintulu   Tubau
SA
Belaga

Tg. Sirik   Oya Mukah
Dalat
SIBU
Sarikei Bintangkor
Selalang   Kanowit
Kabong   Song Kapit
Saratok
Bukit Batu
2012 m
Tg. Datuk
Bako National Park
G. Gading National Park Sematan Kabong
Lundu Tg. Po
Biawak KUCHING
Sambas Asajaya Pendam
Bau Kota Samarahan
Serian Sri Aman
Pamangkat
Singkawang   Lubok Antu
Mt. Betong
1151 m
KAPUAS HULU RANGE
IND
Gn. Penrissen
1329 m
Gn. Kerihun
1980 m
KALIMANTAN

Sabah, Sarawak and Brunei cover the northwestern tip of Borneo, the world's third largest island, with the remainder occupied by the Indonesian territory of Kalimantan. Borneo's huge landmass of almost 750,000km² is set amid the archipeligoes of the Philippines and Indonesia. Sabah and Sarawak have been part of the Malaysian Federation since 1963, while Brunei is ruled by a Malay Muslim monarchy. Much of Sabah, Sarawak and Brunei is covered by rainforest, including large areas of coastal swamp forest. There are mountain ranges, including Southeast Asia's tallest peak, Mount Kinabalu (4,101m) and limestone outcrops with some of the world's largest caves. Forestry and oil account for the majority of revenue in both Sabah and Sarawak. Brunei, with one of the wealthiest populations in Asia, obtains its revenue solely from offshore oilfields.

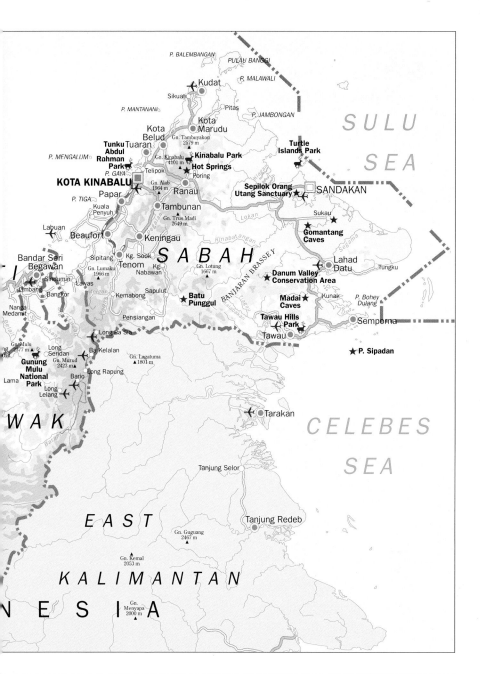

P. BALEMBANGAN
PULAU BANGGI
P. MALAWALI
Kudat
Sikuati
Pitas
P. MANTANANI
P. JAMBONGAN

SULU
SEA

Kota
Marudu
Kota
Belud
Gn. Tambuyakon
2579 m
Tunku Tuaran
Abdul
Rahman
Park
Telipok
P. MENGALUM
Gn. Kinabalu
4101 m
Kinabalu Park
Hot Springs
Poring
P. GAYA
KOTA KINABALU
Gn. Alab
1964 m
Ranau
Papar
P. TIGA
Kuala
Penyuh
Tambunan
Gn. Trus Madi
2649 m

Sepilok Orang
Utang Sanctuary
SANDAKAN

Turtle
Islands Park

Sukau

Gomantang
Caves

Labuan
Beaufort
Keningau
SABAH
Kinabatangan
Lokan

Lahad
Datu
Tungku

Bandar Seri
Begawan
Sipitang
Kg. Sook
Tenom
Kg.
Nabawan
Gn. Lotung
1667 m
Gn. Lumaku
1966 m
Sindumin
Lawas

BANJARAN BRASSEY

Danum Valley
Conservation Area

Kunak
P. Bohey
Dulang

Limbang
Bangkor
Kemabong
Sapulut
Batu
Punggul
Madai
Caves
Semporna

Nanga
Medamit
Pensiangan
Tawau Hills
Park

Long Pa Sia
Tawau

P. Sipadan

Gn. Mulu
2377 m
Long
Seridan
Ba Kelalan
Gn. Murud
2423 m
Gn. Lagatuma
1801 m

Gunung
Mulu
National
Park
Long Rapung
Bario

Tarakan

CELEBES

Lama
Long
Lelang

SEA

WAK

Tanjung Selor

EAST
Tanjung Redeb
Gn. Guguang
2467 m

Gn. Kemal
2053 m
KALIMANTAN

NESIA
Gn.
Menyapa
2000 m

LEGEND

Major Road	○ Village	🏛 Temple	🏛 Museum	Hotel	✆ Telekoms
Through Road	◎ Town	✝ Church	★ Place of interest	▲ Shops/Banks	▲ Mountain
Teritary Road	◉ Bigger Town			● Restaurant	↑ Direction to another town
Int'l Boundary	▢ CITY	☪ Mosque	Reserve	✚ Hospital	✉ Post Office
Provincial Boundary	▣ CAPITAL	✈ Airport	Park Boundary	✱ Police	Railway

EAST MALAYSIA
and Brunei

Edited by
WENDY HUTTON

PASSPORT BOOKS
a division of *NTC Publishing Group*
Lincolnwood, Illinois USA

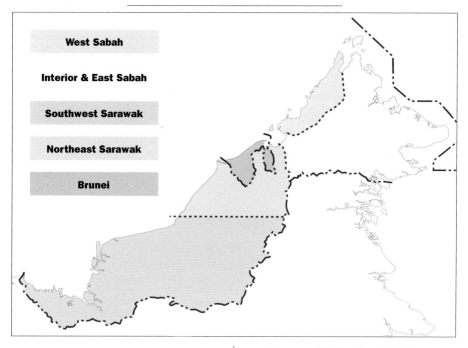

West Sabah

Interior & East Sabah

Southwest Sarawak

Northeast Sarawak

Brunei

Publisher: Eric Oey
Managing Editor: Mike Cooper
Production: Sue Bowles, Mary Chia
Cartography: Regina Wong,
Kathy Wee, Violet Wong

Printed in the Republic of Singapore
ISBN: 0-8442-9890-5

Cover: An Iban man from Sarawak in full ceremonial dress. Photo by Robin Nichols.
Page 1: Adorable young orang-utans in Sabah's Sepilok sanctuary. Photo by Tommy Chang.
Pages 4-5: Rivers function as longhouse "bathrooms" as well as the only highways to the interior of Sarawak. Photo by Jill Gocher.
Pages 6-7: Bajau Laut stilt villages poised off the east coast of Sabah. By Tommy Chang.
Frontispiece: Kayan woman from the upper reaches of Sarawak's Baram River wearing typical heavy earrings. Photo by Jill Gocher.

Passport's Regional Guides

BALI
The Emerald Isle
NEW GUINEA
Journey into the Stone Age
SPICE ISLANDS
Exotic Eastern Indonesia
JAVA
Garden of the East
BORNEO
Journey into the Tropical Rainforest
SULAWESI
Island Crossroads of Indonesia
SUMATRA
Island of Adventure
EAST OF BALI
From Lombok to Timor
UNDERWATER INDONESIA
A Guide to the World's Best Diving
WEST MALAYSIA
and Singapore

The Passport Regional Guides of Indonesia and Malaysia offer an in-depth, region by region look at this diverse and fascinating corner of the globe. Each volume contains over 150 stunning color photographs, as well as authoritative essays on history and culture. Comprehensive, up-to-date travel information round out these books, making them the most practical travel guides available on the region.

Contents

About the Authors

Ann Armstrong-Langub, who has a B.Sc (Hons) in Forestry and a Diploma in Resource Management, worked as a CUSO volunteer for the Forestry Department in Sarawak from 1984-1986. She currently teaches English in Kuching and is married to an Orang Ulu.

Peter Chang, a Sabahan, trained as a marine biologist in the UK. He has worked extensively on marine resources and aquaculture projects, and has also been involved in Environmental Impact Assessement studies.

Daniel Chew, who was born in Kuching, obtained his Ph.D from Murdoch University in Western Australia. Dr Chew is the author of *Chinese Pioneers on the Sarawak Frontier, 1841-1941.*

Jill Gocher is a freelance photo-journalist who has travelled and worked in Southeast Asia for over 10 years. She is happiest when assignments take her away from tourist centers and "civilisation".

Wendy Hutton has worked as a writer and editor in Southeast Asia since 1967, specializing in travel, conservation and cuisine. She has authored books on travel, social history and cuisine. She has frequently traveled throughout Sabah and Sarawak and recently wrote a guide to Sabah, where she has been based for the past 3 years.

Peter M. Kedit received his early schooling in Singapore and his tertiary education in Australia, obtaining his doctorate in anthropology from Sydney University. He is head of ehtnology at the Sarawak Museum.

Victor T. King, Professor of Southeast Asian Studies at Hull University, specializes in the peoples and cultures of Malaysia, Indonesia and Brunei, as well as rural development in Malaysia. He is co-author of *People of the Weeping Forest*, editor of *A Journey among the Peoples of Central Borneo in Word and Picture* and compiler of *The Best of Borneo Travel.*

Clive Marsh, who obtained his Ph.D on climate ecology in Kenya, has worked in forestry conservation in Malaysia since 1978. He has been Principal Forest Officer (Conservation) for the Sabah Foundation since 1981.

Kal Muller, who has a Ph.D in French literature, is a veteran photographer who has authored several books on the Indonesian archipelago, including a guide to Kalimantan.

Heidi Munan is a writer and a private researcher at Sarawak Museum. She takes a keen interest in the varied cultures of her adopted homeland, particularly in the language and literature of the Ibans. Her books include *Culture Shock! Borneo* and *Sarawak Crafts: Methods, Materials and Motifs.*

M. M. Ng has lived in the tropics for the past 17 years, five of them in Malaysia and three in Brunei. Previous publications have primarily focused on scientific studies of rainforest birds and their resources.

Edric Ong, who holds as BA in architecture, is a Kuching-based architect whose professional activities and interests include specialist crafts, costume, fashion and fabric design and choreography. He edited *Pua-Iban Weavings of Sarawak* for Society Atelier Sarawak.

Datuk James P. Ongkili was born in Tambunan, Sabah, and obtained his Ph.D in history from the University of Malaya. He lectured at the University of Malaya until 1976, after which he was active in the Sabah State Government, serving as Deputy Chief Minister from 1976-1983.

Junaidi Payne is project director for WWF Malaysia in Sabah, where he has worked since 1979. He has also been involved in conservation studies in Sarawak and Brunei. Among his previous publications are *A Field Guide to the Mammals of Borneo, Orang-utan — Malaysia's Mascot* and *Wild Malaysia.*

Bob Reece is Associate Professor in History at Murdoch University, Western Australia. He made frequent trips to Sabah and Sarawak in the 1960s and early 1970s while working as a journalist, and subsequently wrote his Ph.D on the end of Brooke rule in Sarawak.

Clifford Sather, who obtained his Ph.D from Harvard, has conducted fieldwork in Sabah and Sarawak since 1964, publishing extensively, chiefly on the Bajau Laut and Iban. Dr Sather is currently engaged in a study of Iban shamanism. Presently at the University of Oregon, he has taught at Universiti Sains Malaysia (Penang) and National University of Singapore.

Dianne Tillotson is currently engaged in writing a Ph.D thesis at the Australian National University on the relationships between art, material culture and ethnic identity in Borneo during the 19th and 20th centuries. Her special interest is the nature of cultural continuity and change in Southeast Asia.

Bruno Vun, a Sabahan economist, is a researcher at Institute for Development Studies (Sabah), in the Economic Development and Planning Affairs Department, He is editorial assistant to the Institute's *Borneo Review.*

PART I

Sabah, Sarawak & Brunei

Borneo, for centuries the embodiment of all things strange and sensational, might have been created expressly for readers of *Boy's Own Annual* and Ripley's *Believe It or Not.* The wildest of fantasies could be realized in this vast island of towering forests teeming with bizarre birds and beasts, inhabited by blow-pipe wielding natives who indulged in the sport of collecting human skulls, with bare-breasted maidens, marauding pirates and even the odd White Rajah thrown in for added glamour.

Long before the West had ever heard of Borneo, however, its reputation as a source of the exotic was firmly established among Chinese traders, who sailed with the monsoon winds in search of rhinoceros horn, edible birds' nests and hornbill casques.

The reality of Borneo today is far from the popular image of the past, yet the powerful fascination of the land and its people is in no way diminished, and most of its stunning natural attractions are now accessible without having to mount a major expedition. Although the erstwhile "wild man of Borneo" might have exchanged his loincloth for shorts or jeans, the peoples of Borneo have retained a sense of pride in their ethnic identity. Traditional skills and ritual observances are maintained. Ancient motifs are woven into fabrics and baskets, repeated in fine wood carvings or vividly painted designs. Although newer gods may be prayed to, the spirits are not forgotten. Shamans and priestesses are called upon in times of need and to maintain the welfare of the community.

Borneo today is divided into four separate states: the independent Sultanate of Brunei; Sarawak, covering the northwest of the island and wrapping itself around Brunei's separate halves; Sabah, which occupies the northwest tip of Borneo, and the Indonesian territory of Kalimantan. Sabah and Sarawak, one once ruled by a trading company and the other by a family of English rajahs, became part of the Malaysian Federation in 1963.

The sheer size and bewildering diversity of Borneo, the world's third largest island, are epitomized by its rainforests, a magnificent if controversial natural heritage, where hundreds of thousands of species act and interact in a perfectly orchestrated symphony of nature. The rainforest contains such extraordinary species as leaves that "walk" (cleverly disguised leaf insects) and flowers that defy the rules of nature (whoever heard of a green orchid with a black lip?).

In Sabah, Sarawak and Brunei, you can find coral islands inhabited by the descendants of sea gypsies; some of the world's most spectacular caves; Dayak longhouses where ancient skulls still hang from the rafters; Southeast Asia's highest mountain; an oceanic isle where divers swim in the company of dozens of sea turtles; emerald paddy fields dotted with megaliths and a wooden stilt village perched over the water within muezzin-call of an Arabian Nights' mosque.

The native name for the island of Borneo, Kalimantan, derives from the word *lamanta*, the edible starch still extracted from the wild sago palm. "Borneo" is a Western corruption of Brunei, the name of the sultanate which held sway over much of northwest of Borneo.

Brunei Darussalam (Abode of Peace) was much diminished in size and power by the end of the 19th century and saved from obscurity by the discovery of oil in 1928.

Sabah and Sarawak, which developed completely independently of each other for both historical and physical reasons (there is no highway linking the two countries), each retain their distinctive character and remarkable cultural diversity.

— *Wendy Hutton*

Overleaf: *A typical suspension bridge seen in an 1847 view of the Sarawak River.* **Opposite:** *An Iban shaman bearing a carved hornbill. Photo by Jill Gocher.*

GEOGRAPHY

Rainforests, Rivers and Mountains

Borneo, the world's third largest island, sprawls its tangled green mass across the equator. In popular imagination, it is a land of humid swamp forests, of massive, slow-moving rivers and dense jungles. But this is only part of the picture, for there are considerable variations in terrain, vegetation and climate, only to be expected in an island of almost three-quarters of a million square kilometers (746,309 to be precise).

Borneo is relatively young as land masses go, formed long after the age of dinosaurs. It began emerging from the sea as the earth's crust buckled and folded around 15 million years ago. Some time during the Pliocene period (perhaps 3 million years ago), tectonic movement caused the raising up of layers of sandstone, mudstone and limestone which had lain on the bottom of the sea. Borneo is outside the "ring of fire" which sweeps

through much of Indonesia, with the only features of volcanic origin being the Hose Mountains and a few volcanic cones in eastern Sabah.

During the last Ice Age, when sea levels were at least 50 meters lower than they are today, Borneo was linked with Java, Sumatra and the Malay peninsula, forming a huge land mass known to geologists as Sundaland. When the ice cap finally melted about 12,000 years ago, Borneo was permanently isolated as an island.

The southwest of Sarawak consists primarily of metamorphic and igneous rock formed by extreme heat and pressure below the surface of the earth. The rest of Sarawak, Brunei and Sabah are composed of particles which accumulated on the surface of the earth, under the waters of the South China Sea, folding and hardening over millions of years to form sandstone and mudstone. It is largely due to this sedimentation that mineral wealth in the form of oil and coal is found in the region.

Southeast Asia's tallest mountain

Over the aeons, the heaving and folding of the earth and differing rates of erosion have created a series of rugged hills in the interior of Borneo, sprawling roughly east and west in Kalimantan and Sarawak, and converging northwards towards the tip of Sabah. One of the most remarkable geographical features in

all of Borneo is Sabah's Mount Kinabalu, a granite core which began as a mass of molten rock squeezed up through the sedimentary rock a mere two million years ago. Mount Kinabalu, already 4,101 meters and still growing, towers above the rest of Sabah's Crocker Range, where peaks average 1,500 meters, and dwarfs the mountain ranges of Sarawak, where the highest peak is only 2,423 meters.

Borneo's unique topography includes frequent limestone outcrops, which often rise above the surrounding forest in a dramatic fashion, the most striking example being the Pinnacles of Gunung Mulu National Park in Sarawak. The limestone is often riddled with caves; many of the more accessible caves have, for centuries, provided a source of wealth with their edible birds' nests, and have also been used as ancient burial grounds.

Most of the coastline of Sarawak and Brunei is fringed by mangrove swamps or covered by peat forests. The large amount of silt carried down Sarawak's rivers, all of which disgorge into the South China Sea, means that white sandy beaches and clear inshore waters are rare.

Mighty rivers and spreading swamps

The many rivers of Sarawak were once the only practical transportation routes between its longhouses, villages and towns, and even today remain important highways.

Only one of Sabah's rivers, the Kinabatangan, is navigable by moderately sized vessels for any distance. Like most of Sabah's major rivers, the Kinabatangan flows down to the Celebes Sea on the east coast, where there are large areas of mangrove and freshwater swamps. The mountains of the Crocker Range give rise to a number of fast-flowing rivers that flow out to the South China Sea on the west coast, building up rich alluvial plains over the centuries.

The narrow coastal plains of the west are often fringed by beautiful white sandy beaches. Sabah's 1,500 km of indented coastline provide the only really good, natural harbors in all of Borneo.

Wet, wetter, wettest

The climate is generally hot and humid, the mean temperature ranging from 23-32° C throughout the year. The mountainous regions are predictably cooler, the mercury even dropping below zero on the summit of Mount Kinabalu on occasion. Although there are regional variations, showers of rain are likely throughout the year. Sarawak is considerably wetter than Brunei or Sabah, especially in Kuching where as much as three meters of rain deluge the city annually.

At the height of the northeast monsoon, which blows from December through March, the east coast of Sabah and most of Sarawak and Brunei are drenched by frequent downpours which swell the rivers dramatically. The southwest monsoon, which blows during the rest of the year, brings showers to Sabah's west coast, Brunei and, to a lesser extent, Sarawak.

Luckily, the region escapes the typhoons which cut an annual swathe of destruction through the Philippines, just north of Sabah.

Variations in normal weather patterns have been noted in recent years, and the severe drought which affected the whole of Borneo in 1982/83 had disastrous consequences. The cause of the recent droughts and periods of severe haze is debated, but many scientists are fearful that the large-scale deforestation of Borneo during the past 20 years is already affecting the climate of the region. It can only be hoped that it is not too late to halt the damage.

— *Wendy Hutton*

Opposite: *Vast areas of coastal Borneo are covered in swamp forests of nipah and mangrove.* **Above:** *The limestone outcrop of Batu Lawi, in northeast Sarawak, is one of many dramatic limestone hills.*

FLORA AND FAUNA

The Bizarre and the Beautiful

Borneo is nature at its most beautiful — and bizarre. It has mammals and reptiles which glide, cats which really do catch fish, fish which "walk" on mud and pigs which climb trees (although the latter can't fly), birds and monkeys which dive, plants which eat insects and insects which cultivate mushrooms, and a highly endangered mammal which sings in the bath and has on its nose an item worth more than its weight in gold. All this and much more goes about its business in northern Borneo.

Although lacking great spectacles of large herds of animals — for it has no natural open plains — Borneo more than compensates for this by containing one of the richest, most complex and diverse arrays of flora and fauna on earth. How about stepping into a forest which contains more valuable timber than almost any other forest in the world, yet where almost every tree you see is of a different species? And another forest which grows in acid and is simultaneously very young and very old?

Some of Borneo's wildlife ranges over wide areas. Flying foxes, with the rather frightening and misleading scientific name of *Pteropus vampyrus*, are actually the world's largest bats, feeding only on nectar and fruits and covering vast distances as they follow the flowering and fruiting seasons in different forests. The bearded pig of Borneo moves from the lowlands to the mountain tops and back again in search of fallen fruits and nuts. When the forest cupboards are bare, the pigs come out into agricultural plantations. Plantation workers have been startled to detect by eyeshine from a reflected torchlight beam the presence of a wild animal in a cocoa tree, and to find on closer inspection that a bearded pig has hauled itself into the lower branches to feast on cocoa fruits.

Life in the swamps

In contrast, most of Borneo's wild plants and animals are restricted to a particular kind of soil or forest. Where there are mudflats subject to periodic inundation with sea water, there are mangrove forests and nipa palm swamps, abode of crabs, lobsters and mudskipper fish. The latter jump around on the open mud with the aid of their flipper-like front fins, taking shelter in holes or on the

lower branches of mangrove trees if danger threatens.

Mangrove and nipa vegetation contains less variety of plant and animal life than the other forests of Borneo, but these areas are vital feeding and breeding grounds for many fish and prawn species. Inland, beyond the tidal influence and especially in eastern Borneo, are freshwater swamp forests of waterlogged clay-rich soils. Some of the swamps contain lakes, home to crocodiles, hairy-nosed otters and waterbirds, including

them by traveling in a small boat.

the Oriental darter, which dives under water and impales fish on its rapier-like beak.

In western and southern Borneo, the lowland zone away from the sea contains extensive peat swamps, where dead vegetation does not rot, but builds up over time and supports its own living forest cover. As the soggy peat builds up, the environment becomes progressively acidic and deficient in minerals and, while in its undisturbed state peat supports a luxuriant and special vegetation, animal life is scarce. The existing peat swamps of Sarawak are all less than 4,500 years old, having extended during this period along with a still-expanding coastline. However, analysis of coal (fossilized peat) not far away under the South China Sea reveals that the same type of forest, with the same kinds of trees, was already in existence more than 20 million years ago.

In areas where there is a combination of open watercourses, riverside trees and swamps, there is a good chance of encountering the peculiar and aptly-named proboscis monkey. This gentle, long-nosed, pot-bellied leaf-eater occurs only in the island of Borneo. It is a skilled swimmer, diving into the water and crossing wide watercourses in order to reach new sources of tender leaves. For reasons which remain uncertain, groups of monkeys always sleep in trees next to open water. This means that wherever proboscis monkeys congregate, it is relatively easy to see

In the dipterocarp forests

In its entirely natural state undisturbed by human activity, most well-drained land in Borneo, up to about 1,000 meters above sea level, supports dipterocarp forest. This name refers to the fact that most of the largest trees (more than 50 meters tall) belong to a single plant family, the *Dipterocarpaceae*. The fruits of dipterocarps are hard, rather oily seeds which bear two or more wings. Dipterocarp forests are home to the greatest diversity of wildlife in northern Borneo.

The tallest of all the Borneo trees occurs in the lowland dipterocarp forests. Known locally as either *mengaris* or *tapang*, it is not a dipterocarp but a member of the legume family. With smooth pale grey bark, this magnificent tree, which grows to more than 80 meters high, is the favorite tree of wild honey bees. Many of the trees bear warty projections up the trunk. In the past, local people climbed the trees by means of ladders embedded in the trunk (hence the warts), to obtain both honey and wax, which was exported to make high-quality candles.

Another noteworthy lowlands tree is the Borneo ironwood, which has extremely hard, dense wood, dark reddish in colour. Lasting out in the open, untreated, for many decades, the wood is much in demand locally to make bridges, fences and the support posts of raised houses.

On the less fertile sandy soils of western Borneo, one may find the Borneo camphorwood, a dipterocarp species, now very rare. In the distant past, this produced a fragrant resin which attracted traders from far and wide, this trade contributing to the early

Opposite: *An enormous diversity of plants and animals is found in the dipterocarp forests.*
Above, left and right: *A* Bulbophyllum *orchid and the green* Coelogne pandurata.

growth of Brunei. On the more fertile lowland soils are forests rich in massive strangling fig plants and trees of the legume (bean) family. In eastern Sabah, these forests are home to an abundance of large animal life, including orang-utan and elephants.

It has been found by zoologists that the abundance of apes, monkeys and some other wildlife species in tropical rainforests is closely tied to the abundance of strangling figs and legumes, which represent important food plants for these animals. While most of the wild fruits of the dipterocarp forests are hard, bitter and inedible to humans, there are quite a few trees with edible fruits, including many wild relatives of the durian, mango, rambutan, jackfruit and mangosteen. There seems to be considerable potential for improving the cultivation of fruit trees through selection of the best wild varieties and grafting existing domestic forms on to wild rootstock.

For most wild species of plants and animals in Borneo, the conservation of large areas of natural forest is the only way to ensure that they will survive in the future.

From singing rhinos to barking deer

Generally, hunting does not pose a threat to Borneo's wildlife except in some particular areas where hunting pressure is intense. One exception is the Asian two-horned rhinoceros, the smallest of the world's five rhino species, the only one which is hairy, and the only one which is exclusively a deep forest-dweller. This rhino is a close relative of larger but otherwise very similar rhinos which inhabited the forests of Europe about 30 million years ago, making it one of the most ancient surviving forms of mammal.

A long-standing Chinese belief that powdered rhino horn, if swallowed, is effective in reducing fever, has caused intense hunting pressure on the Asian two-horned rhinoceros for more than a thousand years. The Asian two-horned rhino has a habit of spending the hottest part of the day bathing in mud-filled depressions, in order to keep cool and to keep biting flies off its thick but sensitive skin. While wallowing, it sometimes utters a plaintive piping song and seems oblivious to the world. As a result, hunters can find them relatively easily and this once widespread species has been severely depleted. The dipterocarp forests of Sabah and Sarawak are amongst the few areas where small breeding populations now remain.

Orang-utans are most common where there is a merging of lowland dipterocarp forests and swamp forests. In their truly wild state, away from "rehabilitation centres" run by wildlife conservation agencies, orangutans are surprisingly shy and cryptic. Often, the only sign of their presence is their nests, looking like small, bushy platforms, which are built daily in the crowns of trees and in which they sleep at night. No other animal of

CED PRUDENTE

the Borneo rainforest makes such nests.

In Borneo, wild Asian elephants occur only in eastern Sabah and the northeastern tip of Kalimantan. Seldom seen outside the forest, they are now under threat from conversion of the natural forest habitat to agricultural plantations. But, for the time being at least, Sabah has one of the largest single populations of this species remaining in the world. Some zoologists believe that the elephant was introduced into Borneo a few hundred years ago by one of the region's sultans.

Other believe that the species is a native, but that its distribution is restricted to areas where there are natural concentrated mineral sources in an otherwise mineral-poor region.

Other large animals include the sun bear, which is reckoned to be the most dangerous mammal in Borneo, but which usually betrays its presence through signs of ripped-open termites' and bees' nests, and the clouded leopard (so named because of the form of the markings on its body) which, although only the size of a goat, it the largest wild cat species in Borneo. The flat-headed cat, an attractive plain-coated wild cat the size of its domestic cousin, lives along river banks and specializes in catching fish at night.

There are five species of deer, all among the favorite targets of local hunters. The largest is the sambar deer, or *rusa*, while the smallest are two species of mousedeer, tiny creatures with a body no larger than that of a domestic cat, but with long, pencil-thin legs. All share a preference for the lowland forests. In the hill ranges, and intermediate in size, are two kinds of barking deer, which are shy and harmless but occasionally startle the unwary traveler with loud, hoarse barks.

Winged beauty

The diversity of two prominent and attractive groups of animal life — the birds and butterflies — is greatest in the lowland dipterocarp forests. Bird-watchers used to spotting birds

through both sight and sound will locate upwards of 50 species of birds during a day in the lowland dipterocarp forests of Borneo.

Most of the birds they see will be members of a grouping of drab little brown insect-eating birds, the babblers, but there will also be bulbuls, drongoes, broadbills, barbets, fly-catchers, trogons, woodpeckers, spider-hunters, sunbirds, flowerpeckers, cuckoos, kingfishers and the occasional spectacular pheasant or hornbill. For the casual observer, other birds to look out for include the shamas (with their melodious song), the racket-tailed drongo (black, with long paired tail feathers) and the paradise fly-catcher (white, with long, ghostly tail). For the specialist, the highlight of an ornithological expedition would be an encounter with the rare Borneo bristlehead, characterized by its bristly orange cap and calls which sound like an attempt at a conversation between a cat and a parrot.

There are always a few butterflies around in the lowland forests, but large numbers are seasonal, often coming with moderately wet weather after a dry spell and an abundance of flowers and new leaves. In order to survive and lay their eggs, butterflies rely on two sources of nutrients — nectar and local concentrations of minerals. The latter occurs both in natural mineral-rich mud and mineral water, such as at Poring in Sabah, and in patches of animal urine on the ground.

The most abundant insects in Borneo forests are ants and termites. Some termite species deposit wads of chewed leaves inside their underground nest and grow tiny mushrooms on top, which they feed to their young. Perhaps because of their sheer abundance, ants and termites form a part of the diet of

Opposite: *The gentle orang-utan is found only in Borneo and Sumatra.* **Above, left and right**: *The Scarlet Sunbird and Rufous-backed Kingfisher are among the many spectacular birds of the lowland forest.*

many forest animals. A toothless mammal known as the pangolin, or scaly anteater, feeds on nothing else.

Climbing plants and animals

Dipterocarp forests contain a variety of lianas (woody climbing plants) and rattans (spiny climbing palms) which grow up, around and through the tree canopy. A liana or rattan plant may consist of one or more stems more than 100 meters in length. Lianas provide convenient pathways through the canopy for a variety of tree-dwelling animals, including monkeys, squirrels, treeshrews, slow loris and a variety of civets (relatives of the cats, which feed on a mixture of fruits and small animals).

Being well-armed with numerous prickles and barbs, the rattans are avoided by most animals. Rattans, however, have for long been one of the natural products of the rainforest which are important for local people. The rough yet flexible canes which can be obtained by stripping off the leaves and spines are used to make baskets, containers, mats and binding material. Rattan canes have become an important economic product during this century for the manufacture of attractive furniture.

In the past, most rattan canes were obtained from wild plants and for many species, cutting the cane means killing the plant. There is now increasing interest in planting rattans as a commercial crop, building on a tradition which in the past was favored by only a few communities in Kalimantan. Paradoxically, rattan is the only plantation crop in Borneo which is helping wildlife because, while the spines of individual plants are a nuisance to most animals, successful cultivation requires that the forest be retained, not cleared.

Swingers, gliders and skydiving snakes

Not all tree-dwelling animals of the Borneo forests make their way around by way of lianas. The Bornean gibbon, a delightful, slender ape which makes distinctive, early-morning, high-pitched bubbling calls in defense of its territory, swings through the forest canopy like a furry pendulum on its extra-long arms. The little Bornean tarsier, a nocturnal primate with eyes that seems enormous for its body, reminding one of a furry frog with a tail, jumps skillfully between saplings and small trees.

Several kinds of animals have evolved the trick of gliding between trees. Rudimentary gliding can be seen when the paradise tree snake coils its body and makes its belly slightly concave, thus becoming an attempt at a parachute. Several species of a little lizard with the generic name of *Draco* expand their ribs, which are linked by web-like skin, and glide between tree trunks.

Amongst mammals, the so-called flying

CED PRUDENTE

squirrels actually glide with the aid of furry membranes between their front and back legs. Thirteen species, all nocturnal, occur in the forests of northern Borneo, ranging from the lesser pygmy flying squirrel (weighing about 20 grams) to the red giant flying squirrel (weighing over 2 kilos), a spectacular animal which often emerges before dusk, and which is nearly a meter long from nose to tail tip. Most bizarre is the colugo, or flying lemur, a mammal which, with teeth like tiny combs, has no close relatives, and has membranes not only between its legs, but extending to the end of its tail.

Up in the mountains

At some point, which varies from place to place but is most commonly at about 1,000 meters altitude, the dipterocarp forest gives way to lower montane forest. Dipterocarp trees became rare or absent, and either conifers or trees of the oak and laurel family begin to dominate the forest. The forest canopy becomes lower as altitude increases. In the lower montane forest, mosses, ferns and orchids become more prominent than at lower altitudes, and lianas are scarce. The forest is often enveloped in cloud, rainfall is generally more frequent and the environment is more constantly damp. The sounds of the forest — made mainly by insects and birds — are different, too, from the lowlands. At the highest altitudes, and typically on ridges above about 2,000 meters, the structure and composition of the forest changes radically yet again. The trees are small and gnarled, eventually giving way to merely bushes on the highest, exposed peaks.

Amazing plants

Borneo is home to a number of particularly interesting forms of plants. In the zone from about 450 to 1,750 meters above sea level is the remarkable Rafflesia, a parasitic plant which manifests itself as massive flowers on the stems and roots of a climbing plant of the grape family. The flower buds take months to develop and the size of the open flower varies, but some are nearly one meter across. The flower withers and blackens after a few days and the fruit, in contrast to the flower, is small and inconspicuous. It is only recently that observations have shown that the fruits are eaten by small mammals, and presumably seeds become stuck to their face and claws and are transferred to the host vine as these animals move around the forest.

Another unusual feature of the Borneo

CED PRUDENTE

rainforests is the pitcher plant, or Nepenthes. These plants bear decorated cup-like structures which accumulate rainwater and serve to entrap insects and other small animals. Nutrients from the dead creatures are absorbed by the plant. All the various species of pitcher plants occur in forests on either white sand, sandstone, or peat, or in the highest mountains, all situations where the soils are especially deficient in nutrients.

The orchid family contains more species than any other single plant family in Borneo. New species are continually being discovered, and it may be that there are around 3,000 native Borneo species in all. Unlike those of domesticated hybrids, the flowers of most wild orchids are often small. Yet close inspection reveals an enormous diversity of beautiful shapes and colors. Only a few species grow on the ground, most occurring as epiphytes growing on the trunks and branches of trees. Some of the most beautiful orchids are highly localized in their distribution, occurring, for example, only on ultrabasic rocks at a particular altitude, making them highly vulnerable to excessive collecting, logging, fires and forest clearance.

— *Junaidi Payne*

Opposite: *The appealing, large-eyed Slow Loris is a nocturnal mammal.* **Above:** *Few people are likely to encounter the handsome but dangerous sun bear.*

THE RAINFOREST

Borneo's Controversial Heritage

Much of Malaysian Borneo is covered in some of the richest and tallest tropical rainforests in the world. However, as the effects of "greenhouse" gas emissions and consequent global warming become increasingly evident, the logging of the world's rainforests has become a highly controversial subject.

Borneo's forests were until recently subjected to relatively low rates of human disturbance because population density was low and agriculture limited by generally poor soils and steep or swampy terrain. In these circumstances, shifting or "swidden" agriculture is probably the only viable means of growing grain crops. Traditionally, patches of up to a hectare per family are cleared and planted with hill paddy ("dry" rice). Usually, only one or two rice crops are taken from a site, after which it is abandoned to a natural succession of fast-growing pioneer tree

TOMMY CHANG

species for 12 years or so. Although this may seem an extravagant use of land, it is quite sustainable at low population densities.

The legacy of logging

Borneo's forests support more than 50% of the known species of *Dipterocarpaceae*, large trees which dominate the forests of Southeast Asia. Surprisingly, up until the 1950s, dipterocarp forests were not considered of special commercial value and only a few heavy hardwood species were cut for local construction or for export as railway sleepers. However, post-war demand for plywood and the revival of the Japanese economy brought light hardwood "South Sea" logs to prominence in world trade. The development of bulldozers and chain saws further set the scene for rapid growth of the timber industry.

Selective logging in Sabah and Sarawak takes place within blocks of land allocated by the government. The licensed operator builds a main road into the area with spur roads off it. Trees are cut (subject to a minimum girth of 60 cm) and the logs hauled out by bulldozer along skid trails to a collection point, where they are measured and identified before being transported to the coast. Throughout this process, the Forestry Department keeps close control of the areas cut and, above all, of the volume, species and grade of logs produced. A hefty royalty is charged, which in Sabah amounts to about 45% of the value of an exported log.

Most timber is still sold in log form to buyers in Japan, Korea or Taiwan, although the proportion processed locally is fast increasing. Although only 6-12 trees are removed from each hectare, most studies find 50-70% of the forest is affected by falling trees, roads, or skid trails. Regeneration to a condition even superficially resembling the original forest takes at least 50 years. Moreover, cutting and infill by tractors also leads to serious erosion and sedimentation of rivers, which in turn affects their value as fisheries and water catchments.

Changing lifestyles

Despite the damage to their habitat by logging, populations of birds and mammals almost always survive, albeit with sometimes major changes in relative abundance.

Rural communities undergo a transformation when logging companies work nearby. The industry brings in roads — at least temporarily — and some locals may obtain employment. However, hunting, fishing, rattan and traditional medicine resources all decline, thus undermining the subsistence economy. Undoubtedly, there are some compensating benefits from general development activities funded, in part, by government revenue from timber. But rural development is often in the form of resettlement schemes or the promotion of commercial plantations.

Unfortunately, state governments heavily dependent on timber revenue have permitted much higher cutting rates than can be sustained. Secondly, as markets have come to accept more "lesser-known" species, extraction intensities have increased, with concomitant damage to young trees and seedlings. "Relogging" to take advantage of changed market conditions within a few years of the original disturbance is particularly damaging. Thirdly, since timber companies rarely have any long-term interest in the land, they have little incentive to reduce incidental damage to the forest or to replant.

Establishing a "balanced" view of the timber industry is difficult but extremely important. The scale and volume of Bornean forests is such that it is unrealistic for outsiders to expect them to remain unexploited, or for traditional forest-dependent lifestyles to stay unchanged. Over 15% of Sabah and a higher proportion of Sarawak is still covered in virgin forest.

Harvesting of timber does not constitute deforestation and a remarkable proportion of wildlife and flora survives the disturbance. Both Sabah and Sarawak have some of the best systems of protected areas in Southeast Asia. Both governments are well aware of their environmental responsibilities and are actively changing in the direction of lower production, greater care during harvesting, greater reinvestment in both plantation forestry and natural forest silviculture.

For example, an exciting new development by Sabah Foundation is the initiation of a program of major dipterocarp and rattan replanting funded by Dutch and US power companies as a means of sequestering carbon dioxide, a "greenhouse" gas which is probably contributing to global warming. Thus, two industries — power generation and timber — may be able to help each other solve their respective environmental problems. This is a far more positive way forward than calls for boycotts of tropical timber, which are viewed by the authorities as a crude attempt to impoverish a developing nation — Malaysia — which happens to have one of the best records in tropical forest management. If rainforests are to be considered a global inheritance, we should all pay for keeping them.

— *Clive Marsh*

Opposite: *The forest is cleared and burned in typical shifting agriculture.* **Below:** *Extraction of logs from the swamp forest requires such alternative methods as this* kuda-kuda.

PREHISTORY

Flaked Tools, Pottery and Ritual Burials

When European explorers investigated the island of Borneo, they found a land of dense tropical forests sparsely inhabited along the river banks by people who still lived virtually in a state of nature. It seemed like a place that could have no prehistory. While there has not been any great intensity of archaeological investigation, excavations and studies in Sabah and Sarawak indicate that the people of Borneo were not forgotten by time.

The earliest evidence for the activities of man was the production of flaked stone tools. Simple flaked tools were discovered at Niah Cave in Sarawak. At Lake Tingkayu in eastern Sabah there has been unearthed evidence for the manufacture of quite elaborate, large bifacially flaked points. These were made possibly around 20,000 years ago and are rather different to stone tools from elsewhere in Southeast Asia, where simple func-

tionality seems to prevail over elegance of design in this era.

The recently re-excavated cave of Gua Sirih near Kuching provided evidence through accumulations of shells and animal bones of a people with a hunting and gathering economy. The existence of hunter-gathers on Borneo at this time does not require an ocean-going technology, for during this period of lower sea level, Borneo was an extension of the Southeast Asian mainland.

Later immigrants arrived by water. It is theorized that these were Austronesian speaking agriculturalists who first arrived from the north around 2,500 BC. There are no hunter-gathers speaking pre-Austronesian languages still surviving; the semi-nomadic Penan are similar in language and racial type to the agricultural peoples of Borneo. An Austronesian culture completely replaced that of the pre-existing inhabitants, but there is negligible information about how this transition took place.

Ritual, technology and trade

Later epochs of prehistory on Borneo have tended to be represented by sites of ritual importance, notably cave cemeteries, rather than by the remains of human habitation. This is largely a feature of the island's climate and of the perishable materials probably used. Niah Cave in Sarawak is the best known of these archaeological sites, but sev-

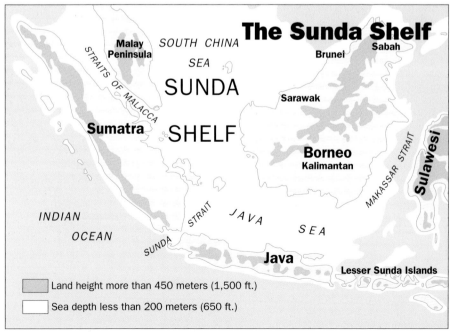

The Sunda Shelf

SOUTH CHINA SEA

Malay Peninsula

STRAITS OF MALACCA

SUNDA SHELF

Sumatra

INDIAN OCEAN

SUNDA STRAIT

Brunei

Sabah

Sarawak

Borneo
Kalimantan

MAKASSAR STRAIT

Sulawesi

STRAIT

JAVA

JAVA SEA

Java

Lesser Sunda Islands

☐ Land height more than 450 meters (1,500 ft.)

☐ Sea depth less than 200 meters (650 ft.)

eral others in Sabah and Sarawak have been investigated. The methods of disposal of the dead were very diverse. Corpses could be buried in the ground, either in log coffins or wrapped in barkcloth or matting, or wrapped bodies left exposed on scaffolding above the ground.

As in other parts of Southeast Asia, complex treatment of the dead, including the use of caves for secondary disposal of bones in jars or coffins, seems to be associated with the spread of iron tools in the first millenium AD. Other evidence for increasing contact around the region is in the form of small trade commodities such as glass, stone or gold beads. Sites of extensive iron working in the Santubong delta region of Sarawak indicate that by approximately 1,000 years ago iron tools were a technological production of the region, not an exotic import.

Cave burial sites during this era contained decorative handmade earthenware pottery. In Sabah's Madai Caves, this pottery greatly resembled that found in similar sites around coastal regions of the Philippines, in the Talaud Islands and in Sulawesi. Niah Cave and Lobang Angin in Mulu National Park in Sarawak, on the other hand, contained locally distinctive forms of earthenware. The three-color ware from these sites is painted in black and red and incised in geometric designs, including angular spirals. These resemble patterns still used on other crafts from Borneo such as Iban *ikat* textiles. Double-spouted vessels uncovered are highly distinctive and intriguingly non-functional, suggesting that they were for the symbolic use of the dead.

Debates about agriculture

Sherds in neolithic levels at Gua Sirih cave had rice hulls and grains mixed in with the clay as temper, which seem to indicate that some of the inhabitants of northern Borneo may have been growing rice by around 4,000 years ago. This small find adds some fuel to the continuing debate about whether the early Austronesian colonizers of the region grew rice, or whether there was a pre-rice agricultural economy. One particular carbon-dated grain found embedded in a potsherd currently tips the balance towards early knowledge of rice agriculture.

Somewhere around 1,000 AD, Chinese porcelain or stoneware items began to appear on the islands around the South China Sea. Colorful, shiny stoneware pottery, in demand for prestige goods and for disposing of the

dead, caused the demise of a skill, as finely crafted and elaborately decorated local earthenware pottery was no longer made.

Occasional finds of carved stone statuary and gold jewelry have suggested long-term relations with the Indianized states of the region. A carved stone bull found not far from Kuching was an object unknown to the local inhabitants, yet many aspects of Bidayuh ritual and language were thought to reflect Hindu influence.

In parts of northern Sarawak and Sabah's west coast, the inhabitants built large ritual constructions of stone, visual manifestations of a stratified social system in which significant members of society were honored and commemorated with conspicuous, labor-intensive memorials. These stone monuments include simple standing stones or menhirs, more complex roofed stone structures or dolmens, seats, bridges and stone urns. Human figures have also been engraved on natural rock faces.

Not all the material evidence for Borneo's prehistoric past has been buried in the ground or embodied in the form of monuments. People of the interior have preserved and cherished certain antique items, which played their part in ritual life and acted as testimony to the social status of the owners. Longhouse aristocrats hoarded Chinese jars, frequently decorated with dragons.

Interior people also hoarded antique glass and stone beads which were traded into Borneo over many centuries. These were worn as girdles or necklaces, or displayed in new contexts as part of caps or jackets. In this way the people of Borneo reworked their past into their present.

— *Dianne Tillotson*

Above: *Glass, stone and shell beads excavated in Sarawak are strikingly similar to those still valued and worn by women throughout Borneo.*

EARLY HISTORY

Ancient Chinese Trading Links

"The King of Puni, called Hianzta, prostrates himself before the most august Emperor and hopes that the Emperor may live ten thousands of years ... My country has no other articles (than camphor, tortoise shell, ivory and sandalwood), and I pray your Majesty not be angry with me."

This message, written on thin bark by the ruler of Po-ni in 977 AD to the Emperor of China, is one of the earliest records of Chinese contact with what scholars believe to have been Borneo. The country known to the Chinese as Po-ni, "forty-five days from Java, forty from Palembang, thirty from Champa", is generally accepted as Brunei. That a relationship between Brunei and China existed would seem to be corroborated by the unearthing of Chinese coins dating from 618 to 1450 AD from Kota Batu, near the site of

Chinese Trading Routes
(15th century)

today's Brunei Museum.

Any history of Sarawak and Sabah must begin with that of Brunei for Sarawak was part of the sultanate until ceded to James Brooke, as was Sabah before being acquired by the enterprising English businessmen who formed the British North Borneo Company.

Two names—Vijayapura and Po-ni—have been given attention in the attempt to locate the center of early Brunei history. Vijayapura was a settled community thought to have existed in northwest Borneo in the 7th century, probably as a tributary to the powerful Sumatran-based Srivijaya empire. Later descriptions of Po-ni in the Sung period suggest that the ruling class was influenced by elements of Hindu civilization, and that the system of writing was the same as the Indian script known to have been used in the Malay world before the arrival of the Europeans.

Archaeological finds at Limbang—now in the far north of Sarawak and half an hour by speedboat from Kota Batu—and at Santubong, near Kuching, all point to Hindu influence. It is, however, believed that this did not come directly from India but through Hindus or Hinduized Malays already long resident in Sumatra and Java. The artifacts unearthed include an elephant, bull and fine *yoni* (phallic sculpture), all in stone, plus several pieces of gold jewelry, beads and figurines.

Po-ni first appeared in Chinese sources in the 9th century, and it seems that a relationship between this state and China continued into the early 15th century. In 1408, the ruler of Po-ni, who had the Hindu name Kala, visited China with his family, and after his death in the imperial capital, his son returned home to succeed him. Marco Polo, who passed through Southeast Asia in 1291, confirmed that trade existed between Borneo and China, with *damar* (resin), edible birds' nests, rattan, camphor, sandalwood, ivory, tortoise shell, pearls, sharksfin and medicinal plants all making their way to the Celestial Kingdom.

Chinese settlement in Sabah?

Brunei annals refer intriguingly to the sister of the "Chinese rajah of China Batangan", who became the wife of the first Brunei ruler to adopt Islam in the 15th century. "China Batangan" is thought to be the Kinabatangan River, on the northeast coast of what is now Sabah, yet evidence of this ancient Chinese settlement is still to be uncovered. Some scholars doubt that it ever existed.

Po-ni had paid tribute to China in an attempt to align itself with the dominant power of the period, against possible interference from the Majapahit empire in Java. On the death of Emperor Yung-lo in 1424, China withdrew from active involvement in overseas affairs, no longer sending fleets to Borneo and to the Muslim kingdom in Malacca. The rulers of Po-ni wisely decided to seek another major ally, and by the middle of the 15th century, had established a close relationship with the powerful Malacca sultanate.

The exact date which the Brunei sultanate, one of the oldest in the Malay world, adopted Islam is uncertain, although according to Brunei annals on the genealogy of its sultans, it was in 1476. The Bruneians accept that their first three sultans intermixed Bisaya, Chinese and Arab origins.

Brunei's golden age

The fifth sultan, Bolkiah, ruled over the most expansionist period in Brunei's history, during what might be viewed as the kingdom's golden age. He subdued the areas now comprising Sarawak and Sabah, voyaged to Java and Malacca, and established control over the Sulu archipelago and the islands off the northwest tip of Borneo. It is probable that most, if not all the riverine and coastal settlements of both Sabah and Sarawak were controlled by Brunei under the reign of Sultan Bolkiah. At no time, however, did Brunei exert control over the people in the interior of Sabah and Sarawak.

The first detailed Western account of Brunei, towards the end of Sultan Bolkiah's rule in 1521, comes from Pigafetta's record of Magellan's voyage. Pigafetta, who is widely accepted as an unbiased and accurate reporter of all he saw on this first circumnavigation of the world, details the pomp and ceremony with which the Europeans were received. They were taken to the city mounted on elephants decked with silk, and found the Sultan guarded by three hundred men with swords and spears. The opulence of the court is evident, with reports of gold-handled daggers adorned with pearls and precious stones, porcelain plates and jars, golden spoons and carpets on the floor.

Certain aspects of Brunei seem to have remained constant even to today. Pigafetta reports that in 1521, "the city is all built in salt water, except the king's house, and the houses of certain chief men... All their houses are of wood, and built on great beams raised from the ground. And when the tide is high, the women go ashore in boats to sell and buy the things necessary for their food."

Inevitably, the power of the Brunei sultanate could not remain at its height, and its influence over the rest of Borneo and Sulu diminished in the 16th and 17th centuries. At one stage, in exchange for the help of the ruler of Sulu in putting down a rebellion, the Sultan of Brunei agreed to cede Sabah (described then as "Kimanis Country") to the Sultan of Sulu. This rather imprecise and nominal overlordship of Sulu was the basis of the Philippines' claim to Sabah when it joined Malaysia in 1963. To be sure of their control over Sabah, the British North Borneo Company signed treaties with both Brunei and Sulu in 1878.

By the time the European colonizers entered on the scene in the 18th century, the Sultanate of Brunei was in a period of decline, with constant problems of piracy and little or even no control over the many minor officials or *pengiran* within its own state. Such a situation made it easy for the Europeans to assert control over most of Borneo: the Dutch in what is now Indonesian Kalimantan; the Brookes in Sarawak and the British North Borneo Company in Sabah, thus irrevocably changing the history of the region.

— James P. Ongkili

Below: *Chinese pottery jars, traded in Borneo for many centuries, are cherished heirlooms in longhouses and homes throughout Sabah, Sarawak and Brunei.*

ARRIVAL OF THE WEST

Adventurers, Traders and Opportunists

Since the first traveler's account in the 16th century, Borneo has continued to excite Western imagination. From Vincenzo Pigafetta in 1521 to Redmond O'Hanlon in 1984, the huge island has promised wealth, adventure and missionary challenge to an astonishing parade of Europeans. Early reports told of fabulous wealth in gold and diamonds, pearls and camphor.

It was Pigafetta, Magellan's chronicler, who set the tone with his description of the two civilizations he encountered on the shores of Brunei Bay—one of them recognizably Malay-Islamic and the other pagan Dayak or Murut. Magellan was interested in saving souls and discovering spices, although later Portuguese, Dutch and English visitors were only interested in the pepper vines cultivated on the hills behind the bay.

Over the next 300 years, "factories" or trading posts were successively built and abandoned along the coast from Balembangan Island in the north to Banjermasin in the southwest, Pepper was almost worth its weight in gold and many a risk was taken to obtain it. The Portuguese were soon discouraged by the unfriendly response of the natives and the English scarcely fared any better, what little trade they did being conducted "sword in hand".

The Dutch were more persistent, however, and by the end of the 18th century had trading posts at Sambas, Pontianak and Banjermasin on the west coast. Hakka Chinese had earlier established themselves in *kongsis* or self-governing colonies in the gold-rich Montradok area, providing the next challenge to Dutch authority.

The first Borneo guidebook

Of these hopeful traders it was Daniel Beeckman, a shrewd English captain, who left the most interesting account of early contact. Visiting Banjermasin for the East India Company in 1714, he wrote a handbook on how to do business with the Islamized coastal people and how to avoid trouble with the pagan Byajos (Dayaks) who lived in an uneasy relationship with them. Invited to the court of Sultan Pannomboang of Caytongee, he was teased and treated to the dancing of four young women "which consisted chiefly in screwing their Bodies into several antick

and lascivious Postures, scarce stirring their Feet From the Ground." Beeckman made a pet of an orang-utan and published a curiously inaccurate drawing of it in his book, together with a more reliable map of the island.

Enthused by the idea of a strategically placed entrepot port serving the new English trade with China, Alexander Dalrymple initiated a disastrous attempt to build a trading post on the island of Balembangan off the northern tip of Borneo. Following Dalrymple's lead, Thomas Stamford Raffles, governor of Java during the brief British interregnum there, also interested himself in Borneo and commissioned a number of people, including John Hunt, to report on its resources.

One of his priorities was to deal with the Dayak pirates who preyed on passing shipping. However, the punitive expedition he sent to Sambas in 1812 was ambushed by the half-Chinese ruler whose cunningly concealed cannons sent the British ships limping back to Batavia.

Enter the freelance imperialists

It was a new breed of adventurer who set sail for Borneo in later years. By the 1820s, British merchants of the industrial era were more interested in selling poplin and iron pots than buying pepper and camphor, and the easternmost islands of what was then called the Indian Archipelago seemed a promising market. Profit was important, but it

was balanced by scientific curiosity and a greater sensitivity to indigenous cultures than that shown by earlier fortune-seekers.

James Brooke was the most successful of these would-be White Rajahs and his story has been celebrated by historians and novelists to the present day. However, other freelance imperialists such as the polygamous Alexander Hare at Banjermasin and the impetuous Erskine Murray at Coti on the northeast coast were no less colorful.

Brooke's foothold on the muddy banks of the Sarawak River was secured only with the help of the British Navy and then extended to its present boundaries by his nephew, Charles Brooke, who succeeded him in 1868. By the end of the century, Sarawak had swallowed up almost all of the river-based communities of Malays, Melanaus and Dayaks on the northwestern coast, who had traditionally accepted the suzerainty of the Sultan of Brunei. Only the establishment of the British Crown Colony of Labuan in 1848 prevented the Sultanate's total demise.

After their ruthless and bloody extirpation of Malay and Dayak opponents (whom they indiscriminately labeled as pirates), and an abortive rebellion by Chinese gold miners in

Opposite: "Wild People at Home," from Carl Bock's The Headhunters of Borneo, presents a romantic image of the Penans. **Below:** The view from Rajah James Brooke's bungalow.

1857, the Brookes and their tiny band of British officers reigned as benign despots, interfering as little as possible with indigenous *adat* (customs) and manipulating the traditional antagonism between different ethnic groups. The only outside company allowed to operate was the Borneo Company, which mined for gold and mercury and established rubber plantations as well as dominating the export and import trade. Anglican and subsequently Methodist and Catholic missions were allowed to proselytize amongst the Dayaks and Chinese, but it was a strict rule that the Muslim Malays be left alone.

Buying North Borneo

From the 1860s, a second wave of adventurers joined in the "scramble for Borneo". The enterprising American consul to Brunei, Charles Lee Moses, purchased a lease of most of what is now Sabah in 1865, selling it to an American trading company in Hong Kong who then disposed of it to the Austrian consul, Count von Overbeck, and an English trader, Alfred Dent. In 1877, Overbeck obtained full ownership of the territory from the Sultan of Brunei but failed to interest his government.

A further bid was made by the Italian government, which wanted to establish a convict settlement on the east coast. It was finally Dent's Chartered Company which obtained recognition to its title and ruled what became British North Borneo from 1881 until 1946.

However, Company rule was not without its challenges. Mat Salleh, a relative of the Sultan of Sulu, saw himself as a powerful leader and sustained his rebellion against its authority on the west coast from 1896 until his death in 1900. Other Bajau and Murut dissidents also caused trouble during the following decade.

Like the Brookes, the Company did not encourage large-scale outside investment and the two territories remained relatively undeveloped until after World War II. Apart from the export of rubber, pepper, sago, timber and jungle produce, the only significant industry was petroleum, which was discovered at Miri in Sarawak and exploited from as early as 1910, and by the Dutch at Balikpapan, on the east coast of what is now Kalimantan.

A new field for naturalists

Under colonial rule, some of the mythology about Borneo was dispelled but its exotic appeal was only heightened by a new rash of travel accounts, the earliest being George Windsor Earl's *The Eastern Seas,* written in 1837. Earl was the first Englishman to visit the goldfields of west Borneo and to describe its Chinese *kongsi* (clan associations) in considerable detail.

James Brooke's journals were also published in 1846 by his friend, Captain Henry Keppel, and were followed by the first com-

prehensive account of Sarawak and its resources by Hugh Low, a botanical collector sent out by his father to find exotic new plants for their London nursery. Low was the first European to climb Mount Kinabalu in 1851, where he discovered new varieties of Nepenthes (pitcher plant), as well as orchid and rhododendron, and gave his name to Borneo's highest peak.

Indeed, Borneo excited considerable scientific curiosity. Alfred Russel Wallace wrote his first paper on evolution at Santubong (Sarawak) in 1856 and the great Italian naturalist, Beccari, wrote extensively about Sarawak after his visit in 1865.

On the Dutch side, the Norwegian collector Carl Bock published an account of his epic journey up the Mahakkam river and down the Barito in 1878, adding to the myths of cannibalism and the existence of *orang buntut* (literally, men with tails). Many others came to emulate the exploits of these travellers, notably the Norwegian explorer Carl Lumholtz in 1915-17, the Dutch pharmacist Dr Hendrik Tillema in 1932 and the German geographer Carl Helbig in 1937.

Keeping the tabloids happy

The Brookes played their part in perpetuating the exotic aura of Borneo. Margaret, wife of the second rajah, became fluent in Malay and wrote extensively of her experiences in Sarawak. Her daughter-in-law, Sylvia, wife of Vyner Brooke, exploited the exotic appeal of Borneo in the salons of Mayfair and two of her daughters, "Princess Pearl" and "Princess Gold", provided good copy for the London evening newspapers. The third and last Rajah was a benign but indecisive ruler who came to rely increasingly on the advice of his private secretary, the mysterious and Machiavellian Gerard MacBryan. Converting to Islam and making a pilgrimage to Mecca with his beautiful Malay wife, Hajah Sa'erah, in 1934, MacBryan dreamed of becoming the Lawrence of the Malay world.

There were few visitors to Sarawak and North Borneo in those times when Singapore was three days away by ship. Government officers, most of them unmarried, had traditionally taken "keeps" or native mistresses in their remote up-river posts, retiring to England at the end of their fourteen years of service. Life flowed on in isolation from the main currents of world activity and any outside challenge was invariably met with the response, "Things are different in Borneo." Somerset Maugham's droll and gently ironical stories captured the atmosphere perfectly.

— Bob Reece

Opposite: *Mount Kinabalu often featured in early views of Sabah, as in this 1840s' lithograph.* **Above:** *The Sarawak River's banks resemble an English park in this 19th-century scene, yet the forest is not far away.*

MODERN HISTORY

WWII and the Birth of Malaysia

The Japanese invasion in December 1941 was a watershed in Borneo's history. Although the island was of primarily strategic importance to the Japanese, they rebuilt the oil fields at Miri and Balikpapan (which had been sabotaged by the Allies) for the use of their navy, and extracted large quantities of timber from the forests.

There was little interference with the people of the interior. By contrast, the Chinese population was treated with suspicion and sometimes extreme cruelty and rebellions against the Japanese at Jesselton and Pontianak were put down with savage brutality.

The main political impact of the Japanese occupation was the damage done to European supremacy. Apart from the destruction by Allied bombing of Victoria at Labuan and Jesselton and Sandakan in North Borneo, few signs of Japanese rule could be seen when

the surrender was taken by the commander of Australia's 9th Division off the Sarawak River on 12th September 1945.

In the meantime, Colonial Office officials in London had been deciding the future of British Borneo. Sarawak and North Borneo were to be ceded to the Crown by the Rajah and the Chartered Company, and a new treaty of protection negotiated with the Sultan of Brunei. By July 1946, new colonial governments had been established in both Kuching and Jesselton.

The people of North Borneo (Sabah) happily accepted the new regime but in Sarawak, most of the Kuching Malays and some Dayaks opposed the annexation by Britain and waged a bitter campaign for its repeal, which only came to an end with the assassination of the second governor, Duncan Stewart, in December 1949.

The oilfield at Seria, in Brunei, was further developed after the war but Sultan Ahmad Tajuddin, whose palace had been destroyed by Allied bombing, went to live in Kuching in protest against what he regarded as shabby treatment by the British government. He also demanded higher royalty payments from the Shell company. When he died in Singapore in 1950, Gerard MacBryan, who had become his private secretary, unsuccessfully attempted to secure the succession for Tajuddin's only daughter, but it was Omar Ali Saifuddin, the Sultan's brother, who was

installed through British official influence as the new Sultan of Brunei.

Uncertain of its hold on its newly acquired colony of Sarawak, the British government commissioned a number of anthropologists to produce the first authoritative studies of the Iban, Bidayuh, Melanau and other groups. The flamboyant curator of the Sarawak Museum, Tom Harrisson, who had parachuted into the Bareo highlands towards the end of the war as part of the Australian reconnaissance operation, also did much to promote Borneo studies.

The role of Britain's debonair High Commissioner for South East Asia, Malcolm MacDonald, was to cement good relations with the Ibans of the Rajang, who had supported the colonial regime from the outset. Adopted as a son by the paramount chief of the Iban, Temenggong Koh, MacDonald made frequent trips to Koh's longhouse, which he recorded in his highly readable book, *Borneo People*.

Under colonial rule, North Borneo and Sarawak were opened up for development and a wider range of social services introduced. The Korean War brought a boom in rubber prices and pepper, timber and other commodity exports sustained a marked improvement in living standards, particularly in the towns. New roads were built into the interior, ending what had been total dependence on river transport. At the same time, the general introduction of outboard motors reduced journeys of several days' paddling to a matter of hours and brought previously remote longhouses within easy reach of traders, officials and ultimately politicians. Air services linking Kuching and Jesselton with Singapore and Malaya helped to break down the isolation of centuries.

Sowing the seeds of federation

Political development was slow during the first post-war decade and it took Tunku Abdul Rahman's Malaysia proposal of December 1961 to galvanize indigenous elites into political parties. Local sentiment favored a Borneo federation as an alternative to, or an intermediate step towards, a wider federation with Singapore and Malaya. Nevertheless, Indonesia's *Konfrontasi* policy (opposing the formation of Malaysia) and the Brunei Rebellion of December 1961 broke down resistance to Malaysia. At the height of this shadowy war, more than 60,000 British and Australian troops were stationed in Borneo and a number of skirmishes took place in bor-

der areas. Sabah and Sarawak achieved independence within the new federation when it was proclaimed in August 1963, but for the next ten years a largely Chinese Communist guerrilla movement was active in the area bordering Sarawak and Kalimantan.

Brunei, which had at first been attracted to the idea of joining Malaysia, retained its status as a British protectorate in order to retain control of its oil revenue. Sultan Omar Ali Saifuddin, father of the present Sultan, successfully courted British protection for his tiny oil-rich kingdom which only achieved full independence in 1984. Renegotiating royalty agreements with Shell, his son and successor, Sultan Hassanal Bolkiah, was rated the richest man in the world by the mid-1980s.

Bandar Sri Begawan, for so long the sleepy river settlement of Brunei town, was transformed within a decade into a modern capital with a splendid new mosque, royal palace and public buildings.

Although the two Borneo states had negotiated their entry into the newly formed Malaysian Federation on special terms, it soon become clear that what the Kuala Lumpur government had in mind was a unitary Islamic state in which the Malay language would be dominant. Resistance to this pattern of centralized control resulted in the dismissal of Sarawak's first Chief Minister and the replacement of Datuk Donald Stephens as Chief Minister of Sabah. More compliant successors agreed to a number of concessions to Kuala Lumpur, including an arrangement which gave the Borneo states only five percent of royalties from off-share petroleum and natural gas. At the same time, federal funds were made available to help build a much-needed economic infrastructure.

In Sarawak, political arrangements reflecting a larger Malay and Muslim native population have continued to favor the maintenance of good relations with Kuala Lumpur. In Sabah, however, the largely Kadazan (indigenous Christian) state government in power since 1985 has been openly critical of what it sees as the erosion of the state's special position within the federation and this has resulted in considerable tension. Rich in natural resources, the two Borneo states are valuable components of the federation, which seems likely to survive the inevitable conflicts of interest between center and periphery.

— *Bob Reece*

Opposite: *The declaration of Independence* (Merdeka) *and birth of Malaysia in 1963.*

ECONOMY

Timber, Oil Fields and Plantations

The popular image of the peoples of Borneo subsisting as semi-nomadic hunter-gatherers is far from the truth today, although roughly half the population of Sabah and Sarawak still depends on agriculture and forestry for a living. Covering three-fifths of the total landmass of Malaysia, with nineteen percent of the federation's population, the Borneo states account for almost seventeen percent of national output. The majority of this comes from the petroleum and forestry industries, with agriculture not far behind.

In the countryside, water buffaloes are still used to plough the fields for irrigated or "wet" rice planting, and in some places even roam the street. In some of the interior areas, "hill" rice is grown on land once covered by forest, cleared, burned, used for a limited period then deserted for 10-15 years, a process known as "swidden" agriculture.

One of the major economic activities in rural areas is the *tamu* or open market, which takes place weekly, bi-monthly or monthly, depending on the location. During these *tamu*, farmers and hawkers present their best harvest and goods for sale.

Although Sabah and Sarawak are neighbors, economic integration is minimal. Trade between the borders is low because of the absence of a connecting road, poor road networks within the states and the vastly similar economic structure. Both are raw commodity producers with a relatively large land mass and a small population base, more than two-thirds of it in rural areas.

Two-way trade with Japan

Japan remains the major trading partner of the two states, consuming most of their logs, and the natural gas produced by Sarawak. In return, Sabah and Sarawak import manufactured goods, machinery and transport equipment from Japan and also from other advanced countries.

Sabah and Sarawak have remained largely agricultural. Sabah is the largest cocoa producer in Malaysia, and has a fair share of the palm oil and timber sectors. Sarawak, on the other hand, is Malaysia's largest producer of pepper and timber. Other crops include rubber, rice, tea, coffee, coconut, local vegetables and tropical table fruits.

Although Sarawak fares slightly better in terms of manufacturing, both states depend largely on the production and export of basic commodities for foreign exchange earnings and state government revenue. Petroleum and forest royalties account for the largest contribution. The vast riches of "black gold" found off the northwestern coasts of Sarawak and Sabah give the impression that these two states must be experiencing rapid economic growth and development through petroleum wealth. In reality, however, the states receive only five percent of total revenue from this resource, as all rights to petroleum are vested with the national oil company, Petronas. In Sabah, petroleum exploration and extraction are enclave activities with little or no linkage to the local economy.

Most of the major industries in Sabah were, until very recently, state-owned, notably Sabah Gas Industries, Sabah Shipyard (both recently privatized), Sabah Forest Industries, and Cement Industries of Sabah. Others are largely small and medium-scale enterprises, with food processing and saw mills dominating. Sabah is the sole copper producer in

Malaysia. All the copper concentrate mined, together with traces of gold and silver, is shipped to Japan for processing.

In Sarawak, major industries are mainly oil and gas related. It has the world's largest granular urea plant located in Bintulu, producing some 1,000 tonnes of ammonia and 1,500 tonnes of urea (used for fertilizers and plastics) per day. Another huge plant is also in the pipeline. Bintulu also houses a massive liquefied natural gas plant with a maximum capacity of 6.5 million tonnes a year. Other industries comprise mainly food and wood-based processing.

With a fairly centralized economic planning, the future of Sabah and Sarawak is largely shaped by the central power at the Federal capital. Vision 2020 is a plan aimed at turning Malaysia into an industrialized nation by the year 2020. The two Borneo states are expected to benefit from this move. The respective state governments are already pursuing the value-added, further downstream strategy to diversify their economies. In line with the call for privatization, a number of state-owned entities have been identified for this purpose. Among other things, this exercise will further reduce the financial burden of the governments.

There are plans to build a pan-Borneo highway linking the northern-most tip of Sabah with the western-most part of Sarawak, thus enhancing greater economic, social and political integration between the two regions.

Awash with oil

With an area of 5,765 square kilometers and a population of about a quarter of a million, Brunei is among the richest countries in the world in terms of per capita income. Much of this is contributed by petroleum and natural gas, which account for about three-quarters of national output. Reserves of oil and gas are estimated at 1.5 billion barrels and 5,134 billion cubic feet respectively. The huge reserves of natural gas hold the promise of sustaining Brunei's future economic growth when oil reserves run dry. It already has one of the world's largest gas liquefaction plants at Lumut, which produces 5 million tonnes of natural gas a year.

With no personal income tax, the government derives most of its revenue from petroleum royalties, a 30% corporate tax, and receipts from overseas investment. Surplus government revenue is banked or invested elsewhere to maintain a steady source of earnings.

— Bruno Vun

Opposite: *Although agriculture is dominated by oil palm and cocoa, smallholders grow the majority of rice produced in Sabah and Sarawak.* **Below:** *Revenue from logging provides almost half of the states' revenue, with Japan being the major purchaser.*

CED PRUDENTE

PEOPLES

The Ethnic Diversity of North Borneo

Borneo tends to conjure up an image of tropical forests and "wild men" living in savage isolation. From ancient times, however, Borneo has been a major crossroads of trade and cultural contacts, and its peoples have never lived in total isolation. In Indonesian Borneo (Kalimantan), "Dayak" is commonly used as a general term for all indigenous, non-Islamic interior peoples. In Sabah, Sarawak and Brunei, where this term has never gained the same currency, the inland peoples are far from homogenous.

Long before Western exploration of the region began, the influence of commerce and of outside contacts brought about an increasing differentiation of cultures and society between the peoples of coastal and interior Borneo. The influence of traders from China, mainland Southeast Asia, the Philippines, Indonesia and as far away as India and the

Middle East clearly had their greatest impact along the coast.

By the 14th century, Islam had reached Borneo and was adopted by the great majority of its coastal peoples. While the lives of the coastal dwellers were transformed and increasingly oriented by religion and trade to a wider world, those living in the interior defended their local political independence and maintained a pattern of smaller-scale, non-centralized societies. They also continued to preserve their own highly varied cultures and religious beliefs, even though a number of trade goods, such as brassware, gongs and Chinese porcelain were eventually adopted as status symbols and objects of spiritual power.

Coastal control of trade

Despite their differences, there was a bond of interdependence between inland and coastal peoples, with products of the interior traded downriver through coastal and estuarine settlements, and foreign goods passing upriver along the same channels.

When Magellan's ships halted there in 1521, Brunei was the most powerful kingdom in Borneo. Its capital was situated on the sheltered Brunei Bay, where a number of river mouths disgorged. The kingdom began its ascent by gaining early control of these, securing access to their interior watersheds and thus dominating the flow of forest and

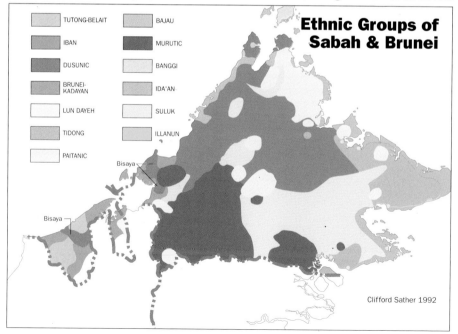

Ethnic Groups of Sabah & Brunei

TUTONG-BELAIT

IBAN

DUSUNIC

BRUNEI-KADAYAN

LUN DAYEH

TIDONG

PAITANIC

BAJAU

MURUTIC

BANGGI

IDA'AN

SULUK

ILLANUN

Bisaya

Bisaya

Clifford Sather 1992

agricultural produce from the interior, and the reverse flow of foreign goods coming from the coast.

Rice: physical and cultural mainstay

The great majority of Borneo's indigenous people, despite growing urban migration, continue to live in farming communities situated mainly along rivers, coastal plains and inland valleys. Inland people are frequently shifting cultivators, although this is rarely the sole method of farming practiced.

The Kelabit of the interior Bario highlands of Sarawak, for example, perform notable feats of engineering in their diversion of streams to irrigate their fields or to drain excess water; by keeping water levels high throughout the growing season, they largely eliminated the need for weeding and were probably the most productive of all traditional rice-growers in Borneo.

For all Borneo's people, each stage of rice cultivation is bound up with ritual observances. Rice is both the staff of life and an object of sanctity, with rice plants believed to be animated by a spiritual personality or soul (*semangat padi*).

For the Iban of Sarawak, rice and human existence have an even more fundamental connection. After death, the soul of an individual is believed to return to the world in the form of dew, which falls to the earth where it nourishes growing rice plants. The ancestral dead are therefore eventually transformed into the lifestuff of rice, with rice and man conjoined within a single chain of existence.

While the great majority of coastal people are Muslim, the people of the interior generally practice a variety of indigenous religions, although Christianity and, to a lesser extent, Islam have also gained adherents. Religious specialists include bards, priests, shamans, priestesses and priestess-mediums.

Shadowy, complex worlds

Cosmologies are complex, but generally include a distinction between this world (inhabited by humans, natural species and spirits), a shadowy otherworld of the dead, and an upper world inhabited by the gods and deified heroes.

Spirits are of major concern, with rituals intended to attract the favor of well-disposed spirits, while placating or expelling those that threaten harm. Bird augury is widely observed and the flight and calls of birds may be interpreted as signs of spiritual encouragement or as warnings of possible ill-luck.

The vast majority of indigenous people of northwest Borneo subsists by rice agriculture, coastal fishing and trade, or by sago cultivation. However, in the past, nomadic bands of forest dwellers occupying the remote headwaters of the great river systems of Sarawak and Kalimantan once lived on game and wild plants. Only a few of these people remain

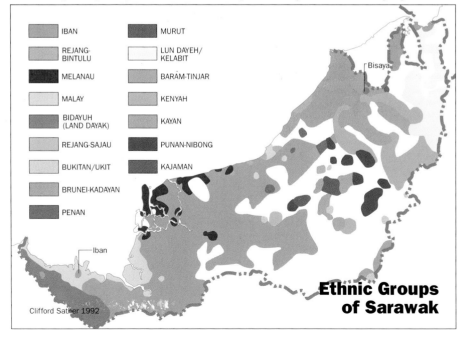

IBAN

REJANG-BINTULU

MELANAU

MALAY

BIDAYUH (LAND DAYAK)

REJANG-SAJAU

BUKITAN/UKIT

BRUNEI-KADAYAN

PENAN

MURUT

LUN DAYEH/KELABIT

BARAM-TINJAR

KENYAH

KAYAN

PUNAN-NIBONG

KAJAMAN

Bisaya

Iban

Clifford Sather 1992

Ethnic Groups of Sarawak

fully nomadic today.

In Sarawak, nomads and former nomads are distinguished variously as Punan, Penan, Sian, Bukitan and Ukit. Small numbers of Penan, now largely settled, extend from the headwaters of the Baram river into present-day Brunei. The term "Punan" has come to be used as a general term for all hunter-gatherers, but more correctly refers to the Punan Bah, who are settled agriculturalists in Kalimantan.

The mystery of the missing nomads

In Sabah, the presence of forest hunter-gatherers has never been reported, and in historical times, the vast rainforests of the state have been completely devoid of forest foragers. Why this is so remains a mystery. Evidence of Stone Age hunter-gatherers has been found in cave sites in eastern Sabah from up to 20,000 years ago, but it is unclear what became of their descendants, or how these early foragers might be related to those living in other parts of Borneo.

In Sarawak today, the last partially nomadic groups are limited to Penan communities living chiefly in the upper Baram, northward from the Baram headwaters to the Medalam. The last fully nomadic groups live today along the Sepayang tributary of the Limbang river and on the Magoh and Tutoh tributaries of the Baram. The Penan of Niah, like the Ida'an of east Sabah, engage in birds'-nest collection.

Many formerly nomadic groups like the Ukit, Bukitan and Sian of the upper Rajang, have adopted rice agriculture and longhouse life from the settled interior groups living around them. Others have been assimilated by their settled neighbors. Scattered bands of Bukitan, for example, once lived along the Skrang and Saribas rivers.

During the first great Iban migrations into Sarawak, these bands allied themselves with the advancing settlers, serving as forward scouts, and as a result of this relationship, most were eventually absorbed, becoming part of the continually expanding Iban population of the region.

It is believed by some observers that assimilation has gone on for a very long time and that possibly some settled groups, like the Kenyah, were once forest nomads. Others have argued that nomadism is comparatively recent and that the ancestors of people like the Penan were formerly agriculturalists who abandoned a settled life and moved into the forest.

Whatever the case, it is clear that the nomads and their agricultural neighbors have long been bound to one another by ties of trade. For more than a millennium, trade in forest products such as wild gums and resins, bezoar stones (a medicine found in monkeys' gall bladders) and rattan has linked the two. Nowadays, partially nomadic groups continue to make excellent rattan mats and containers for trade, receiving in return a variety of goods including salt, tobacco and metal tools.

Camps and class systems

Among traditional forest nomads, local groups are small, averaging some thirty persons. Each group builds a main camp in the area it exploits, then moves from one temporary camp to another, using the main camp as its collection base while breaking into smaller family units for hunting and collecting. Each local group is headed by a recognized elder, who commands little real authority; in addition, every local band is under the dominance of the headman of a nearby longhouse.

The longhouses that monopolize trade are typically stratified communities, and individual families are subject in turn to upper-class patrons. In the past their patrons tended to express contempt for the nomads, often referring to them as animals and claiming them as their "property". In order to remain nomadic, foragers had to trade with settled people, while the goods they supplied were a source of considerable profit to their settled partners.Today these relationships have lost much of their former importance.

Guardians of the forest

The principle dietary staple of all Borneo forest-foragers is wild sago (*Eugeissona spp*), a characteristic that distinguishes them from other tropical Asian hunter-gatherers. The palm is felled and its trunk grated and washed to extract the starch. Felling may be done at any time of year, and an average palm yields some four kilos of sago flour, enough to feed a single adult for a week.

Penan methods of felling are designed not to interfere with natural regeneration; they never fell the rootstock of the palm, allowing it to sprout new trunks. Local bands of Penan tend to orient their movements around known sago stands, and by marking young sago, individuals secure rights to future harvest. A similar system of marking applies to rattan, ensuring an orderly supply of forest resources.

Wild pigs are the preferred game, but virtually all wild animals are hunted, with monkeys being the most common fare. The skill of Penan hunters with their main weapon, the blowpipe, is legendary and a poisoned dart can travel as far as 100 meters, and is often used to bring down game from the upper canopy of the forest. Blowpipes are fashioned from an ironwood shaft, bored through its length, topped with a spear-blade.

The Penan look upon the forest with special reverence as it provides all the necessities of life, and they see themselves as its stewards, carefully managing their sago stands, wild game and other resources so that they remain sustainable. For even semi-settled groups, the forest is an integral part of daily life, a source of food, shelter and trade. Today, logging activities have reached many Penan areas and threaten to end this age-old stewardship of the forest.

Boat dwellers

While Sabah is without forest nomads, the southeastern coast of the state was the traditional home of sea-going boat people, in some respects the maritime counterparts of the Penan. Without crops or landed property ashore, these boat-dwelling people gained their livelihood by fishing, using mainly spears and driftnets to work the enormously rich coral gardens of the region.

Each boat housed a single family; local groups comprised those families that regularly returned between fishing voyages to the same anchorage site. Membership in these groups was fluid, with families readily shifting affiliation from one anchorage group to another. Neighboring groups shared a common burial site.

Linguistically, the boat nomads of Sabah, —commonly known as the Bajau Laut— belong to a large congeries of Bajau-speaking peoples, the great majority of whom now live in settled island and coastal villages.

There is a widespread myth known throughout coastal Sabah and the southern Philippines that the ancestors of the Bajau were once commissioned to escort the Princess of Johor (at the tip of the Malay peninsula) to Sulu, where she was to wed the Sultan. At sea, however, they were attacked by a fleet led by the Sultan of Brunei, who carried off the Princess. Fearful of returning to Johor, they instead scattered northward, their descendants becoming both boat people and coastal villagers.

Contrary to this myth, the Bajau (or Sama) appear to be an early population of the

islands south of Mindanao. Boat nomadic groups are probably the descendants of more generalized coastal foragers who, with the rise of regional trading states, evolved into a highly specialized population, linked to neighboring settled communities by trading ties.

Trade and protection

Thus, boat groups in the past supplied their settled patrons with maritime trading commodities including pearls, pearl shell, seaslugs, tortoise shell and sharks' fins, receiving in return agricultural foodstuffs, metal tools and protection from attack by other settled groups ashore. Similarly, like the forest foragers, the sea nomads were generally looked down upon in the past as pariahs.

Today, these former trading ties have disappeared, and in the decade before the formation of Malaysia, the last boat-nomadic groups in southeastern Sabah began to construct permanent pile-house villages. Today, almost all of them are settled, some in Sandakan and Semporna, living in semi-urban communities and engaged in a variety of occupations in addition to fishing.

— *Clifford Sather*

Below: *A Dusun priestess or* bobohizan *from the interior district of Tambunan, in Sabah. These people are also skilled in the use of herbal remedies.*

CHINESE

Changing the Face of North Borneo

The Chinese are a very visible ethnic group in Sabah, Sarawak and Brunei, found not only in the cities and urban centres but—unlike overseas Chinese elsewhere—in much of the countryside. Today, the Chinese (who form about 30% of the population in Sarawak, 20% in Brunei and 12% in Sabah) play an important role in state government and politics and are influential in business, especially the lucrative timber trade. As well as being engaged in other trades and professions, a high percentage of Chinese work as urban manual laborers, tradesmen, farmers and fishermen.

Archaeological evidence points to Chinese trade and settlement in this part of Borneo since around the 7th century. However, it was only in the 19th and 20th centuries that large-scale Chinese migration transformed the demography, landscape and economies of

northwestern Borneo. The establishment of the Brooke dynasty in Sarawak in 1841 and the formation of British North Borneo (Sabah) in 1881 created a need for labor In order to develop the area economically. The Chinese were brought in as pioneer traders, laborers, miners and planters, to conduct trade and work on the land.

Hokkien and Teochew traders followed in the wake of Brooke officials, setting up bazaars and conducting long-distance riverine trade with the natives in Sarawak. In British North Borneo, Hakka, Hokkien and Cantonese traders set up trading centers following the establishment of law and order and provided much-needed labor to keep the urban economies functioning.

Working the land

It was in agriculture that the Chinese made the greatest impact, the social and economic effects of which are still being felt today as many Chinese continue to eke their livelihood from the land. The Brookes encouraged the Chinese to plant pepper and gambier (used in tanning) in Sarawak in the 19th century, and at the beginning of the 20th century, Charles Brooke (the second rajah) urged the Foochows to grow rice. However, they became attracted to the more lucrative rubber planting. After initial government encouragement, a tide of Foochow immigrants arrived of their own volition.

In North Borneo, the Chartered Company recruited Hakka laborers from Hong Kong to work on the land, especially to plant rubber plantations. Many of them stayed on after the expiry of their contracts. Between 1920 and the outbreak of World War II there was a government-sponsored immigration program of providing peasant settlers with free passage and generous land grants. This, coupled with private recruitment, sponsorship and individuals coming in on their own, was responsible for rapid growth in the Chinese population.

The familiar push-pull factor

In Sarawak, too, many Chinese arrived on their own, sponsored or encouraged by their own clan, district or occupation associations in the all too familiar story of the "push" factor of escaping poverty in China and the "pull" factor of searching for a new livelihood in Borneo.

Life for the early Chinese pioneers was by no means easy. Traders in Sarawak faced restrictions, such as not being allowed to stay overnight in longhouses, but a lack of enforcement prevented this law from being effective. Stories concerning the hardships of the early pioneers have become part of the oral folklore of the Chinese. Still, whichever part of Sarawak, Sabah or Brunei the Chinese lived in, they established closely knit communities with associations, clubs, guilds and schools.

A distinct group

In the 19th century, when the flow of Chinese migrants was still small and mostly confined to men, many of the rural traders in Sarawak and urban shopkeepers of North Borneo took native spouses and maintained good social relations with the natives. This was good business sense, accentuated by another factor—traders in Sarawak could literally loose their heads to the Dayaks if not on good terms with them.

Close social relations and continuing intermarriage with the indigenous population have resulted in the emergence of a distinct Sino-Kadazan group in Sabah, who can fit into either community.

By the 20th century, as more complete Chinese communities with women and children came over and increased in numbers, like the Foochows in Sarawak and the Hakkas in North Borneo, there was less inter-marriage and consequently fewer opportunities to interact with and understand the native way of life.

From Brooke and Chartered Company rule to the Japanese Occupation, British colonial rule and finally independence within Malaysia, the Chinese—especially those locally born—have become a permanent and significant presence.

Today, the Chinese are spread throughout Sabah and Sarawak, their numbers as significant minorities making it possible for them to maintain their culture and values. In both states, Chinese schools still enjoy the support of the community. Many Chinese in Sabah and Sarawak can speak their respective dialects and Mandarin. There is a conscious striving to maintain Chinese culture, although the Chinese are also cognizant of their Malaysian national identity.

Brunei has a record of ancient trading links with Chinese, and the Chinese have settled here at different periods, but it was not until well into the 1930s that large numbers of Chinese came as skilled and unskilled laborers to work on the newly opened oil fields. The Chinese, who are concentrated in trade, business, the professions and within the Shell Company, form a well-to-do community in a wealthy Islamic nation.

— Daniel Chew

Opposite: *The first Chinese came to Sarawak to seek their fortune in the goldmines at Bau.*
Below: *Chinese work on the land as well as being engaged in professions and trade, like this laid-back shopkeeper.*

CRAFTS

Intricate Art Created from the Jungle

The people of Borneo have lived in and off the jungle for generations. Shelter and clothing came from the forest. Food was hunted in the jungle and planted in clearings which reverted to the wild after a season. Skilled fingers fashioned jungle produce into every item of daily use, from the profane to sacred. "Borneo art" was recognized by all 19th-century travelers who had eyes for anything other than bare bosoms.

"The majority of men and women are capable of producing works of art without any tuition other than watching their elders," the Dutch explorer Dr Nieuwenhuis wrote in 1899. "It appears to be members of upper-class families, however, who have the necessary leisure to apply themselves to artistic craftwork seriously."

Nieuwenhuis traveled mostly in what was then Dutch Borneo, among the peoples known as Orang Ulu in Sarawak, whose works of art include spectacular murals and funerary monuments. The good doctor didn't meet the Iban, Bidayuh and Kadazan of British Borneo, democratic societies where everybody lends an energetic hand with all kinds of work. Yet their articles of daily use, ornament and worship are as beautifully finished as any aristocrat's.

Besides using more or less the same materials, the peoples of Borneo created their artwork with similar, simple tools, some of which even hark back to the Stone Age. Bark-cloth, used for rough wear by some people until quite recently, is beaten pliable with a stone mallet.

The indigenous cloth of Sarawak and Sabah is made from wild cotton and woven at a backstrap loom. Malay brocade (*songket*) is produced at a cottage loom. Rods lie on top of the warp threads and are lifted in sequence for each shot of the beautiful gold and silver brocade. The Iban produce superb *ikat* textiles at a simple backstrap loom (see Pua-Kumbu, p. 107).

The long-handled multi-purpose knife is a very common tool. It is used today in the kitchen, but before scissors were easily available, it also served at the loom, for finishing basketry, cutting out appliqué decorations, gold embroidery patterns, and even for shaving and trimming hair. For woodcarving, the handle is tucked firmly between the carver's

rib cage and elbow to give the blade more purchase.

Besides three-dimensional carving there is a form of bamboo decoration practiced by most Borneo tribes. The skin of fresh bamboo is carved in decorative designs, then the whole piece of bamboo is rubbed with color which adheres to the exposed parts. The deer horn handles of *parang* (machete) are carved with a small knife; the artist has a stone handy for honing the blade frequently

The *parang*, worn at the waist by men and

carried in their baskets by women. is used for the shaping and blocking of wood before the finer carving is done. Both large and small blades are essential to many daily tasks; some *parang* hilts have a pocket for carrying the small working knife.

The Borneo craftsman doesn't despise modern aids in his work. Large pieces are roughly shaped with the ubiquitous chain saw before the more detailed carving begins. Chisels, awls and gouges are skillfully used, sandpaper and polishers are employed to give a good finish.

Before iron—local and imported—began to be used in Borneo in the first millennium AD, stone axes and adzes brought jungle trees crashing down. A wedge-shaped iron blade is still used in the same way: it is lashed parallel to the axis of the shaft to form an axe, for cutting. Lashed at right angles it forms an adze, used for hollowing boats, containers, food dishes or musical instruments.

Wind orchestras and pig-traps

Besides drums, gongs and a type of softwood guitar, wind instruments are much used. They range from the plain flute to a complicated "mouth organ" that has six or eight pipes attached to a dry gourd as wind chamber. The Kelabit and Lun Dayeh have evolved a type of wind orchestra, an assembly of anything from tiny piccolos bass flutes.

Food dishes and serving spoons were made either of wood, or coconut shell. Rice huskers, rice mortars and their heavy pestles were made of good wood to withstand daily use. Water was carried in hollow gourds or bamboo tubes, purely utilitarian vessels with no decorations.

One characteristic piece of Iban carving is the "pig-trap" charm, a human figurine crouching on top of a stick used to measure the height of a trap's trip-wire. The little carved fellow, with his oddly simian features, is familiarly known as *wat* and is supposed to attract prey towards the trap.

Human settlements were protected by wood carvings in the old days: god-figures, often grotesque, were placed by the path or at the stairhead. Some doors were carved to represent frightening faces and contorted quasi-human shapes, designed to ward off evil spirits.

Taking care of the dead

The dead were kept very near the living by many communities, in elaborately carved and painted coffins, tomb-huts or ossuaries. The Orang Ulu and Melanau specialized in the construction of tall hardwood pillars, beautifully decorated, to hold the coffins of departed aristocrats.

Earth burial is now the norm in most of Borneo, but in the past a high-ranking family had to take every care that the deceased's memory should be worthily preserved with the most expensive monument that money (and beads) could buy.

Some Kadazan communities living along the west coast of Sabah made a special memorial to a person who died childless. A wooden effigy of the deceased was erected in his or her *padi* fields, perpetuating the memo-

Opposite: *Colorful mats woven by the Cagayans.* **Above, left and right:** *The Rungus are the only people who do needle weaving, while the Kayan are skilled at all crafts.*

ry of the aunt or cousin who had left this piece of land to their heirs.

High fashion

Hats are worn in Borneo for protection against the sun and for elegance. Wide shady hats may be fashioned of sago leaves like the Melanau or Orang Ulu styles, one finished as a cone, the other with a flat, bead-embroidered top. The Iban make hats using the same technique as diagonally woven mats, so do most Kadazans. Sabah hats come in a variety of cones, from very flat (Tuaran) to steep-sided (Papar) and hexagonal (Pensiangan).

The Lun Dayeh and Lun Bawang of West Sabah and East Sarawak make a hat that is not woven: a plant fibre is coiled and sewn over a conical leaf base, and the hat decorated with stencilled or painted designs. For everyday wear, the Chinese "coolie hat" is cheaply available in shops and commonly worn. The mania for suntans has yet to hit Borneo.

Besides giving shade, hats can confer status. Some Bidayuh ladies of West Sarawak wear a black, white and red cloth cap with long streamers as part of their traditional costume, others a tall conical hat made entirely of beads topped with a flat palm-leaf cone. As "good" beads are getting more and more difficult to find, the same hat can be made of bamboo strips. Another fashion is to cover the head with a piece of black cloth hemmed with antique silver coins.

Iban ladies wear one of the most spectacular headdresses, a tall comb of silver shivering with attached leaves and platelets. Orang Ulu ladies keep their hair in order with an artistically plaited reed headband which may be replaced by an intricate bead circlet for formal occasions. Their Kelabit sisters wear a magnificent cap made of antique beads, a fashion shared by the Lun Dayeh and Lun Bawang of the lowlands.

Kadazan priestesses wear a tall beaded headdress for ceremonies while their menfolk drape their heads with splendid kerchiefs woven on a backstrap loom. Rungus and Bajau men share this style of artistically tucked and pleated headgear, woven or embroidered by skilled fingers.

Multi-purpose mats

The mats of Borneo are made in three ways: on the bias, on the square, or by parallel threading. Square woven mats are usually coarse and very large. The Bidayuh weave them of split rattan and bark cloth strips for the purpose of strengthening a floor if a large crowd is expected, or for drying agricultural produce. The Orang Ulu and some Dusun make strong mats woven from whole rattan canes, pierced at regulars intervals and threaded, the ends frayed and plaited to make a tough edge.

Mats are commonly used for sleeping or sitting on, but also for many other purposes.

JILL GOCHER

Pandanus mats may even serve as packing materials, or as makeshift sails if the engine of a small boat has broken down. One kind (sometimes called a "Bajau mat" in Sabah, although also made by Illanun and Cagayan women) is made of a layer woven in a colorful patterns stitched to a plain base. These large (1.75 m x 2.5 m) mats are popular souvenirs. Sleeping mats are made from a type of reed woven in beautiful designs by the Iban women of Sarawak. A fine reed mat is a work of art and must be rolled up carefully rather than folded for storage or transport.

A bounty of baskets

Then there are baskets: seed baskets, harvesting baskets, winnowing baskets, fishing baskets, storage baskets, ladies' tobacco and betelnut baskets, and huge carrying baskets that dwarf the men who carry them.

Baskets are woven in the three basic matmaking techniques; some are reinforced with bark, cane struts or animal pelt strips Others are embellished by the use of colored strands, or applied decorations after they are finished. Storage baskets may have a pelt lining and pelt lid, making them water resistant.

Many of the traditional designs found on mats and baskets have names, although not all modern weavers understand their meanings. Some "typically Iban" designs also appear in Lun Dayeh basketry. It is difficult to determine whether one tribe borrowed from another, or whether all draw on a common Bornean heritage.

Outside influences

Immigrants from the eastern sea have brought their traditions and crafts to enrich Sabah's culture. The Bajau, dubbed "Sabah cowboys" because they prefer riding to walking, have long used a homemade saddle plaited of coconut rope or made of wood (their ponies evidently have thick hides). Cast brass stirrups and bridle fittings date from the time when Brunei and the adjoining districts of Sabah were centres of an indigenous metalwork industry.

Brass-casting was once a famous Brunei industry, with the products of the Sultanate's backyard foundries traded all over Borneo and beyond. Cannon, gongs and domestic utility goods were made until the turn of the century when the old industry gave way to an influx of mass-produced, cheaper imports. Much of the need for craftwork has been eliminated by the advent of cheap cloth and hats, containers, cooking vessels, and mat-

tresses. Today's carver, weaver, or mat-maker works for personal satisfaction or for the souvenir market.

The future of the ancient crafts

New tools and raw materials are readily employed; aniline dyes and enamel paints are used enthusiastically and sometimes indiscriminately. In Lawas (northeast Sarawak), some enterprising Lun Bawang villagers have started making beads out of clay; plastic beads realistically modeled to represent antique ones are filtering into Sabah from the Philippines.

Brunei, Sabah and Sarawak are making efforts to preserve the old skills and encourage craftworkers to sell their work on a commercial basis. Handicraft courses are run in the main centers, where knowledgeable elders pass on their knowledge. So far, these efforts have resulted in an increased productivity; "native crafts" are available in souvenir shops in most towns and bazaars, and many longhouses or *kampung* frequented by tourists. The future will show whether a new, educated generation of craftworkers can maintain the proud tradition of their elders.

— Heidi Munan

Opposite: *Both the Kayan and Kenyan create swirling patterns in paint and woodwork.*
Below: *Prized antique beads worn with typical modern Rungus beads.*

LONGHOUSES

Daily Life in a Borneo Condominium

Having escaped from the hustle and bustle of the city, you might expect to find peace and quiet in the heart of the Bornean jungle. You're in for a surprise if this is what you anticipate at a longhouse, especially if you arrive during a festival, or your tour operator has arranged a *gawai* just to celebrate the arrival of guests.

The resounding brass gongs and the beat of drums set the rhythm for the swirling and twirling *ngajat* dance of the Iban as they welcome the visitor in a ceremony typical of most traditional longhouses, regardless of ethnic group. The best female dancers of the Iban longhouse, dressed in glittering silver headdress and belts of silver dollar-coins, move in graceful coordination down the long, wide enclosed verandah. Tattooed men in feathered headdress, sword in one hand and wooden shield in the other, yell out war cries.

The welcome procession leads the visitor down the entire length of the longhouse, passing forty or more doors of the family rooms, where the walls are hung with precious *pua-kumbu* weavings as a sign of celebration. Passing in front of the door, the visitor is halted as family members pour out welcome drinks of rice wine (*tuak* or *tapai*). By the time they're half way down the *ruai*, the kick of the rice wine already has most visitors ready to join in the *ngajat*.

The procession stops in front of the headman's room, under a canopy of woven cloths. The headman delivers a welcome speech and introduces the visitors to his people. A white cockerel is brought forward by the shaman, together with plates of food and rice filling a brass tray. Reciting a chant, the shaman raises the cockerel over the visitors' heads and in one quick move of his sword, slaughters the bird, thus ensuring spiritual protection for the longhouse.

More wine is poured as food is served: wild boar's meat, jungle-fern tops and bamboo shoot. The men congregate around the visitors on the verandah, while the women retreat to the family quarters for their meal. As the musicians stop to eat, the dogs start scuffling and chasing each other down the verandah.

After food, it's time for a smoke. Home-grown tobacco rolled in the dried leaves of a reed is passed around, setting the right

JILL GOCHER

atmosphere for some serious discussions, which might range from the hottest political issues to the latest Yamaha outboard engine.

And so to bed

By this time, feeling weak in the knees and light in the head, you are ushered by the headman into his *bilek*, where mosquito-nets have been hung over the mattress. As you lay your throbbing head on the pillow, within the privacy of your own mosquito-net, none of the noise seems to bother you any more.

The headman's family has sacrificed the main living space in the *bilek* for visitors, and moved up the notched-log stairs to sleep among the baskets and old jars stored there.

The cock crows early in the longhouse, though throughout the night, there may be the sounds of barking dogs, which disturb the pigs which disturb the cocks which disturb a crying baby—all of which disturb the light sleeper!

Cock-fighting is a favorite longhouse pasttime, and every family keeps two or three prized cockerels. As these feathered pets duel for loudness, the women are up making the fire to boil water and to cook. The day begins early as the people of the longhouse prepare to journey to their farms, which may be a few hours away on foot or by canoe. Packed lunch of rice and a few salted fish plus some very sweet coffee is standard fare.

Every able-bodied man and women does his or her fair share of work on the farm, planting hill-*padi* and other crops such as cocoa, pepper or rubber. Life in a Malaysian Borneo longhouse is fairly similar, whatever the ethnic community. The Iban, Bidayuh and Orang Ulu of Sarawak, and the Rungus and Murut of Sabah share a similar concept of communal life, living in a closely-knit society that predates the modern concept of condominiums. The architectural style of the longhouse varies slightly depending on the ethnic group. Traditional iron-wood shingles (*belian*) or thatch (*attap*) roofs, which vary in pitch, are increasingly being replaced by zinc-aluminum sheets throughout Borneo.

A different concept of privacy

The physical separation of wooden walls identifies each family group, and the individual's privacy within the family may only be the thin enclosure of the mosquito-net. The communal verandah space or *ruai* in front of each apartment, though built and maintained by the family, is used by the whole community. Accepted levels of privacy, tolerance and communal care within the longhouse are indeed quite different from modern Western expectations.

The urban drift of the past two decades has seen a decrease in the population of longhouses. The educated young have found jobs in the towns and cities; school-age children leave their longhouses to stay at government boarding schools, leaving only the very young, the aged, and those still farming the land at the longhouses.

The present agrarian lifestyle of the longhouse often loses out to the town lifestyle with the young educated Iban, Bidayuh, Orang Ulu, Murut or Rungus. The logging industry, offering quick money and a higher income, has drawn many young men into timber camps. It is not that longhouse lifestyle has lost its appeal; family ties and communal feelings remain strong, and it is primarily economic necessity that is threatening the continued existence of longhouse life. If the trend away from the longhouse continues, the pulsating beat of the gongs and the rich ceremony of its festivals may simply fade away.

—Edric Ong

Opposite: *Longhouses consist of a communal verandah and private family quarters (*bilek*), where these men are enjoying a meal with tea and rice wine.* **Below:** *A notched log leads up to the longhouse.*

JILL GOCHER

FOOD

Fern Tips, Pickled Boar & Rice Wine

If you were invited to a traditional meal in Borneo, you might feast upon juicy fern tips and bamboo shoots braised with fermented prawn paste, a leaf-wrapped packet of boiled hill rice, smoked river fish and wild boar pickled in a bamboo tube, washed down with rice wine from an antique Chinese ceramic jar.

Don't expect to encounter much traditional local food on a visit to north Borneo, unless you eat in private homes or at festivals. Food stalls, coffee shops and restaurants in Sabah, Sarawak and Brunei dish up the typical Malay/Indonesian, Chinese and Indian food found throughout Peninsular Malaysia, although you may find some regional specialities at simple stalls in the smaller towns and villages.

Mornings in the towns begin at the local coffee shop (*kedai kopi*), that ubiquitous institution which is not just somewhere to refuel but a place to relax and discuss the issues of the day. In many coffee shops, you can help yourself to the hard boiled eggs, cakes and various steamed savouries wrapped in banana leaf placed on the table. Or order noodles; most common for breakfast is *kon loh mee*, noodles tossed with soya sauce and often enlivened with shreds of roasted pork. In Sarawak, don't miss the Kuching *laksa*, noodles, chicken, prawns and shredded omelette swimming in a spicy coconut-milk gravy.

If you prefer something a little less challenging first thing in the morning, ask for toast and *kaya* (a sinfully rich coconut-milk jam) in any coffee shop. Alternatively, you might like to try a range of steamed dumplings and buns (*dim sum*), especially popular in Sabah's Chinese coffee shops. In the mornings, most local markets sell local cakes and snacks, as well as packages of noodles tossed in sauce or *nasi lemak* (rice cooked in coconut milk, served with chilli *sambal*, egg and fried fish).

Where to go for lunch? Simple, open-fronted restaurants as well as coffee shops offer either ready-cooked food or will prepare to order. A menu is virtually non-existent (or written in Chinese) except for in the more formal restaurants. Standard procedure is to look at the range of raw ingredients and ask the cook to whip up whatever you fancy; for example, you might order stir-fried vegetables with oyster sauce, salted cabbage soup

with beancurd and shredded pork, steamed fish or prawns in a spicy *sambal* (chilli-based sauce).

An inexpensive way to sample a variety of tasty Malay and Indonesian food is to ask for *nasi campur* (pronounced champur). Point to three or four of the prepared dishes on display (they're invariably less chilli-hot than their Peninsular Malaysian equivalents). A spoonful or two will be added to a plate of steamed rice for the princely sum of around M$3. Look for Borneo favorites such as hot sour pineapple (*pacheri nanas*); fern tips stir-fried with dried shrimp and chilli paste (*pakis sambal belacan*) and *sayur manis*, an asparagus-like vegetable popular in Sabah.

Noodles of all types, served either in soup or fried (*goreng*) with various vegetables and meats, are a great lunchtime favorite. Wheat-flour noodles are known as *mee;* thin dried rice-flour noodles are *meehoon* while wide fresh rice-flour noodles are *kway teow.* Chinese throughout Borneo will generally agree that the best fresh noodles are those made by the Foochow Chinese in Sibu, Sarawak. If you're tired of noodles, you might try *nasi ayam*, a simple but surprisingly tasty dish of chicken, rice, cucumber and served with a bowl of chicken stock.

A change from noodles

Indian Muslim food can be found in most towns, and offers a change to sometimes endless offerings of Chinese noodles. Be sure to try *roti canai*, an ultra-light flaky pancake eaten with curry gravy, or sample the version filled with minced meat or chicken and onion (*murtabak*). Another southern Indian speciality, *dosai*, is a very thin crisp lentil pancake eaten either plain (*kosong*) with fresh coconut chutney, or stuffed with spicy potato.

One of the nicest ways to enjoy Borneo's soft tropical evenings is to dine outside. Many non-air conditioned restaurants move their tables out onto the pavement around sunset. There are also clusters of open-air stalls offering of Malay *satay* (skewers of charcoal-grilled meat served with a thick peanut sauce), all kinds of noodles and other quickly cooked dishes. Sarawak's night markets are a particularly good spot to look for tasty inexpensive food.

If you're a lover of seafood, you're in for a treat, especially in Sabah. The range of fresh fish, prawns, lobsters, crabs, scallops and squid is matched only by the number of ways they can be cooked. One of the favorite methods is seasoning the seafood with sour

tamarind juice, slathering it with spices and grilling it over charcoal. In Sabah, a wrapping of banana leaf is generally added, further improving the flavor and succulence.

Another fish preparation that merits seeking out is a good *ikan asam pedas,* fish simmered in a sour, fragrant and slightly chilli-hot gravy. Raw fish marinated in lime juice and mixed with various herbs and seasonings is traditionally prepared by a number of coastal peoples, especially the Sarawak Melanau (who call their version *umai*), and Sabah's Kadazan (who call it *hinava*).

Almost all Borneo's non-Muslims (except for some of the fundamentalist Christians in Sarawak) enjoy rice wine (depending on where you are, known as *tuak, lihing, tapai* or *borak*). To refuse an offering of this would be considered impolite, although you could get away with just touching the glass. But why refuse? Just relax and enjoy the very real hospitality that the people of Borneo are certain to lavish upon you. With a little rice wine inside you, you might even become adept at one of the traditional dances invariably performed when the wine begins to have its mellowing effect.

—*Wendy Hutton*

Opposite: *Rice is the staff of life, although there are endless versions of Chinese noodles.*
Below: *Fish range in size from these small fry up to enormous tunas.*

JILL GOCHER

PART II

Introducing West Sabah

Possibly the most beautiful region in all of Sabah, the west coast's plains are a shimmer of green backed by steep mountain ridges, with the great bulk of Mount Kinabalu standing sentinel. The coastline, fringed by sandy beaches washed by the South China Sea, eventually bulges out into the Klias Peninsula, which still has vestiges of its original peat swamp forest.

West Sabah is, like the rest of the state, peopled by an incredible mixture of ethnic groups, and is the heartland of the Kadazan - Dusun tribes (who form 17% of Sabah's population). Traditional lifestyles can be witnessed in a wide variety of locations, including a Bajau fishing community living in thatched houses perched above the sea; a Kadazan village where megaliths dot the rice-fields; a coastal Illanun community where the women weave beautiful mats; a Bisayan village where sago is extracted from palms growing in the swamp, and a Rungus longhouse where the women create fine strong baskets, weave cloth on a backstrap loom and produce intricate beadwork.

The narrow strip of flat land running along Sabah's west coast is isolated from the rest of the state by the formidable mountains of the Crocker Range, which march north towards Marudu Bay. Contact with the Sarawak district of Lawas to the south is likewise restricted by the Maligan Range, which left the west coast to develop in relative isolation until recent times.

Natural geographic barriers helped the carving up of Sabah into neat administrative regions, known as Divisions. In this guide, West Sabah includes not only the West Coast Division (Kota Kinabalu, Mount Kinabalu and the fertile river plains of Ranau), but also the Kudat Division. A large percentage of Sabah's population of 1.7 million lives in the west: 30% in West Coast and 7% in Kudat. The two divisions cover only 17% of Sabah's total land area.

The Klias Peninsula and the town of Beaufort, both west of the Crocker Range, are also included in the West Sabah section, although administratively they are part of the Interior Division.

British North Borneo

Once controlled by the Sultan of Brunei, the northwest coast of Borneo was gradually sold off. Labuan was bought by the British Crown in 1846, then a sizeable chunk went to an American who attempted to found a settlement in Kimanis Bay, just north of the Klias Peninsula.

By 1880, Englishman Alfred Dent had taken over the rights for what constituted most of today's state of Sabah, ceded by both the Sultan of Brunei and the Sultan of Sulu (who controlled northeast Borneo). In 1881, Dent founded a company which obtained a Royal Charter, becoming formally known the following year as the British North Borneo Chartered Company.

The first capital of British North Borneo was established in Kudat, but after a couple of years and frequent pirate attacks, it was moved to Sandakan Bay on the east coast. The west coast, reached from Sandakan only by several days' sailing through reef-strewn seas, had long been inhabited by a considerable mixture of peoples. In the Klias Peninsula, Muslim Bruneians and Bisayans lived together with Kadazans. Further up the coast, the rich rice-growing plains of Papar and Penampang districts were farmed by the pagan Kadazan, most of whom have since converted to Christianity.

The estuary of Mengkabong, just north of Kota Kinabalu, was home to a large community of Muslim Bajau who made their living by fishing, salt making and the odd spot of

Overleaf: *Dawn on the summit of Mount Kinabalu. Photo by Morten Strange.* **Opposite:** *This Rungus woman belongs to Sabah's most traditional ethnic group. Photo by Jill Gocher.*

piracy. The district around Tuaran, full of beautiful orchards and fertile fields, and the adjacent, equally rich land of the Tempasuk plains around today's Kota Belud was farmed by Bajau and Illanun, both groups believed to have arrived in Sabah from the southern Philippines during the 18th and 19th centuries.

Frequent fights between the Bajau and Illanun, together with raids by Sulu pirates and the taking of slaves, forced many of the indigenous Kadazan/Dusun people to flee further inland, where they farmed in the river valleys and on the slopes of Mount Kinabalu. One Dusunic group that remained, the Lotud, are found in the Tuaran area and near Tamparuli even today.

Originally coastal people, the Bajau adapt-

ed well to the plains around Kota Belud, becoming adept at raising cattle and ponies. Spenser St. John remarked in 1886 that the Bajau never walked if he could ride, even if it was only astride a water buffalo. (The water buffalo should not be despised as a mount; British North Borneo's native police used them in lieu of ponies in the early days!) Today, Bajau horsemen in ceremonial dress still ride their gaily caparisoned ponies at most festive events held in Kota Belud and in the capital.

The Kudat Division, the northern tip or "ears" of Borneo, is more sparsely populated than the rest of West Sabah, particularly in the Bengkoka Peninsula on the eastern side

of Marudu Bay. Kudat is dominated by a sub-group of the Kadazan/Dusun people, the Rungus, who traditionally grew rice, tobacco and cotton, and traded in rattan, wax, camphor and tortoiseshell. The Rungus have remained the most traditional of all Sabah's ethnic groups, the majority of them still living in communal longhouses.

Gaya and the Chartered Company

Sailors traveling along the west coast of north Borneo knew they could find safe haven in the perfect harbour of Gaya Bay. Acknowledging its ideal location, the Chartered Company founded a settlement on Gaya Island in 1882, where there was already a Bajau fishing village. A traveler visiting Gaya just nine months later accurately predicted that "for its admirable harbor and for other reasons, Gaya is likely to prove the most important post on the west coast of the Company's territory."

The area was to become much more than that, but not before a Bajau, Mat Salleh, rose up in protest at the British presence and burned the Gaya settlement to the ground in 1897. The Chartered Company decided to transfer to the more easily defended mainland, to the narrow strip of land already chosen for the terminus of the Trans-Borneo Railway. Started in 1896, this railway was intended to link Brunei Bay with Gaya Bay, and to run right across the interior of North Borneo to the east coast.

The railway was never completed, but the new settlement of Jesselton (named after a director of the Chartered Company) grew as the railway pushed through to reach the Interior by 1905. This enabled rubber, previously brought out on horseback, to be transported by rail from the huge estates planted in the wide, fertile valley around Tenom.

Development of British North Borneo was concentrated on the east coast until the total destruction of the capital, Sandakan, at the end of World War II. Unable to afford the rebuilding of North Borneo after the war, the Chartered Company transferred its possession to the British Crown, and the capital was moved to Jesselton. This was renamed Kota Kinabalu four years after North Borneo reverted to its old name, Sabah, on joining the Federation of Malaysia in 1963.

— *Wendy Hutton*

Left: *Lotud priestesses performing the* Magavau, *a ritual dance invoking the rice spirit during the annual Harvest Festival. The Lotud are a sub-group of the Kadazan/Dusun.*

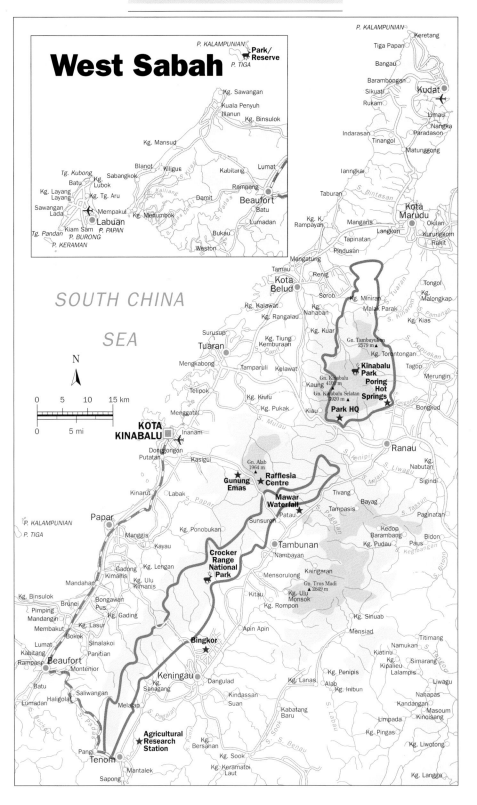

West Sabah

P. KALAMPUNIAN

Park/Reserve

P. TIGA

Kg. Sawangan
Kuala Penyuh
Ilanun
Kg. Binsulok
Kg. Mansud
Blanot
Kilugus
Kabilang
Lumat
Tg. Kubong
Sabangkok
Kg. Lubok
Kg. Tg. Aru
Batu
Kg. Layang Layang
Kg. Menumbok
Damit
Rampang
Beaufort
Sawangan Lada
Mempakul
Batu
Kiam Sam
P. PAPAN
Labuan
Bukau
Lumadan
Tg. Pandan
P. BURONG
Weston
P. KERAMAN

SOUTH CHINA

SEA

N

| 0 | 5 | 10 | 15 km |
| 0 | | 5 mi | |

KOTA KINABALU

P. KALAMPUNIAN
P. TIGA

P. KALAMPUNIAN
Keretang
Tiga Papan
Bangau
Barambongan
Sikuati
Kudat
Rukam
Limau
Nangka
Paradason
Indarasan
Tinangol
Matunggong
Iaringkai
Taburan
Kota Marudu
Kg. K. Rampayan
Mangaris
Langkon
Okilan
Kurungkom
Rakit
Tapinatan
Pindusan
Mangatung
Tamau
Renig
Kota Belud
Sorob
Kg. Miniran
Malak Parak
Tongol
Kg. Malongkap
Kg. Kalawat
Kg. Nahaban
Kg. Rangalau
Kg. Kuar
Gn. Tambuyukon
2579 m
S. Kinorom
S. Pamitan
Surusup
Kg. Tiung Kemburaan
S. Bintasan
Kg. Kias
Tuaran
Tamparuli
Kelawat
S. Torontongan
Tagop
Mengkabong
Gn. Kinabalu
4101 m
Kinabalu Park
Poring Hot Springs
Merungin
Telipok
Kg. Kiulu
Kaung
Gn. Kinabalu Selatan
3920 m
Menggatal
Kg. Pukak
Kiau
Park HQ
Bongkud
Inanam
Donggongon
Putatan
Kasigui
Ranau
Kg. Nabutan
Sigindi
Kinarut
Labak
Gn. Alab
1964 m
Gunung Emas
Rafflesia Centre
Tivang
S. Kenipir
S. Liwagu
Papar
Mawar Waterfall
Patau
Tampasis
Bayag
Paginatan
Manggis
Kg. Ponobukan
Sunsuron
Kedop
Barambang
Kg. Pudau
Bidon
Paus
Kayau
Mensorulong
Tambunan
Nambayan
Kaingaran
Mandahan
Gadong
Kimanis
Bongawan Pus
Kg. Ulu Kimanis
Crocker Range National Park
Kitau
Gn. Trus Madi
2649 m
Kg. Ulu Monsok
Kg. Sinuab
Mensiad
Kg. Binsulok
Brunei
Pimping Mandangin
Kg. Lengan
Kg. Gading
Kg. Rompon
Titimang
Namukan
Membakut
Kg. Lasur
Bokok
Apin Apin
Kg. Kipalieu
Simarang
Lalampis
Liwagu
Lumat
Kabitang
Rampang
Beaufort
Sinalakoi
Panitian
Bingkor
Kg. Lanas
Alab
Kg. Penipis
Kg. Inibun
Nahapas
Batu
Montenior
Keningau
Dangulad
Masoum
Kinoisang
Haligolat
Saliwangan
Kg. Sanagang
Kindassan
Suan
Kabatang Baru
S. Sook
Limpada
Kg. Pingas
Lumadan
Melalap
S. Pagalan
Kg. Liwotong
Pangi
Agricultural Research Station
Kg. Bersanan
Kg. Sook
S. Benau
Tenom
Mantalek
Kg. Keramatoi Laut
Kg. Langga
Sapong
S. Buck
S. Padas
S. Kalilang
S. Klias
S. Damit
S. Papar
S. Mulau
S. Pegalan
S. Melati
S. Tassus
S. Kegabangan
S. Bitoon
S. Labak

KOTA KINABALU

City of the Sacred Mountain

As a plane circles over the islands in front of downtown Kota Kinabalu, coral reefs paint the sea in colors ranging from deepest sapphire to tender jade. Mushrooming stilt villages march on shaky wooden piles away from Gaya Island towards the modern buildings of the city opposite. To the north, a curving bay is dominated by a tall needle of a building, its mirrored walls reflecting the encircling green hills. And in the background, its presence always felt even when veiled by clouds, broods the huge granite mountain after which the city is named: Kinabalu.

Although it has all the amenities of a city, Kota Kinabalu still behaves like a big *kampung* or village—relaxed, friendly, and blissfully free from the stresses and strains of big-city life. Kota (City of) Kinabalu began life as the British North Borneo Company's Jesselton.

The company had been forced to abandon its first settlement on Gaya Island by a Bajau rebel who burned to the ground in 1887.

Ironically, the site chosen for the new settlement was known to the natives as "Api Api". Since the word *api* means fire, it is sometimes erroneously claimed that this name commemorates the burning of the Gaya settlement. In fact, *api-api* is the name given to the mangrove swamps around Gaya Bay, which were filled with fireflies.

Owing to the shortage of flat land in Jesselton, most native housing perched on stilts over the sea. The town also constantly pushed back the sea by land reclamation, a process which continues today, with a highway now isolating most of the remaining water villages (*kampung air*) from the sea.

Kota Kinabalu (now home to around 200,000) became capital of Sabah by a quirk of history when the previous capital, Sandakan, was totally demolished by bombing at the end of World War Two. Although itself badly damaged, with just three of its original buildings left standing, the new capital grew phoenixlike out of the ashes of war.

Kota Kinabalu is best treated as an introduction to rather than the sole focus of a visit to Sabah. The city itself has several attractions worth seeking out, including the truly idyllic islands of the Tunku Abdul Rahman Park, just minutes away by speedboat. You can walk from one end of downtown KK (as

it's affectionately called by the locals) to the other in about 15 minutes.

Strolling the streets

The northeast area, tucked against a hillside, is known as KK Lama (Old KK). Its main street, **Jalan Gaya**, was once the heart of Jesselton and known as Bond Street. It now houses the city's banks, upmarket offices and shops. On the other side of the busy Jalan Tun Abdul Razak nearby, is the **Segama** shopping complex.

Further southwest are two other complexes, **Sinsuron** (nearest the sea) and **Kampung Air.** The end of Sinsuron is marked by the large Centrepoint complex. Some of these older shopping complexes (particularly Segama) could do with a good cleanup but are nonetheless worthwhile exploring by those in search of local color, food, and a wide range of moderately priced goods.

For an overview of the city and harbour, head for the **observation point** on Signal Hill (Bukit Bendera). If you decide to walk (which will take 15-20 minutes) rather than taking a taxi, there's a short cut up the hill beside the quaint old **Clock Tower,** just beyond the Police Station. Built in 1905, the tower was one of the three structures that survived the bombing during World War Two. From the Observatory, you can gaze down on the city and across the coral-studded bay to the stilt villages of Gaya Island.

A renovated colonial-era building in Gaya Street is home of the **Sabah Tourism Promotion Corporation,** with brochures on tours and accommodation as well as news of any special cultural events; there's also a good souvenir shop in the lobby.

Sabah's incredible ethnic mix makes people-watching a fascinating occupation in the streets of downtown Kota Kinabalu, especially around the Central Market and in Segama and Sinsuron. On the **covered pedestrian bridge** leading from the Post Office to the

Central Market, blind Filipino musicians perform for the passers-by, while tobacco-chewing Rungus women, clad in traditional black sarong and dozens of beads, sit with their bare feet thrusting out as they gossip and string bright plastic beads for sale.

Although Kota Kinabalu boasts several multi-storey shopping complexes — the biggest of them all, **Centrepoint,** complete with Japanese department store — the traditional focus for shoppers has always been the market. KK's **Central Market** sells everything from fish, orchids and grapes imported from the USA to asparagus grown on the slopes of Mount Kinabalu. There's everything you need for a betel nut chew (a local confection which leaves the mouth bright red), strange jungle fruits, nose-tingling spices and fresh herbs.

Located by the water's edge, where massive brightly painted fishing boats tie up, are separate buildings for poultry and fish. Brave the wet tiled floor of the fish market and you'll be rewarded by the sight of baskets of crabs, mounds of prawns, moon-white squid, clams and fish in every size and color.

Bargains and bajau boats

Near the Central Market is a rabbit warren of stalls known as the **Filipino Market.** Specializing in inexpensive handicrafts from the Philippines, as well as offering a few items from Sabah and Sarawak, plus Indonesian batik cloth, the stalls open at around 10 am daily. As you duck your head to avoid the cascading macrame hangings and curtains of cowrie shells, keep an eye out for bargains in basketware, sun hats, shells, wood carvings and a host of other souvenir items. Be sure to bargain and

Opposite: Kota Kinabalu's fishing boats tie up alongside the fish market. **Above, left:** *The Central Market is full of interesting faces as well as food.* **Above, right:** *Mamutik's beaches are only minutes from downtown KK.*

you may get the price down by up to 30%.

To find out more about things truly Sabahan, be sure to visit the **Sabah State Museum,** located in a complex of buildings strikingly designed to reflect local cultural elements. Before entering the Museum proper, turn right at the car park to the gardens where five traditional houses are located. Built by the villagers of each ethnic group represented, these houses offer a unique chance to see traditional architecture, cooking and farming implements, and even kitchen gardens together with medicinal plants. There is also an interesting collection of plants in the ethnobotanical garden.

The main museum building, which has a carved wooden *lipa-lipa* or Bajau boat at one end, has an interesting ethnography section to the left of the entrance. The gift shop, to the right, has one of the best selections of Borneo books found anywhere in Sabah. Just beyond this is are fascinating historical photos of Sabah, while behind is a reproduction of a birds' nest cave. Upstairs there are small sections on Sabah's natural history and archaeology.

Within five minutes' walk of the Museum is the striking **Sabah State Mosque**, with its dove-grey walls, delicate minaret and series of golden domes. Inspiration seems to have run dry when it came to the interior of the mosque, which doesn't really merit a visit.

Exquisite tropical islands

There aren't many capital cities that are literally within minutes of unspoiled tropical islands, where talcum-powder sand is bathed by translucent waters and where the loudest noise is likely to come from the honking of hornbills flying overhead. Kota Kinabalu is indeed fortunate that as early as 1923, the greater part of the largest of these islands, Gaya (from the Bajau word *goyoh*, meaning big), was declared a forest reserve. In 1974, the tiny island just off Gaya's tip, Sapi, and three other equally picturesque islands were preserved as the **Tunku Abdul Rahman Park**, honoring the first Prime Minister of Malaysia.

Although rights to Gaya's timber reserves had been given to a Mr White in 1879, there is little evidence today of the forest having been exploited. Most of **Gaya** is still covered by the type of lowland rainforest that once grew over large areas of the west coast. There are also a couple of patches of interesting mangrove swamp and many secluded bays and sandy beaches. A fishing village still flourishes on the site of the original Bajau settlement of Gaya, although this is dwarfed in size by the spreading stilt villages, home to several thousand Filipinos who started arriving here in the 1970s.

The five islands of the Tunku Abdul Rahman Park are administered by Sabah Parks, and can be reached by boat from the jetty in front of the Hyatt Hotel or by more expensive ferries leaving from the marina at Tanjung Aru Resort (see Practicalities). Visitors to Gaya usually focus their attention upon the deep inlet of Bulijong Bay, better known as **Police Beach.** The strong northeast winds which blow from December through March sometimes make it difficult to land here, but at other times of the year, Police Beach is undoubtedly the loveliest location in the group of islands.

The fine white beach is long enough to ensure privacy, while trees fringing the beach provide shade for rests between swims in the crystal-clear water. Unfortunately, dynamite fishing in the past has damaged most of the coral in the bay, but the onshore vegetation remains unspoiled.

Take a hike along the trail leading behind the picnic area, with its large palm-thatch shelter, and in less than five minutes, you'll come to a small river with a mini-fall tumbling into a boulder-strewn pool; this is a good spot to sit in the shade and watch out for the many birds and butterflies seen on Gaya. Although there is no Sabah Parks' accommodation on Gaya, it is possible to bring your own camping gear and stay overnight at Police Beach. A more comfortable alternative is the private Gayana Resort, next to the Park's boundary.

There are still a few wild pigs on Gaya, as well as macaque monkeys and large monitor lizards, some of which cheekily explore the trash cans after visitors have departed. The black and white Pied Hornbill can often be seen and heard here, although the strange Megapode bird, which incubates its eggs in the sand, is much harder to spot.

Snorkeling amid blue starfish

On the other side of Gaya, not far from **Camp Bay** (where many of the Parks' staff reside), is a raised walkway leading above a patch of mangrove swamp. This walkway is just part of the 20-km trail system that criss-crosses Gaya, and links Camp Bay with Padang Point. This point is a thigh-deep wade at low tide, or a 50-meter swim from Sapi Island.

Popular throughout the year for its sheltered position and safe beach, **Sapi** is a delightful place to spend the day. Picnic tables, barbecue sites, toilets and a jetty make for maximum comfort, while trails leading around the island and patches of shallow coral (most interesting at the southwest tip) provide ample diversion. Although the corals themselves have suffered from dynamiting, they are slowly regenerating and snorkelers may be rewarded with the sight of vividly colored reef fish, delicate feather stars, sea fans and bright blue starfish.

The most developed of the islands, **Manukan,** offers several small beaches, chalets —which can be rented through the Sabah Parks office in Kota Kinabalu—a restaurant, swimming pool, squash court and conference center, as well as picnic shelters, barbecue pits and a hiking trail around the island. Manukan is the most popular island with local visitors and consequently quite busy at weekends. If you're seeking privacy, try another island.

Nearby **Mamutik**, its two perfect little beaches fringed by coral reefs that drop off dramatically, is much smaller and more peaceful than Manukan. It has the usual picnic facilities and toilets. You can camp here if you bring your own gear and obtain permission in advance from Sabah Parks. There is also a two-storey resthouse, once a private holiday home, which can be rented through Sabah Parks and offers the wonderful chance of having a tropical island entirely to yourself

for the evening.

The most remote island, **Sulug,** consists of a long spit jutting into the sea from a round green-covered hump. Erosion has caused the loss of several large casuarina trees from the sand spit, and also of some of the picnic tables. Sulug's major charm is its isolation and, for scuba divers, the best coral of all the islands found at a depth of 10-15 meters off the southwest corner.

Kota Kinabalu's nightlife generally focuses on eating, and for many locals begins with a sunset stroll along the long casuarina-fringed beach of **Tanjung Aru**. The beach is also popular at weekends for swimming, sailing, walking through the small Prince Philip Park, and for snacking at the food stalls set up along the waterfront.

Another late-afternoon option is to take a **sunset cruise** around the island on the romantic Buginese sailing schooner, *Mata Hari* (book at the Marina at Tanjung Aru Resort or call 011-810227).

Weekend diversion is provided by the **Gaya Street Fair**, an urban version of the famous *tamu* or weekly market held in other towns and villages of west Sabah and the Interior. From 8 am to midday every Sunday, a cheerful collection of stalls selling everything you might possibly want — and a lot more besides — is set up along the lower end of Gaya Street.

— *Wendy Hutton*

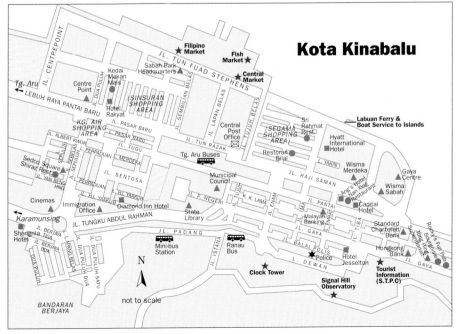

Kota Kinabalu

KINABALU PARK

A Most Remarkable Mountain

The massive bulk of Mount Kinabalu, crowned by a series of peaks shooting upwards like petrified flames, seems to have erupted from the center of the earth only to find itself into the wrong landscape. More than twice the size of the surrounding green velvet ridges of the Crocker Range, this ridiculously large hunk of granite dominates not only the landscape but the folklore of western Sabah.

The bald facts are impressive enough: at 4,101 meters, Mount Kinabalu is the tallest mountain between the Himalayas and Indonesian New Guinea; it is one of the world's youngest mountains and still growing at an estimated rate of five millimeters per annum; the vegetation on its flanks constitutes possibly the richest and most remarkable assembly of plants in the world.

The facts, however, simply don't prepare you for the dramatic power of Mount Kinabalu. The Kadazan/Dusun people, understandably impressed by its towering presence, have long regarded the mountain as the abode of spirits; it is generally accepted that its name derives from the Dusun "Aki Nabalu," or "Sacred Place of the Dead," although many more fanciful derivations of the name exist.

The mountain is the most striking feature of Kinabalu Park, which covers some 754 sq km ranging from an altitude of around 600 m to more than 4,000 m. Standing on the summit of Mount Kinabalu as the sun creeps up over the rim of mountains to the east, bringing to life wave after wave of forest-clad ridges, ranks high on the list of Borneo's most rewarding experiences. But the challenge of scaling Southeast Asia's tallest peak is only one aspect of Kinabalu Park.

Park Headquarters are just 90 km by sealed road from Kota Kinabalu. The road passes through the village of Tamparuli then begins its climb up the Crocker Range. Not long before you arrive at the park, a straggle of stalls, **Nabalu** village, is particularly colorful on Thursday mornings during the weekly *tamu* or market. Here betel-chewing Dusun women unload their bamboo back-packs (*wakid*) and spread out green and red-skinned bananas, wild honey, brown "hill" rice and pineapples.

To the right as you enter Kinabalu Park is

a **reception centre**; the **souvenir store** next door has an excellent range of books on sale. Below this is a **restaurant** with a fine view of the mountain from its wide verandah, and a limited range of foodstuffs and other useful items in the small shop. **Accommodation,** ranging from inexpensive hostels through twin-bed cabins to luxurious chalets complete with fireplace, is tucked away along the road leading down to the **Park Administration Building**. This houses an interesting display centre on the first floor, a theaterette and

another **restaurant** with a range of good local and Western food.

An excellent introduction to some of the plants of Kinabalu Park is found in the **Mountain Garden**, located behind the Administration Building. Of particular interest are the insectivorous pitcher plants or Nepenthes, and some of the 1,200 or so varieties of orchid found in Kinabalu Park.

Guided walks leaving from in front of the Administration Building at 11:15 am daily are another way to discover more about the flora and fauna of Kinabalu Park, some of which are endemic, found nowhere else in the world. As you walk, you may well encounter tree shrews, squirrels, frogs, stick insects up to 30 cm in length and innumerable beetles. Along the river on the Silau Silau trail, watch out for the magnificent iridescent green butterfly, Rajah Brooke's Birdwing.

You could encounter up to 20 of the 280 species of birds found in Kinabalu Park during an early morning stroll along the roads of Park Headquarters, which experts claim is probably the best region in all of Borneo to see montane species such as noisy laughing thrushes, liquid-toned barbets, bulbuls, blackbirds and drongoes.

The first foreigner to climb Mount Kinabalu was a British colonial officer and ardent botanist, Hugh Low, who made his first attempt in 1851. Poor Low was let down by a faulty barometer and failed to identify

the summit; he returned in 1858 with the indefatigable Spenser St. John, yet once again, his barometer failed. The honor of being the first man to scale the true summit was the zoologist, John Whitehead, who, in gentlemanly English fashion, named it after the dogged Low.

Scaling Southeast Asia's tallest peak

Although climbing Mount Kinabalu today does not require any mountaineering skills, and a well-marked trail leads all the way to the summit, don't be misled into thinking it's an easy stroll. As the trail leads relentlessly upwards, with frequent staircases to be negotiated, the demands on your legs, heart and lungs are strenuous to say the least. As the temperature can drop below freezing, be sure to bring warm clothing (see Practicalities for check-list).

The fastest time from the start of the trail at the Power Station to the summit and back is 2 hours 42 minutes, recorded by a Gurkha during the annual Kinabalu Climathon. Most climbers prefer to take a minimum of two days, and ideally, should arrive at Park Headquarters the day before they start the climb to acclimatize themselves and enjoy the surroundings.

On the day of the climb, it's best to be at the reception centre as soon as it opens at 7 am to register, obtain a climbing permit and arrange a compulsory guide. Porters can also be found. A 15-minute ride by shared pick-up takes you to the start of the trail at **Timpohon Gate**, opposite the Power Station. Bring along high-energy snacks and perhaps an apple or two to keep you going during today's 4-5 hour climb, and for fuelling the following morning.

Opposite: *Looking down from the highest point, Low's Peak, towards South Peak.*
Above, left and right: *Climbers pass from the lush lower regions of the mountain to the stunted scrubs at around 2,500m.*

WENDY HUTTON

Headache tablets are recommended as many climbers suffer from the altitude around 3,000 m. Don't bother bringing water on the first day of the climb as taps are located at all rest stops along the trail. Be sure, however, to carry an empty water bottle to fill the following morning and take on the final ascent.

An eerily beautiful expedition

The first part of the trail leads through montane forest, where the height of the trees (many of them oak and chestnut) is markedly lower than that of typical lowland forest. Watch out for some of the 25 species of rhododendron growing on the mountain, especially the huge golden blooms of the *Rhododendron lowii* and the orange *R. javanicum*. As you continue climbing, the vegetation changes to an eerily beautiful moss forest, with festoons of moss dripping from the trees, thickets of bamboo and tree ferns.

Seven shelters, located roughly every 45 minutes along the trail, not only inform you of your progress but contain interesting information panels. When you reach around 2,700 m, there's a change in soil which produces a much more open vegetation with an abundance of pitcher plants, including the huge *Nepenthes raja*, which holds up to two liters of water in its cups, and *N. lowii*, with a waist like a corsetted Victorian lady. As you climb, look carefully on trees and rocks for orchids, many of which have tiny inconspicuous blooms in white or yellow.

Paka Cave, at 3,200 m, is just a 10-minute walk from the main trail and well worth the diversion if you're interested in birds and plant life. Both Low and Whitehead slept in the cave, where the sunlight never penetrates, together with their miserably cold lowland guides.

The first day of the climb ends, for most people, at **Panar Laban** plateau (3,300 m), where there is a comfortable resthouse (Laban Rata) with heated rooms, warm showers and a restaurant. Nearby is a more spartan, unheated hostel, Gunting Lagadan. Some hardy climbers push on for another hour to stay at the very basic Sayat Sayat hut, which offers cooking facilities and bunk beds.

Panar Laban is surrounded by the last straggling vegetation on the mountain, including the Heath Rhododendron with its tiny red bells, white leptospermum and wild raspberries. The dramatic bare granite rockface looming above Panar Laban reminds you that there are going to be serious challenges on

ANTHONY LAMB

your reserves of energy tomorrow.

Your guide will urge you to get up at 2.30 am the following morning for an early breakfast and a torchlit climb up to see the sunrise from the summit. While the view of sunrise is often an unforgettable experience, you could alternatively start at around 5.30 am, so that by the time you start pulling yourself up the ropes of Panar Laban rockface you'll no longer be wishing for a third hand to hold your torch, and the often-icy wind will be loosing its chill as the day breaks. Another bonus is that most climbers will already have come down from the summit, leaving you to enjoy your achievement in blissful solitude.

Yawning chasms and aching bones

The last part of the trail leads across great slabs of bare granite, still bearing gouges made by glacial movement during the last Ice Age. Seen from the lowland, sunlight glinting off the granite gave rise to legends of diamonds embedded in the mountain. Yet another myth goes by the board as you struggle breathlessly across the treeless slopes, that of the *lagundi* tree believed to grow on the summit and whose fruit restores you (oh, that it could, at this stage) and promises longevity.

As you finally struggle up Low's Peak to gaze down over all of north Borneo, take care as you turn towards the east: the vast, yawning chasm of Low's Gully, which almost splits the mountain in two, drops down a sickening

1,500 m. Hopefully, you'll feel some of the elation experienced by St. John who scaled South Peak, just 69 m lower than the true summit. He confessed to feeling "some shortness of breath and disinclination to bodily exertion, but as soon as I sat on this lofty point (...) a feeling came as if the air made me buoyant and long to float away."

The descent of the mountain, with a pause at Panar Laban to eat, rest and compare experiences and aching muscles with fellow climbers, is almost an anti-climax. When you return to Headquarters (which should take about 3 hours from Panar Laban), you can pick up a certificate as proof of your achievement.

Hot baths with butterflies

The wise traveller then heads straight for **Poring Hot Springs**, on the eastern edge of Kinabalu Park, for a long, therapeutic soak in a hot pool. The springs, developed by the Japanese during the occupation of World War Two, are a great attraction for local visitors, who throng the area to picnic and bathe during the weekends (take note and avoid this time if possible).

Poring, named after the giant bamboo that grows in the locality, has undergone considerable development in recent years, with the installation of private bathing huts, a landscaped cold-water pool, a second resthouse (to add to the existing resthouse and two chalets offering accommodation to visitors), a canopy walkway and a butterfly park; a restaurant was due to open end-1992.

Strung high above the floor of the forest and anchored by three giant trees, the 140-m long canopy walkway consists of a series of horizontal aluminum ladders covered with planks, steel cables, ropes and strong netting at the sides for maximum security. The walkway offers a unique view of typical lowland rainforest canopy and some of its birds and animals. Although the walkway can be used anytime, it's best during the early hours of the morning, as the inhabitants of the forest awaken.

Thousands of butterflies attracted to the seepage of mineral-rich water around the hot springs make a butterfly park a natural addition to Poring's charms. A small stream runs through the huge landscaped enclosure, which is filled with vivid blooms and other plants providing food for the butterflies. An on-going breeding and research program makes this more than just a delightful way to view some of the rare and beautiful butterflies, stick insects, massive rhinoceros beetles and other insects of the Kinabalu Park.

— *Wendy Hutton*

Opposite, left and right: *Orchids range from Poring's vivid lowland species to inconspicuous blooms growing at around 3,300 m.*
Below: *A dramatic swirl of clouds forms a halo around the summit of Kinabalu.*

TRIPS NORTH

Longhouses, Fisherfolk and Cowboys

Sabah's most traditional ethnic group, the longhouse-dwelling Rungus, Bajau fishing villages, Dusun communities tucked away in river valleys and the state's most glorious beaches all lie north of Kota Kinabalu.

The way north, Tuaran Road, passes Soon Yii, a pottery in **Telipok** (on the left shortly after the "Tuaran 9 km" sign), where a traditional Chinese "dragon" kiln is used to fire handmade pots made in a variety of styles, with both local and Chinese motifs, including replicas of antique jars.

To explore a beautiful valley farmed by the Dusun on the lower slopes of the Crocker Range, take the road to Kinabalu Park, turning off where indicated towards Tamparuli; just before the river, turn right into Jalan Kiulu. The sealed road winds over steep hills for about 15 minutes, giving glimpses of the river, occasionally spanned by delicate-looking suspension bridges.

Take the unmarked left fork over the bridge to **Kiulu village.** There's an attractive flat area along the river bank here, and as you continue up the valley, rapids where the Dusun fix bamboo fish traps, deep pools and shady spots with only birdsong, the rushing of the river and flitting butterflies to disturb the peace.

For a total change of culture, take the road to **Tuaran** through postcard scenery with *padi* fields, neat little houses, groves of fruit trees, water buffalo and, if the weather is clear, Mount Kinabalu forms a spectacular backdrop. A large community of Bajau fishermen has lived in the stilt village of Mengkabong, a little south of Tuaran, for over a century. Today, the village is unromantically modern, unpleasantly littered with plastic, and suffers from having been visited by busloads of tourists. Forget it and head on through Tuaran (which has an interesting Sunday market or *tamu*) towards Surusup.

An upriver village and 365 hairpins

Where the road ends by Sururup's jetty, ask for a boatman to take you upriver to **Kg Penambawan**, a Bajau fishing village where time seems to have stood still. The boardwalks connecting the hundred or so houses perched over the river are mostly rounded *nibong* palm trunks and the simple houses made of palm thatch. Cats and kids wander

past trays of drying fish; women weave pandanus-leaf mats or winnow the rice for the next meal, while the men repair their fishing nets. The friendliness of this rather poor but very welcoming community make it well worth the ten-minute boat ride.

Tamparuli, where there's a lively market each Wednesday, marks the start of the road up the Crocker Range towards Kinabalu Park or on to Kota Belud. This road is notorious for its 365 hairpin bends, alternately snaking up and down and around endless hills and plunging into picturesque valleys before finally arriving in the heart of Bajau country, **Kota Belud**.

Sabah's "cowboys"

Over-enthusiastic tourist literature has led some visitors to expect to see Bajau horsemen, splendidly decked out on equally decorated ponies jingling with bells, trotting down the main street of Kota Belud. Although many Bajaus are indeed keen horsemen, they don their ceremonial dress only for special cultural events, as well as for a "photo opportunity" around 10 am during the Sunday *tamu* or weekly market. While men discuss the merits of the water buffalo and ponies on sale under the trees nearby, Bajau and Dusun women sell fresh local produce alongside vendors of clothing, shoes, plastic kitchenware and gaily striped conical food covers made of pandanus leaf.

The road north of Kota Belud leads through a **bird sanctuary**, an area largely covered by freshwater swamps between the Tempasuk and Kawang Kawang rivers. With its thousands of tall slender birds and grazing cattle, it could almost be the Camargue in the south of France, except that they're egrets and not flamingos, and the wild cattle are actually docile water buffalo. There are sadly no facilities for bird-watching in the area; hides and walkways above the swamps are non-existent, limiting serious exploration to all but the dedicated enthusiast.

Kota Marudu, the major center for the area south of the deep inlet of Marudu Bay, is the last chance to buy fuel and food before driving on to Kudat, on the northwest tip of Borneo. On the east side of Marudu Bay, the small centre of Pitas serves the Bengkoka Peninsula, a largely arid and poor region.

The Rungus of Maruda Bay

Rarely visited by tourists, Kudat district on the western arm of Marudu Bay is a particularly rewarding region for those with their own transport and a spirit of adventure. The coastline has some spectacular beaches and beautiful lagoons, while there are dozens of

Opposite: *A timeless view along Sabah's west coast.* **Below:** *The "real" Bajau horseman contrasts with ceremonially dressed men and horses seen during festivals.*

JILL GOCHER

Rungus longhouses, reached by rough dirt roads where a 4-wheel drive is advisable.

The Rungus are a sub-group of the Kadazan/Dusun, with a distinctive language, dress, architecture, *adat* (customs) and oral literature. Most Rungus live in longhouses, each family group having their own separate quarters off the main hall. At the edge of this hall a raised split-bamboo platform, backed by an outward sloping wall of widelyspaced poles, provides a well-ventilated and comfortable area for relaxation and socializing.

There are probably less than half a dozen thatch-roofed longhouses in existence today, the traditional *attap* having been replaced by more durable corrugated zinc roofing. Rungus longhouses are usually single storey, although more modern two-storey buildings can be found. It is now quite common to find one or two single-family dwellings built alongside the longhouses as some Rungus eschew the communal lifestyle.

Finding a longhouse

It is unfair to recommend one particular longhouse, as an influx of tourists could affect the genuine hospitality with which the visitor is currently greeted. Whether you decide to ask permission to stay overnight at a longhouse (naturally armed with suitable gifts of fruit, biscuits, cigarettes and balloons or picture books for the children) will depend on your ability to adjust to only rudimentary comforts, a lack of toilet facilities and your facility in Malay. You may be lucky and find a community where someone speaks English, but the two-way cultural exchange will be much richer if you have a Malay-speaking guide or are fluent in the language yourself.

Daily life in most longhouses involves getting up early to go out to the fields, or perhaps to tend the beehives that provide additional income for many. Home-grown "hill" rice is husked daily in wooden mortars in the common hall.

Many women weave sashes on backstrap looms, make fine trays and containers from a vine covered with a strong type of grass, and string together glass or plastic beads. Others rip the husk from the interior of coconuts and fashion them into brooms, to be sold for M$1 at the weekly *tamu*.

The older women, their wrists encircled by brass coils with white, black and coral-colored bracelets at either end, wear the typical black home-spun sarong. Their daily dress often includes hundreds — even thousands — of dollars worth of antique heirloom beads, of the type traded in Borneo for centuries.

One major longhouse community can be found at **Mattungong**, with another, **Mompilis** (popular with a number of tour operators) reached by an unmarked dirt road to the right of the highway a few kilometers north of Matunggong. At the sign for **Kg Pinawantai**, a road right leads towards Marudu Bay, passing several longhouses (one of them still with a thatch roof) before **Nangka,** where two spectacularly large longhouses perch high on a ridge.

At the Pinawantai turnoff, a track on the opposite side of the main road leads to **Gambiau**, while further north along the main road, the left turn to Kg Indarasan leads into **Tinangol** and on to a number of other isolated longhouses such as **Rita** and **Pomudahan**.

A surprise awaits those persistent enough to follow the Indarasan road right to the coast: a picturesque little fishing village, its *attap* houses clustering around a lagoon at the end of a fine long beach. **Indarasan Laut** is home to a handful of Muslim Illanun people. Less than a kilometer north, there's another settlement of Obian fisherfolk.

A rough journey to two lagoons

About 22 km south of Kudat town, before Sikuati village, there's a rough road to the left at the SAFODA sign for "Stesen Badarag". If you turn in here, take the left fork 25 m on, drive past the estate's houses and on to a bluff, you'll be rewarded with a superb view over two lagoons and the magnificent long **Sikuati beach.**

Kudat, like Tenom in the Interior, is one of the few Sabah towns with a sense of history. It was the first capital of British North Borneo, and Guillemard, who visited in 1886, remarked that "its situation is far prettier than that of Elopura (Sandakan). It is neater and cleaner and the bungalows have walls of wood... There is a splendid beach extending for miles, and, wonderful to relate, we actually found some attempts at gardening."

The gardening still goes on, with lawns and trees, and a 9-hole golf course so close that you could drive a ball right down the main street. The little port and inlet with stilt houses, and the old warehouses or *godowns* nearby make for a pleasant stroll around Kudat. About 12 km out of town, there's the popular Bak Bak beach, although it's nowhere near as good as the beaches on the west coast.

— *Wendy Hutton*

TRIPS SOUTH

Megaliths and Wild Water

For many visitors, the main reason for heading south is to ride the railcar through the Padas Gorge, or to experience the thrills of white-water rafting down the often-raging Padas River. If you're prepared to go off the beaten track, you'll find there's a lot more south of Kota Kinabalu than the Padas. Minibuses ply the main road to Beaufort, doing the trip in around 1 1/2 hours. They also go to Kuala Penyu and other major villages south of the capital. Needless to say, a hire car gives you a lot more flexibility to explore.

The area stretching from Tuaran, north of KK, and almost 50 km down to Papar has been referred to as the "megalithic belt" of Sabah. In the early 1960s, more than 100 upright stones (menhirs) still existed, embedded in the bunds of the rice fields. Although many of these have been moved or have fallen, several can still be seen around the vil-

lages of Tampasak and Punsuk, less than 20 km from Kota Kinabalu.

The megaliths, generally about 1.5 meters high and of coarse-grained sandstone, were dragged from 3-4 days' distance and erected as a symbol of bravery and power, as a memorial or as property markers. Even more impressive are the carved male and female wooden figures used to establish property rights when the owner died without heirs.

The finest of these, a seated female wearing a conical hat, was moved to the Sabah Museum in 1965, where it can be seen in the ethnography section. A cement duplicate was erected in the original site, the owners of the original statue receiving in exchange one water buffalo, one pig, one chicken and M$50.

The perfect way to explore this beautiful district of *padi* fields cradled between hills thick with spiky *nibong* palms and stands of bamboo, is on horseback. No special riding skills are needed on the "*kampung* trail ride" offered by **Kinarut Riding School**; provided you can just sit on a horse Contact Dale Sinidol on (088)225525.

Alternatively, hire a car and follow the road past the airport and Lok Kawi Army Camp. Continue straight at the junction where a right turn leads to Kinarut Laut vil-

Below: *A replica of an original statue now in the Sabah Museum stands in the fields of Kg Tampasak, part of Sabah's "megalithic belt".*

TOMMY CHANG

TOMMY CHANG

agriculture, except for the end of the peninsula near Kuala Penyuh. Located near the mouth of an estuary, Kuala Penyuh is the ideal departure point for Pulau Tiga. Several tracks off the main road to Kuala Penyuh, after the left fork to Menumbok, lead down to one of Sabah's loveliest beaches, over 20 km of pure clean sand, totally deserted and as yet undeveloped.

Around 20,000 people — Kadazan, Bruneian, Bajau, Bisayan and Chinese — live in this area, which still has a few swampy regions ideal for the wild sago palm. During the last Sunday in July, the Pesta Rumbia or Sago Festival offers a glimpse of rare Bisayan dances and local sports, as well as demonstrations of the versatility of the sago plant. You can see how the trunk of this versatile tree is grated, washed, and the edible starch extracted in the traditional fashion. Be daring and sample the gluey staple made from boiling the starch with water (*amboyat*), its unusual texture and bland flavor enlivened by spicy side dishes and sauces.

Burping mud volcanos

Pulau Tiga, a reserve run by Sabah Parks, is a fascinating spot rarely visited by tourists, although there is a comfortable chalet for 6, and a camping ground. Tiga, which has particularly interesting flora and fauna, also has rich marine life, with good scuba diving and snorkeling over the reefs to the southwest. Within the borders of the Park are another couple of nearby islands: Kalampunian Besar, with its sugar-white sand spit and clear waters, and Kalampunian Damit, known as Snake Island because of the poisonous sea snakes breeding there.

Tiga's marked trails wind through subtly different types of forest where many birds, macaque monkeys and monitor lizards may be spotted. One trail leads to the bizarre mud volcanoes, a metre or so high. Pulau Tiga itself is thought to have grown from a similar type of eruption, with the last impressive outpouring in the early in 1960s. Today, the mud volcanoes are cones of very fine mud, not at all hot to the touch, which give a desultory burp and flip up a bubble of mud from time to time. Weird if not spectacular.

The best way to Pulau Tiga is to charter a boat in Kuala Penyuh to take you to the island and stay overnight so that the next day you can explore the other two islands before returning to Kuala Penyuh.

Beaufort, the last town of any consequence on the west coast of Sabah, is most

lage just beyond the marker "Papar 34 km". After you pass the "Papar 31 km" post, take the marked turn left to Kg. Tampasak/Labak. Turn right across the wooden bridge at the sign painted on a car tyre for **Kg Tampasak**. About 150 m beyond the bridge is the remains of a quarry on your right. Park and walk down the hillock to your left, cross the covered wooden bridge and before you are *padi* fields with the cement replica of the Museum's fine wooden female statue, as well as a megalith.

The main road south passes the unremarkable beach of Kinaraut and continues on to **Papar** through irrigated rice lands, with great, docile water buffalo and flocks of white cattle egrets.

Beyond Papar, which also has a large community of Muslim Bajau, the road follows the coastline of shallow **Kimanis Bay,** where ships anchor far off awaiting the timber carried here from the Interior. Kimanis today gives no hint of its former beauty, when it was surrounded by forests of cinnamon trees (*kayu manis*) which gave it its name.

On the road to Pulau Tiga

Just before Beaufort, a road to the right leads out across the Klias Peninsula to **Kuala Penyuh**, and to Menumbok where ferries depart for Labuan. Much of the swamp forest originally covering this peninsula has been cleared, but the acidic soil is unsuitable for interesting for the way its shop houses are built high above the roads to avoid flooding when the Padas River overflows its banks. You might even spot a canoe tied under the wooden boardwalk of the houses immediately opposite the railway station.

Riding the railcar

Beaufort Station has been in operation since 1905, when, in an impressive feat of engineering, a line was hacked through the forest and into the steep hillsides along the Padas Gorge to Tenom. This gorge is the only natural pass through the Crocker Range; prior to advent of the railway, the only way into the fertile plain of the Interior region was by bridle path across the mountains. Although a slow train to Beaufort travels from the Tanjung Aru station in Kota Kinabalu, the journey is not very interesting. Instead, take a mini-bus to Beaufort where you can board the railcar. Looking like something from a child's Lego set and carrying around a dozen passengers, the **railcar** runs only between Beaufort and Tenom.(See Practicalities).

Try to take a seat (in front if possible) as soon as the railcar comes into the station. You'll know you're about to depart when the driver (generally as diminutive as his railcar) comes on board with a chain saw, essential for coping with any trees which may have fallen on the track.(Sabah is Borneo, after all!)

The railcar shakes its way cheerfully through tunnels of green, startling handsome chestnut and black coucals as big as hens at the side of the tracks. As the gorge narrows, the river reacts in protest, hurling itself around massive boulders, boiling in chaotic rapids and spinning in dizzying whirlpools. It all looks pretty impressive from the railcar, but infinitely more so as you try to remain inside a furiously bucking rubber dinghy, paddling frantically to get clear of a 3-metre wall of water.

A white-water escapade

Rafting on the **Padas**, especially after heavy rainfall inland, is an experience that should not be missed, initially terrifying for the novice but ultimately exhilarating. In tranquil stretches between rapids, you drift past the forest, soothed by the wall of green forest suddenly slashed with turquoise as kingfishers dart by.

If you're rafting, your tour operator will take you back to Kota Kinabalu. Independent passengers on the railcar will arrive in Tenom, not long after passing the Panggi

Hydroelectric Station, which produces most of the West Coast's electricity. It is possible, although not recommended, to return immediately by shared taxi from Tenom via Keningau and Tambunan to the capital. Rather than exhaust yourself, why not stay overnight in Tenom and enjoy something of the Interior before returning.

Stepping stone to Brunei

The island of **Labuan,** just off the Klias Peninsula, was a British colony from 1846 until after World War II, when it became part of Sabah. Labuan became part of Malaysian Federal Territory in 1984, and current efforts focus upon making it a financial and industrial centre. It already has free-port status, and attracts hundreds of Bruneian visitors who relax in the easy lifestyle of Labuan. Physical and commercial links still tie Labuan closely to Sabah, with regular ferries and flights from Kota Kinabalu.

Despite its pleasant, old-style Malay *kampung* in the north, and its relaxed ambience, Labuan has little to attract visitors stopping over between Brunei and Sabah.

— *Wendy Hutton*

Opposite: *A warm smile from a woman in a village near Papar.* **Above:** *Braving the Padas River after a railcar ride provides plenty of excitement, especially when the river is in full spate after the rains.*

PART III

Interior and East Sabah

The green heart of Sabah — evocatively known since colonial days as "The Interior" — is traditionally home to rice farmers and hunters living in its fertile valleys and rugged mountains. It contrasts dramatically with the east of the state, where coastal villages and coral islands are frequently peopled by descendants of sea gypsies, where swamp forests teem with a bewildering diversity of birds and apes, and birds' nests are still gathered in the very caves which once supplied the Imperial court of China.

The Interior offers two levels of exploration for today's visitor. Much of the region's scenic beauty and remarkable plants, particularly the Rafflesia and hundreds of native orchids, are surprisingly accessible in the valleys and hillsides in the northern region of the district. Further south, the terrain becomes more mountainous and challenging, accessible only along rough logging roads, by canoe or on foot.

Although Kadazan/Dusun people are nowadays found as far south as Keningau, a number of tribes known collectively as Murut (Hill People) dominate the Interior from Tenom on down to the highlands near the Sarawak border. In the past the Murut were renowned warriors and rebelled against the British in 1915.

The Interior is relatively underpopulated, with only 15% of the State's population in 25% of the total land area. Agriculture is the main occupation in the Tambunan and Tenom areas, while Keningau is the centre of the forestry industry in the Interior.

East Sabah includes both Sandakan and Tawau Divisions. Sandakan sprawls from the swampy northeast coast right across to the geographical centre of Sabah, covering 39% of the entire state, inhabited by only 19% of its total population.

Despite large-scale logging in much of the division, Sandakan still has areas densely populated by birds and other wildlife, making Sandakan town an ideal base for exploration.

The Sepilok Orang-utan Rehabilitation Centre has been attracting visitors for almost thirty years. An hour or so by boat and you can be in the Turtle Islands Park, where year round, turtles drag themselves ashore to lay their eggs. Another short trip brings you to the swamp forests of the Kinabatangan River, where you are virtually guaranteed to see the proboscis monkey and a magnificent array of birds, with the possibility of also seeing elephants, wild cattle, crocodiles and otters.

Although occupying only 19% of the total land area of Sabah, Tawau Division houses almost 29% of the state's population. Much of Tawau's coastline, washed by the Celebes Sea, fringes the huge Darvel Bay. On the northern side of the bay, Lahad Datu is the gateway to the Danum Valley Conservation Area, which preserves a large tract of lowland rainforest for scientific research, and gives the visitor an opportunity to discover the most complex ecosystem on earth.

Archaeological finds show signs of human habitation as much 20,000 years ago in the region of Tingkayu, not far from Madai Caves. Many of the limestone caves around Darvel Bay have been used as burial grounds in the past millennium, and are still harvested for birds' nests by the Ida'an.

Darvel Bay, right down to its southern tip at Semporna, is dotted with exquisite coral islands. Far to the south of Darvel Bay lies Malaysia's only oceanic isle, the stunning Pulau Sipadan, which rises straight up for 600 meters (2,000 ft) from the floor of the Celebes Sea and offers some of the finest scuba diving in the world.

— *Wendy Hutton*

Overleaf: *Pulau Sipadan, the most exquisite island off Sabah's east coast. Photo courtesy Sabah Air.* **Opposite:** *The tiny tarsier is one of the many bizarre creatures of the rainforest. Photo by Alain Compost.*

A Heartland of Cultural Complexity

Recent linguistic research has established that nearly all of Sabah's indigenous people speak languages of a single major stock, the Bornean, comprised of four principal families: the Dusunic, Murutic, Paitanic and Tidong.

Dusunic-speakers, numbering around 300,000, comprise the largest single ethnic community in Sabah. The term "Dusun" covers a large number of separately named communities, living chiefly in the West Coast and Interior Divisions. These are divided between upland groups (notably the Ranau and Tambunan Dusun), practicing mainly slash-and-burn cultivation, and more populous lowland and plains communities, growing mainly irrigated rice.

"Dusun" literally means "orchard" and so, by connotation, refers to "upcountry people," those living between the coastline and the interior highlands. It is not a term traditional-ly used by the Dusun themselves, but appears to have originated with coastal trading groups. The term "Kadazan," originally used by the Dusun of Penampang and Papar, has today become the most widely accepted general term for all Dusun-speakers.

High priestesses and spirit mediums

The Rungus, living in the Kudat and Bengkoka Peninsulas on both sides of Murudu Bay, represent one of a large number of distinctive upland groups. Like others, they cultivate hill rice, chiefly by shifting methods, supplemented with maize, cassava and a variety of vegetable and orchard crops. The Rungus also trade with coastal peoples, from whom they formerly obtained heirloom wealth in the form of gongs, brassware and jars, whose acquisition served as a primary measure of family prestige.

Although not isolated, the Rungus, represent one of the least acculturated Dusun communities in Sabah, many of them continuing to live in longhouses. Despite recent inroads by Christianity, many families continue to practice indigenous religion. The principal religious figures are women priestesses and spirit mediums called *bobolizan*.

Priestesses are similarly the central religious figures in most lowland Dusun societies as well. The *bobolizan* communicate with the spirit world in trance and perform sacrifices accompanied by complex ritual chants. They look after family prosperity, individual health and fertility, perform life-crisis rituals, including marriage and death rites, lead family and longhouse renewal rites and conduct public sacrifice to safeguard village well-being.

A dozen different languages

In Sabah, the Bisaya comprise a Muslim community of wet rice agriculturalists who live, interspersed with other groups, along the lower reaches of the Padas and Klias rivers and in the Kuala Penyuh region. Although considered a separate ethnic group, the Bisaya speak a Dusunic language.

Murutic-speakers are found throughout southwestern Sabah, chiefly in the Keningau, Tenom, Spitiang and Pensiangan districts, extending southwards into Kalimantan. There are also scattered Murut communities in the Beaufort district and in Tawau and Kinabatangan on the east coast. In all, the Murut number some 50,000 in Sabah.

Linguistically, the Murut are a highly diverse group, speaking at least 12 languages. The most widely distributed are the Sum-

JILL GOCHER

ambu-Tagal Murut who inhabit the whole southwestern region. The Murut are divided between lowland and hill groups. The lowland Murut, including the Timugon, Nabay, Baukan and others, are plains-dwellers, inhabiting mainly the coastal plain of Klias Peninsula and the intermontane plains of Tenom, Keningau and Sook.

The Timugon Murut, whose name means "People of the River," are a lowland group living chiefly along the western banks of the Pcgalan river, which runs through the fertile

Tenom valley; along the eastern banks of the Padas, and at the confluence of these two rivers, below Tenom town. The Timugon grow both "wet" and "dry" rice, and cultivate sago and cassava. Rice is also brewed into wine (*tapai*), the consumption of which traditionally formed a central feature of Timugon culture and ceremony.

From drink to dry

Like other Murut groups, drinking alcohol was an essential accompaniment to public rituals including funerals and marriages, to planting, harvesting, house building and the settlement of disputes. Except at funerals, drinking was accompanied by gong music, singing and dancing. With the spread of fundamentalist Christianity and its prohibition on drinking, much of this once-rich ceremonial and artistic life has been lost.

In the past, the Timugon lived in longhouses, although almost all of these have now been replaced by single-family dwellings. One of the most striking features of the hill Murut culture was a spring platform called the *papan* or *lansaran*, set beneath the surrounding floor level of the common area of the longhouse. This acted as a trampoline and was used for religious singing, dancing and for jumping contests.

Paitanic-speaking peoples live scattered throughout the northern and west-central regions of Sabah. They are generally an

inland people, living mainly along interior rivers. No consistent term is used to refer to these people. In the upper Kinabatangan, the term "Orang Sungei" ("River People") is now being adopted by Paitanic groups. However, in the lower river, the same term is used by unrelated people, including coastal Ida'an communities. Linguistically, the Paitanic peoples are highly diverse, speaking chain languages with only limited intelligibility between them.

The Tidong are Muslim by religion and live chiefly in coastal or sub-coastal settlements, particularly in the Tawau District. Eastern Sabah forms the northern edge of the traditional area of Tidong settlement, most of which lies in east Kalimantan.

Exceptions to the rule

Not all the indigenous people of inland Sabah speak languages of Bornean stock. The Banggi, a small population on Pulau Banggi off the northern tip of Sabah, are one exception, speaking a language believed to have its closest links to the Molbog language of southern Palawan in the Philippines.

Another exception are the Lun Dayeh, who inhabit the southwestern border of Sabah, Brunei, Sarawak and Kalimantan. They are relative newcomers to Sabah, believed to have first settled the Ulu Padas area of Sipitang a century ago. "Lun Dayeh" means "Upriver People," in addition, the Lun Dayeh also call themselves Lun Lod ("Downriver People") and Lun Bawang ("Local People" or "People of this Area". These terms have only recently become ethnic labels.

— Clifford Sather

Opposite: *An exuberant Murut man in a bark jacket.* **Above, left:** *Dusun women on the slopes of Mount Kinabalu carry huge loads in their rattan backpacks.* **Above, right:** *Making yeast for rice wine in a Rungus longhouse.*

EXPLORING THE INTERIOR

A Wealth of Wondrous Flowers

The Interior, once isolated from the west coast by the knife-edged and densely forested mountains of the the Crocker Range, can now be reached by the rail linking Beaufort with Tenom, (see Part II) and by sealed road. This road passes through **Penampang**, today virtually a suburb of the Kota Kinabalu but for generations, an important center for the rice-growing Kadazan.

Winding sharply and steeply up the Crocker Range, the road affords dramatic glimpses of both Mount Kinabalu and the city and nearby islands. Just before the Sunsuron Pass (1,649 m), the **Gunong Emas** restaurant (the most popular between Keningau and Kota Kinabalu) also offers the chance to view some of Sabah's native animals and birds in a rather cramped private zoo.

As you cross Sunsuron Pass, on the right of the road is a small visitors' centre, the northern boundary of the **Crocker Range Forest Reserve**. A number of wild orchids have been transplanted here, and can be spotted along several short, easy trails.

Be sure to stop at the attractive and informative display centre in the **Rafflesia Reserve**, where you can learn about the weirdest flower imaginable, a parasitic plant which takes months to develop a flower up to almost one metre in diameter and which smells like rotten meat. You may be lucky and have only a five-minute walk to see a Rafflesia in bloom, or you may have to walk for up to 1 1/2 hours in very steep terrain.

The best rice wine in Borneo

Tambunan Plain nestles in a Shangri-La setting at 1,000 m, its terraced *padi* fields watered by sparkling streams and dotted with picturesque villages. The largest of the seventy villages in Tambunan district, **Sunsuron** is renowned for its split-bamboo houses, which sadly don't benefit aesthetically from their rusty zinc roofs. The forests of bamboo growing on the hills around Tambunan are the result of the colonial government edict that twenty bamboo clumps must be planted for every pole cut.

A sign to the right of the road at Kg Tibabah indicates the **memorial to Mat Salleh**, the Bajau rebel who burned the settlement on Gaya. East of Tambunan looms Sabah's second highest mountain, **Trus Madi** (2,642 m), sometimes tackled by climbers who prefer less beaten tracks to those leading up Mount Kinabalu. The many side roads leading off the Tambunan-Keningau road also invite exploration; one of the prettiest regions is around **Kg Makatip**, while the valley of the **Kaingaran River** is also worth visiting.

The **Mawah Falls** are reached via Kg Patah, off the Tambunan-Ranau road; the rough road eventually peters out, leaving you with a 20-minute walk to what is perhaps the most beautiful waterfall in Sabah (except for the stunning seven-tier falls in the Maliau Basin, in the very heart of north Borneo, accessible only by helicopter).

You can discover how to make rice wine —except on Sundays — at **Tambunan Village Resort Centre** (to the left at the Shell Station, just beyond the small Tambunan Handicraft Centre). The undiluted *lihing*, a Tambunan speciality, is probably the finest rice wine in all of Borneo. The resort has a number of simple bamboo huts and longhouses where it is possible to stay, but as

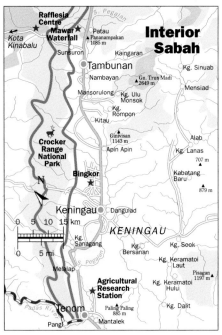

the resort is neither fully completed nor properly maintained at the time of writing, better stay in the government resthouse in Pekan Tambunan. The **weekly markets** or *tamu* are worth visiting; on Thursday, the market is held in Pekan Tambunan, while on Sunday, it awaits churchgoers outside Holy Cross Church at Kg Toboh.

Keningau town is a sprawling, unappealing centre for the timber industry. Visitors should head on south to **Taman Bandukan**, a small park near Bingkor, which attracts

hundreds of butterflies, some of which will even land on your hand. Take the marked road to Bingkor, just north of Keningau, and turn right at the old wooden shophouses of Bingkor village towards Taman Bandukan. There's a clean river ideal for splashing about in, as well as picnic shelters; best avoid the weekends, when it gets crowded with people as well as butterflies.

From Keningau, a secondary road leads ever deeper into the Interior to Nabawan and on to Sapulut and Pensiangan, while the main road continues south to Tenom. Two vast rubber plantations, one north of Tenom at Melalap, and the other south at Sapong, were once the lifeblood of Tenom district, especially after the railway came all the way through to Melalap in 1905.

A record-breaking orchid collection

Rubber has diminished in economic importance, and **Tenom** is now a mixed agricultural center, famous above all for its coffee. The narrow plain around Tenom is dotted about with small farms, all of which benefit from the work of the **Agricultural Research Station** at Lagud Sebrang, some 20 km from Tenom. An Agricultural Park devoted to education and recreation is planned to open to the public around 1994, but the nucleus of it, the Orchid Centre, has been drawing visitors since 1976.

Set in a lovely (but mosquito-ridden) gar-

den, the **Orchid Centre** houses the world's biggest collection of Borneo orchids, with around 450 of an estimated total of 3,000 species. The center also grows hundreds of orchids from other countries, in a truly astonishing variety of sizes, colors and shapes.

Request permission to visit at the entrance checkpoint at the Agricultural Research Station, or call (087)735661 in advance if you intend coming after 1 pm, when officially the Orchid Centre is closed. Although there's an infrequent bus service from Tenom, it's best to hire a taxi to take you to and from Lagud Sebrang (around M$20). (The locals and even a sign board still refer to the Agricultural Research Station by its old name, the Cocoa Research Station.)

Food, then south to an old rock riddle

Tenom itself is a pleasantly relaxed town with a sense of continuity absent in many other towns of Sabah. With a tourist-standard hotel on a hill overlooking the town, and good food to be enjoyed in its restaurants, Tenom is worth a stopover. If you're traveling in a group, it is possible to arrange with a tour operator in Kota Kinabalu for a fascinating evening of Murut and Lun Dayeh cultural dances and music, plus the opportunity to see the *lansaran* (springy bamboo or rattan platform) in action at **Kg Kemabong**, south of Tenom.

Further south of Kemabong, at the village of **Ulu Tomani,** there are some mysterious carvings on a massive boulder, with smaller carved rocks nearby. The swirling, stylized faces and figures, Sabah's only rock carvings, were created within the past millennium, but archaeologists are unsure of the exact date.

To venture deeper into the Interior, it is necessary to take the unsealed road from

Above, left and right: *Growing up to one meter in diameter, the Rafflesia can usually be found blooming in the Rafflesia Forest Reserve.*

Keningau to Nabawan, through countryside devastated by excessive logging followed by forest fires in 1983. The road, used by dozens of loaded logging trucks, is dangerous and only one rule is observed: might is right. Logging trucks are always given absolute priority, even if they're on your side of the road.

The administrative center of the Pensiangan district, bordering Kalimantan, was transferred from remote Pensiangan (then accessible only by river) to **Nabawan** in 1974. Unfortunately, the poor soil around Nabawan makes it unsuitable for farming, and although the village (your last chance to eat in a restaurant) is relatively busy, there's little to support it apart from government operations.

The dead, a bridge and a head

The burial customs of Murutic peoples vary. Those living near Keningau either buried their dead directly in the ground permanently, or else exhumed the bodies some time after burial and kept the remains in a large jar in a special burial hut. The Muruts living around Sapulut placed their dead in either a jar or, more commonly these days, a coffin, which is never exhumed, and erect a grave hut over this. Between Nabawan and Sapulut, a number of interesting **Murut grave huts** dot the roadside; if you come shortly after a funeral or at Christmas, when the graves are often decorated, they are remarkably colorful and photogenic.

Sapulut is a scattering of houses, a school and a small hospital on both sides of the Sapulut river. A suspension bridge for pedestrians spans the river near the simple shops, but a solid vehicular bridge, which four different contractors failed to complete owing to inexplicable collapses, remains unfinished. Locals mutter about the old legend that a head must be buried to appease the spirits when a bridge was constructed; perhaps it's as well it remains incomplete!

The main reason for coming to Sapulut is

to continue by river to either Batu Punggul or Pensiangan. Although a rough, relatively new road leads to **Pensiangan**, to see the Murut longhouses in the area and appreciate the scenery, hire a boat in Sapulut and go by river. Ask at the shops; you should get the return trip for about M$300, and it will take from 1 1/2-3 hours, depending on the height of the river. If you have an Indonesian visa, you can continue by river into Indonesian Kalimantan, and follow the Sembakung River all the way to Tarakan on the east coast. It is

also possible to take a public 4-wheel drive vehicle from Keningau and Sapulut across to Tawau, by private logging road.

The Muruts around Pensiangan and Sapulut, once renowned for their skill with a blowpipe, are still keen hunters and can often be seen heading off with a gun and at least one dog to look for deer, wild pig or some other tasty morsel. A Murut without a dog is unthinkable, yet these animals are generally scruffy beasts which act as if perpetually starved. At least they don't attempt to eat your shoes, like the dogs which Alfred Russel Wallace encountered in Sarawak's Dyak longhouses in the 1850s!

To virgin forest by motorized canoe

If you want to visit **Batu Punggul**, a limestone pinnacle in the heart of virgin rainforest, you can arrange boat hire in Sapulut and stay at Tataluan longhouse, about 10 minutes before Batu Punggul. It is, however, cheaper and more convenient to stay at the **Batu Punggul Resort**, which will arrange your boat transport (see Practicalities). The trip by long wooden canoe gunned along by an outboard engine can be anything from 2-5 hours.

During the dry season (especially January to March), everyone has to get out of the canoe and help haul it over the shallow rapids. After heavy rain, the rapids become a boiling mess of water and rocks which the boatman, with the help of a lookout with a pole in front, negotiates with reassuring skill. Expect to get splashed, and have everything well wrapped in plastic; don't forget hat and sun cream.

The banks of Sapulut River are dotted by isolated longhouses, until you reach the last settlement at Tataluan. From here on, the river is enclosed by beautiful virgin rainforest. About 10 minutes upriver from Tataluan, the forest canopy is pierced by a sheer limestone outcrop, Batu Punggul. Although it presents a formidable vertical face towards the river, Batu Punggul can be scaled by a slightly less challenging route by those who don't suffer from vertigo, while less adventurous souls can content themselves with exploration of two networks of caves within the limestone massif.

According to Murut folk tales, the two caves complexes of Batu Punggul and nearby Batu Tinahas were once longhouses, which were turned to stone. Murut guides point out a massive wooden beam, mystifying wedged more than 10 m high in the roof of one cave, claiming it to be a rafter of one of these mythical longhouses.

Batu Punggul has a small cave with the usual complement of bats, while Batu Tinahas, about 20 minutes' walk from Batu Punggul, is a much larger and more interesting complex. Here, you may be lucky to see mossy nest swiftlets (whose nests are not edible) nesting low down on the walls of the cave. Although not yet surveyed, Batu Tinahas is thought to have at least three levels of caves. Be sure to bring a torch and take care as you explore, as there is a least one very dangerous drop off.

Cool nights in longhouse country

Surprisingly for such a remote location, there is a range of accommodation and simple food available at Batu Punggul Resort. If you don't mind sleeping on a mattress on the split bamboo floor, you can stay in the traditional Murut longhouse at the Resort, or can opt for more conventional accommodation. Be prepared for cool nights, thanks to the combination of forest, river and altitude.

Apart from jungle trekking (with the chance to see a Rafflesia), climbing and cave exploration, you can also arrange for an evening of Murut cultural dances, performed by the people from nearby Tataluan longhouse, who come up to Batu Punggul Resort and enjoy the evening just as much as their audience. The evening will, of course, be accompanied by rice wine (*tapai*), which the

Muruts take seriously, solemnly sitting down to a huge jar which is topped up for each drinker. You're obliged to sip the *tapai* through a reed straw until an indicated level on a floating marker is reached. Go easy on the number of sessions you have at the jar unless you want to feel decidedly seedy the following day.

Trekking into Sarawak

The country around **Long Pa Sia** a small village of very friendly Muruts, to the far southwest of the Interior, has been popular with a few intrepid trekkers in recent years. As the village is surrounded by forest which is being progressively logged by Sabah Forest Industries (which runs Malaysia's only paper mill at Sipitang, on the southwest coast), there are now logging roads close to Long Pa Sia and subsequent disturbance to the virgin rainforest.

There's a weekly rural air service flight to Long Pa Sia, where you can find a local guide to take you on a trek down to Long Semado, in Sarawak; from here, you can fly to Lawas, near the coast, and return to Kota Kinabalu by minibus.

— *Wendy Hutton*

Opposite, left and right: *Heading up the Sapulut River to Batu Punggul entails passing under bridges made of as many as eight layers of massive logs.*

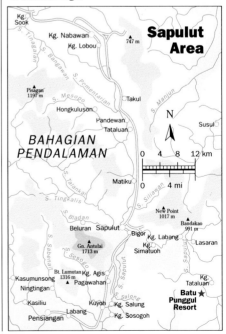

SANDAKAN

Gateway to Borneo's Wildlife

Vast salt-water swamps sprawl along Sandakan District's coastline, while fresh-water swamp forests spread like a green stain along the lower reaches of Sabah's largest rivers. Gently rolling hills, many covered by plantations, stretch as far as the eye can see.

Sandakan town faces eastwards, both geographically and historically, with the nearest Philippines' island less than 20 nautical miles away. Wander around its seafront market and the links with Sulu are tangible in the amazing mixture of faces and languages.

When Spenser St. John sailed past in 1858, he reported that "Sandakan Bay itself is a splendid harbor, with a good supply of freshwater. It used to be well inhabited but on one occasion, the villages were surprised by the Balignini pirates, and sacked and burnt by them." The villagers fled elsewhere, but every year, assembled "to collect the valuable products of the place, which consist of large quantities of white birds' nests, pearls, wax, sea-slug and the best kind of camphor."

These products were sold primarily to traders from the Sulu islands, whose then-powerful sultan exercised control over northeast Borneo. As Sulu's power waned during the latter part of last century, a group of German and British adventurers — at least one of whom was known to be supplying guns to the Sultan of Sulu — set up a base on Sandakan Bay. This became known as Kampung German, and was where the first Resident of the east coast district was based on the formation of the British North Borneo Company in 1881.

"The place which was pawned"

After Kampung German accidentally burned down, a new site was chosen and a town fancifully known as Elopura (Beautiful City) founded at Buli Sim Sim, near the mouth of Sandakan Bay. The locals persisted in using the older Sulu name for the region, Sandakan ("The place which was pawned"), and Elopura was eventually dropped.

The industry which was to give Sandakan what was claimed as the greatest concentration of millionaires anywhere in the world in the 1970s began almost by accident. A group

Below: *Villages perch above the sea or estuaries around Sandakan Bay.*

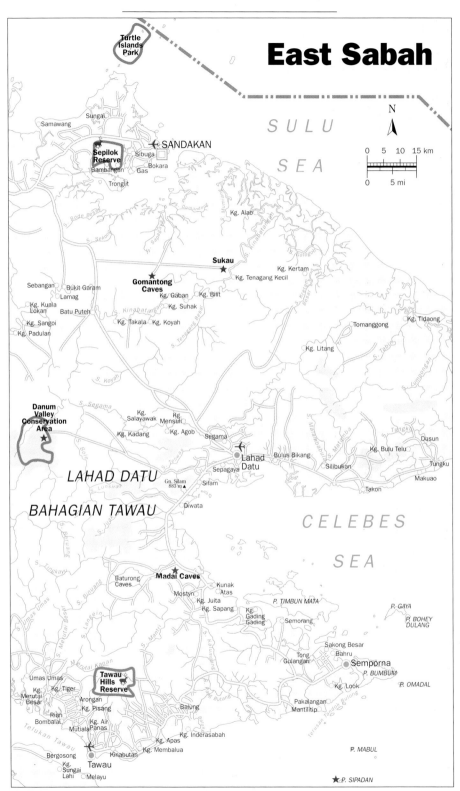

East Sabah

Turtle Islands Park

Samawang

Sungai

Sepilok Reserve

Sibuga
Gas   Bokara

⭐ SANDAKAN

Bambangan

Tronglit

S U L U

S E A

N

| 0 | 5 | 10 | 15 km |

| 0 | 5 mi |

Kg. Alab

Sukau ⭐

Kg. Kertam

Kg. Tenagang Kecil

Sebangan   Bukit Garam
Lamag

Gomantong Caves ⭐

Kg. Gaban   Kg. Bilit

Kg. Kuala
Lokan   Batu Puteh

Kg. Suhak

Kg. Sangoi

Kg. Takala   Kg. Koyah

Kg. Padulan

Tomanggong

Kg. Tidaong

Kg. Litang

S. Koyah

Danum Valley Conservation Area

Kg. Salayawak   Kg. Mensuli

Kg. Kadang   Kg. Agob   Segama

Bulus Bikang

Kg. Bulu Telu   Dusun

Silibukan   Tungku

LAHAD DATU

Sepagaya

● Lahad Datu

Makuao

Gn. Silam
883 m ▲   Silam

Takon

BAHAGIAN TAWAU

Diwata

C E L E B E S

S E A

Baturong Caves

Madai Caves ⭐

Mostyn

Kunak Atas

Kg. Juita
Kg. Sapang

P. TIMBUN MATA

P. GAYA

Kg. Gading Gading

Semorang

P. BOHEY DULANG

Sakong Besar

Umas Umas

Kg. Tiger

Tawau Hills Reserve

Tong
Gulangan

Bahru

● Semporna
P. BUMBUM

Kg. Merutai Besar

Arongan
Kg. Pisang

P. OMADAL

Kg. Look

Rian
Bombalai

Kg. Air
Mutiala Panas

Balung

Pakalangan
Mantilitip

Kg. Inderasabah

Kg. Apas

Bergosong

Kg.
Sungai
Lahi

Kinabutan

Tawau

Kg. Membalua

Melayu

P. MABUL

⭐ P. SIPADAN

of Australians, who'd cleared land to plant sugar cane in 1885, altered their plans when the price of sugar plummeted. They decided to export the timber they had felled, thus beginning the forestry industry in Sabah. The timber boom peaked between 1960 and 1980, but now that the best timber has been extracted, Sandakan Division is dominated by huge oil palm and cocoa estates.

Exploring the town

The town of Sandakan, in its heyday referred to as a mini Hong Kong (but only by the locals), is small and undistinguished, yet has a certain elusive charm, with its feet washed by the sea and its back sheltered by hills still covered with a few stands of tall trees. You can get a good overview of the town from the **Observation Point** on Jalan Bukit Merah.

Opposite this point, walk up the overgrown drive to the sadly neglected but atmospheric white wooden bungalow on the ridge. This was once the home of the Conservator of Forests in British North Borneo, and his American wife, **Agnes Keith**. She wrote three books about her life in Borneo between 1934 and 1952, the first of which popularized the old seafarers' name for Sabah in its title, *The Land Below the Wind*.

At the southern extremity of Sandakan, the huge **Puu Jih Shih Buddhist temple** sprawls across a hilltop above Tanah Merah. The dazzling gold and vivid primary colors of this relatively new temple (completed in 1987) are enough to scare away even the most malevolent spirits, and although it lacks the air of mystery and magic permeating some old Taoist temples, it has an unrivaled panoramic view down over Sandakan town and across the huge bay.

St Michael and All Angels Church, a stone building with narrow Gothic windows, seems to have been directly transplanted from an English village. Begun in 1893, this church miraculously escaped destruction during the bombing of Sandakan in 1945.

Just north of the large, starkly simple **Sandakan mosque**, completed in 1988, is the orderly stilt village of **Buli Sim Sim**, built on the original site of Sandakan town. Take a stroll down any of the walkways (*jambatan*), past the spacious wooden houses, their wide verandahs decorated with pot plants and strings of drying flowery *sarongs*, their spotlessly clean sitting rooms graced with cabinets full of bric-a-brac, sports trophies and the best china reserved for festivals. The people of Kampung Buli Sim Sim are very welcoming, but it is courteous to ask before photographing them.

History, seafood and crocodiles

A curious historical footnote can be seen in a corner of the main cemetery at the end of Jalan Istana. Tucked away on the hillside near a clump of bamboo (you'll need a guide to find the spot), the **Japanese cemetery** houses a memorial to the Japanese soldiers who died in Borneo during the war. More unusually, it also has a number of graves of Japanese girls, victims of a prostitution racket, who died in Sandakan. None of the grave markers faces the east, towards the Land of the Rising Sun, in deliberate rejection of the country felt to have so ill-used some of its girls.

The **Australian Memorial** erected in 1986 on the site of a prisoner-of-war camp at Taman Rimba, Labuk Road, commemorates those who lost their lives in the "Death March," when over 2,500 already ill prisoners were marched across the jungles of north Borneo to Ranau. Only six of them survived.

Be sure to set aside some time to wander about **Sandakan market**, and don't miss the separate fish market, Sabah's largest, where the fishing boats pull right alongside to unload a bewildering range of seafood.

If you have the time, take a taxi or Labuk Road bus to the **Forestry Department Headquarters** (Ibu Pejabat Perhutanan), next to Sandakan Golf Club, and go upstairs

to the exhibition center (open during normal government office hours). This little museum is devoted to the history of the forestry industry in Sabah, and is full of interesting information and displays.

The **Crocodile Farm** on Labuk Road, some 12 km outside of the town, is a favorite spot with some tour operators, though few visitors are impressed by the endless cement tanks containing up to 2,000 generally immobile crocodiles of all sizes.

Meeting the man of the forest

As an adorable baby looks at you with trusting eyes while reaching out his long-fingered hand to clasp yours, you cannot fail to fall in love with Sabah's orang-utans. Gentle and highly intelligent, these animals gaze at you with such intensity that you begin to wonder just who is observing whom. At the **Sepilok Orang-Utan Rehabilitation Centre**, 25 km from Sandakan, the visitor is privileged to be able to meet these fascinating primates.

When the keeping of this remarkable "man of the forest" (for this is what orang-utan means in Malay) was outlawed, it was necessary to find somewhere to put the once captive animals. Sepilok, a reserve of 43 sq km of beautiful lowland rainforest, was chosen in 1964 as the site for a program that trains once-captive orang-utans to live the way nature intended, in the forest. Over the years, around 100 animals have returned to fending for themselves in the forest, some mating with wild orang-utans and producing young.

The health of the orang-utans is carefully monitored, and to avoid their catching diseases from humans, visitors are not permitted to touch them within the forest. A couple of hopeless cases, orangs that refuse to be rehabilitated and much prefer human company, are generally brought out to meet visitors and pose nonchalantly for photos before the visitors enter the sanctuary.

It's best to arrive at Sepilok around 9 am and sign in at the Registration Centre, where the daily program is chalked up on a notice board. Provided they are in good health, Judy and Jo-Jo will be brought out to socialize before you proceed to an area where young orphaned orang-utans are literally learning the ropes, taught by Wildlife Department rangers rather than their mothers how to climb. Then it's a five-minute walk to feeding platform A, built around a giant dipterocarp tree. Here, orang-utans are fed twice daily with vitamin-laced milk and bananas, a deliberately monotonous diet which encourages them to forage in the wild.

Another feeding area (platform B) deeper into the forest, where more independent

Below: *In the rehabilitation center at Sepilok, just outside Sandakan, visitors are able to view a program teaching orphaned orang-utans to live in the wild.*

CED PRUDENTE

orang-utans come to feed before quickly melting back into the forest, is open to a restricted number of visitors to assist in speeding up the rehabilitation process; request permission for this privilege when registering if you're prepared for a reasonably strenuous hike.

Feeding times are at 10 am and 2.30 pm, with an excellent video film shown at 11 am and 3 pm. There is also an interesting Nature Education Centre. Be sure to visit the rare and highly endangered Asian two-horned (Sumatran) rhinoceros kept at Sepilok. It is hoped that the pair kept here may breed and establish a captive population. A very small number of elusive rhinos are known to live in Danum Valley Conservation Area and in Tabin Wildlife Reserve.

There are some good trails through the forest at Sepilok; it's well worth going with a guide who can identify many of the magnificent dipterocarp trees, birds and the countless varieties of insects (including voracious mosquitos) you'll encounter.

A profoundly moving experience

It's hard not to feel ambivalent as you crouch on the sand at night watching a nesting turtle, privileged to witness a stage in the life cycle of this ancient species yet guilty at intruding upon such an intimate event. The huge turtle — so swift underwater — drags herself laboriously ashore, choosing a spot above the high-tide line to dig a hole with her flippers, pausing from time to time with a human-like sigh before continuing her work. When the hole is deep enough, she lays around 100 ping-pong ball sized eggs, carefully covering them with sand before lumbering slowly back into the sea.

Just 40 km north of Sandakan lie three small islands, Selingan, Gulisan and Bakkungan Kecil, which were, together with the surrounding reefs and seas, gazetted as the **Turtle Islands Park** in 1977 and are among the most important in all of Southeast Asia for

sea turtles. To prevent over-exploitation of their edible eggs and a subsequent drop in the turtle population, hatcheries were first established on the Turtle Islands in 1964.

Visitors can stay overnight in Sabah Parks' accommodation on Pulau Selingan to watch the turtles coming ashore. By some instinct which no one understands, the turtles always return to the beach where they themselves were hatched to lay their eggs. They start breeding at around 20-25 years, and since a conservation program has been in

action at Pulau Selingan since 1964, a large number of turtles is now returning to lay their eggs: you can be certain of seeing them any night of the year.

The island, so small you can walk around it in 30 minutes, is surrounded by lovely clear waters and has a pleasant beach. Around dusk, when the temperature drops, the hatchlings start emerging from the sand where the eggs were buried, safely surrounded by wire mesh, during the incubation period. After dinner in the restaurant, visitors wait in their chalet until the rangers advise them when the turtles begin arriving (generally after 8 pm) and conduct them to the beach to watch the turtle digging her hole and laying.

The turtles are tagged, the eggs gathered and quickly reburied in the hatchery. You may be able to help take newly emerged hatchlings by bucket down to the water's edge to release them. Watching them race for the sea is a bitter-sweet experience when you consider that only 3% of them will reach maturity, owing to natural predators and disease.

Rich in rare wildlife

Sabah's biggest river, the 560-km **Kinabatangan**, begins in the mountainous center of Sabah, snaking down through the forest and leaving oxbow lakes in its wake as it changes course over the years. The lower reaches of the Kinabatangan hold the greatest concentration of orang-utans, proboscis monkeys and elephants in Malaysia, and acknowledging the importance of the region, the Sabah State Government has plans to make it a protected area.

It was only in 1988 that tour operators began taking visitors to the region, initially on an afternoon trip by speedboat across Sandakan Bay and up the Kinabatangan as far as the first Orang Sungei village, Kampung Abai, with guaranteed sightings of Borneo's unique proboscis monkey en route. It is now also possible to go by road (via the Gomantong Caves or Suan Lamba) to the village of Sukau, staying overnight in a simple but comfortable riverside lodge less than five minutes by boat from the Menanggol River, unrivaled for close-up viewing of the proboscis monkey. (There's no public transport to either Gomantong or Sukau, and it might be difficult to try to arrange a boat along the river, so it is advisable to use a tour operator.)

A curious creature

Found only in Borneo, the proboscis monkey is undoubtedly the most extraordinary of all the apes. The large males have a huge pendulous nose (hence the name), fat "beer belly" and long white tail. Their markings makes them look as if they're wearing grey tights, white underpants and an orange jacket. The male's permanent erection simply enhances his bizarre appearance.

The proboscis monkey, whose partially webbed hind feet make him a strong swimmer, is also a prodigious jumper; launching off into the air enthusiastically, seemingly without a thought of where he's to land, only to crash in an explosion of breaking twigs into a neighboring tree.

Smaller, with more delicate noses and minus the beer belly, the females have less dramatic coloring than the males. Highly sociable animals, proboscis monkeys always come to the riverside at night to see and be seen (by each other rather than by the tourists) before going to sleep. This predictable behavior makes it almost certain you'll be able to observe them.

Noisy macaques, silver and red leaf monkeys or langurs, and even the shy wild orangutan may all be seen in this region, while if you're very lucky, you could spot an elephant, otters or a crocodile.

The bird life around Sukau and the oxbow lakes further upriver is stupendous. In one week, an ardent bird-watcher spotted 72 different species. Even a 2-hour trip along the Kinabatangan and Menanggol will produce slender egrets, jewel-bright kingfishers, eagles, hornbills sometimes as numerous as sparrows on a city street, the glorious Asian

Opposite, left: *Turtle hatchlings ready for release into the sea.* **Opposite, right:** *Traveling by boat up a tributary of the Kinabatangan.* **Below:** *Borneo's unique proboscis monkey.*

CED PRUDENTE

Paradise Flycatcher with its trailing tail feathers and the Oriental Darter, which plunges like an arrow into the river to impale fish on its rapier beak.

Edible birds' nests in profusion

The limestone massif of **Gomantong Caves**, set in a forest reserve almost the size of Sepilok, is an excellent area for bird-watching and for clouds of brilliant butterflies that often cluster on the track leading into the caves. But the main attraction here is — as it has been for centuries — edible birds' nests made from the saliva of two types of swiftlet.

Located en route for Sukau, about 1 1/2 hours from Sandakan, the Gomantong Caves consist of the easily accessible Simud Hitam Cave, where so-called "black" nests (which have feathers mixed in) are gathered, and the more remote and larger Simud Putih complex where the much more valuable pure "white" nests are found. Despite considerable opposition from locals harvesters, the North Borneo Company managed to take control of the Gomantong Caves, which are today administered by Sabah's Wildlife Department. One WWF expert has claimed that Gomantong is "the best managed edible birds' nest cave in the world."

The Wildlife Department has constructed an information center on the cave ecology, as well as chalets and a simple picnic area. Visitors interested in the forest as well as the caves will find exploration the Gomantong area richly rewarding; the large-scale planting of oil palms in the surrounding region has resulted in a concentration of wildlife in this remaining patch of virgin forest.

In the Simud Hitam cave, only 5 minutes' walk from the picnic area, light streams through holes in the roof, illuminating areas of the floor of the cave which is cushioned with guano, droppings from the thousands of bats which share the cave with the swiflets. This guano absolutely seethes with beetles, spiders, cockroaches and other insects one might prefer not to know about. Be sure to wear sensible footwear.

The most spectacular time to visit the caves is undoubtedly during the harvesting season. Some time between February and April, as soon as the swifts make their nests, collectors are permitted to gather them before the birds have laid their eggs. The birds then make a second nest, and after their eggs have hatched and the young birds flown away — between July and September — the used nests are harvested. Government-licensed contractors employ collectors, who work using rattan ladders, poles and suspended ropes, risking death to earn, for the pure white nests, at least US$500 per kilo.

To check whether harvesting is in progress during your visit to Sabah, phone the Wildlife Department at Sandakan: (089)-666550.

— *Wendy Hutton*

COASTAL PEOPLES

Diverse Yet United by Faith

Surrounded on three sides by sea, the coastal and island communities have powerful links, reflecting historical and cultural affinities, with Brunei, the Sulu archipelago, Sulawesi and eastern Kalimantan. Under the the influence of Brunei and Sulu, Islam arrived in the 14th century coastal Sabah; today, virtually all of the state's coastal peoples share Islam as a common faith.

Sabah's coastal peoples include the Brunei and Kadayan of the southwestern coast; the Illanun of the west coast; the Suluk, Tidong, and Ida'an of the east coast; and along both coasts, the Bajau, the most numerous and diverse of all these groups.

Historically, the Suluk or Tausung ("Men of the Current") formed the dominant population of the Sulu Sultanate. Although the Bajau, a once-nomadic people who lived in small covered boats, may be grouped with the Suluk and Illanun as coastal Muslims, all three groups speak different languages and are culturally distinct from one another. Unlike the Suluk, the Bajau have no history of past political cohesion and are divided into an array of regional speech communites, each identified with a separate, chain-related dialect and a named home area.

The Bajau are the most sea-dependent of Sabah's coastal peoples, although many are well settled ashore. This is particularly so on the west coast, where the majority of Bajau work the land, cultivating crops and rearing cattle, buffalo and horses. Bajau market women and traders are a major fixture in most local *tamu* or markets of the Kota Belud and Tuaran districts.

Substantial fishing populations are also present along both coasts of Sabah and over half of the state's native fishing communities are Bajau. Around the coral-fringed islands and deeply embayed coasts of southeastern Sabah, the Bajau regularly fish the area's rich reefs and "coral gardens."

Throughout the 19th century, the Illanun constituted the most feared piratical community in the eastern Malay world. The Illanun are originally a people of the Lake Lanao region of southern Mindanao. During the Spanish colonial period, Illanun communities spread as far as Sumatra, through the Sulu Archipelago and along the north Borneo coast. The present Illanun population of Sabah is small, numbering only 5,000, and lives chiefly along the western coastal plains and in a small enclave at the mouth of the Tungku River on the east coast.

The Ida'an appear to be part of an early population that once inhabited a much greater area of the eastern Sabah coast than they do at present. Today, Ida'an communites are found throughout the Dent Peninsula at the southern edge of Darvel Bay. Numbering around 6,000, they include both Muslims and a small pagan community at Ulu Tungku, the latter calling themselves Bega'ak. For centuries, the Ida'an have owned exclusive collection rights to the limestone birds' nest caves of the region, notably those of the Madai complex.

— *Clifford Sather*

Opposite: *The danger of collecting birds' nests at Gomantong caves is outweighed by the enormous profit. Nests fetch up to US $500 per kilo.* **Below:** *Many Bajau on Sabah's east coast were semi-nomadic until about 30 years ago, living in boats covered with thatch.*

TOMMY CHANG

CORAL REEFS

An Amazing Underwater Ecosystem

Coral reefs, as well as being one of the most beautiful environments on this planet, form some of the largest natural structures in existence and represent one of the most complex and most productive ecosystems on earth. Coral polyps, usually only a few millimeters in size, are interconnected with neighboring polyps and thus share nutrients rather then complete with each other. These interconnections determine the skeletal pattern which is unique to each species of coral.

Reefs occur in different formations, depending on certain factors. The most common form, a fringing reef, extends from a slope up to several hundreds meters seawards, developing around islands and bordering continental land masses. Where irregularities cause the sea bed to rise up close to the surface, reefs may develop if the substrate is suitable. If the top of the reef is irregularly exposed, it is a platform or patch reef; if it lies beneath the surface and is never exposed, it is a bank reef.

Barrier reefs are separated from the adjacent land mass by a relatively deep trench or lagoon. Atolls are reefs that surrounds a central lagoon where portions of the reef can emerge to form an island, with breaks in the reefs allowing access from the sea. Atolls are thought to have began as fringing reefs around islands which subsequently subsided. As long as the rate of subsidence is slow enough, the corals can keep the pace by growing upwards.

Growth-form variations in corals are very readily seen on a reef slope. Corals on the upper slope, exposed to continual pounding from ocean waves, are small, stunted and solidly constructed. Further down the slope, where wave action is less, coral colonies became larger and more delicate, and a much wider range of forms occurs. Still deeper, where there is no wave action but where light availability is reduced, the shapes of the colonies are different again; broad delicate tables and plates and lightly structured branching forms become more common.

Sabah's coastal waters have many coral reefs around numerous islands lying in shallow waters. But there is restricted reef development along the mainland coastline itself.

Unlike Sabah, Sarawak lacks diverse coral communities. Reasons for this include the

TOMMY CHANG

existence of large tracts of muddy shorelines caused by the outflow of a large number of rivers carrying silt, which eventually settles on the sea beds. Coral larvae has to find the right substrate to adhere to before it can establish, and muddy, shifting sea beds are not suitable. Silt also causes very turbid waters which prevent proper penetration of light, eventually clogging the coral's feeding mechanism.

Reefs cannot develop in areas that are periodically inundated with river water, a primary factor controlling coral distribution along the coastlines. Sarawak's coast is lined by a number of major rivers which bring large quantities of fresh water into the coastal areas, thus ensuring a low level of salinity unsuitable to coral growth.

Just minutes away from Kota Kinabalu in Sabah is a group of islands, making up the Tunku Abdul Rahman Park, where it is possible to discover the wonders of coral reefs. This location offers a range of fringing, platform and bank reefs suitable for both snorkelers and scuba divers.

Sabah offers a range of other locations including Pulau Tiga, south of Kota Kinabalu, and Pulau Sipadan, Malaysia's only oceanic island and rated one of the world's top dive spots. Layang Layang, in the middle of the South China Sea, offers the only coral atoll diving in Malaysia and is a diver's dream.

A world of breathtaking beauty

From the basic framework sculptured by the minute coral polyps evolves an assemblage of animals and plants that is hard to equal in terms of abundance and diversity. Amid the gaps, crevices and spaces of the reef live a bewildering range of organisms, the more conspicuous ones being colorful sponges, soft corals, gorgonian fans, brittle stars, feather stars, starfishes, sea whips, sea urchins and snails which occur in every possible hue.

Less noticeable are the sea squirts, coral polyps, snails, crabs, shrimps, lobsters, copepods, worms, sea slugs and a host of others. It is the pelagic or free-swimming organisms, however, that usually attract swimmers' attention — fish in a dizzying display of colors, shapes and sizes.

Reef communities are sadly disappearing. Natural factors such as storms, which usually cause extensive localized damage, are rarely catastrophic as recovery soon takes place. Reefs are, however, very susceptible to the often sudden stresses imposed by large-scale

human activities. These include sedimentation from unplanned land use, land reclamation, fish bombing, coral mining, sand dredging, the collection of corals, and pollution from coastal populations and industries.

Nature's irreplaceable heritage

Not only is the destruction and deterioration of reefs from these causes more serious than from natural causes, it is much more widespread, and usually continuous, thus limiting or even preventing reef recovery. The rich diversity of coral reefs also represents a vast bank of genetic information which has yet to be investigated.

Reefs continually release nutrients into the pelagic food web, indirectly supporting stocks of commercially important fish and crustaceans for the fishing industry. Reefs are also important tourist attractions, and act as a buffer, dispersing wave energy and thus protecting the adjacent coast from erosion. Like Borneo's rainforests, its coral reefs represent a natural heritage that can never be replaced and whose loss might have immeasurable consequences for future generations.

— *Peter Chang*

Opposite: *Coral reefs vie with rainforests as the world's most diverse ecosystem.* **Above left and right:** *An astonishing variety of corals, fish, hard and soft sponges and other organisms provides a vital source of food for fish.*

TAWAU

Exquisite Isles, Caves & Rainforest

Tawau Division, occupying the southeast corner of Sabah, cradles the huge, shallow Darvel Bay and finishes in a maze of swamps around Wallace Bay to the south. The border with Indonesian Borneo (Kalimantan) runs right through the center of Pulau Sebatik across the bay from the town of Tawau.

Although archaeological research has uncovered evidence of human habitation near Darvel Bay some 20,000 years ago, these early people have disappeared. Coffins and shards of pottery found in the region's many limestone caves testify that descendants of the Austronesians, who began arriving in Sabah around 2,500 BC, lived in the region at least 1,000 years ago.

Tawau district is peopled by a mixture of coastal Muslims (Bajau, Suluk, Ida'an and Tidong) with thousands of Indonesians, most of them Buginese from Sulawesi, who work on the area's plantations.

Tawau town is orderly and businesslike, it's main businesses these days being timber logged in the rainforest far to the west. A softwoods plantation, part of a reforestation program, located at the head of Wallace Bay, made it into the *Guinness Book of World Records* with one of its *Albizia falcataria* trees recording the fastest growth of any species, an amazing 30.5 meters in just over five years.

Cocoa plantations once stretched over Tawau's gently rolling hills as far as the eye could see, but these are being increasingly replaced by oil palm, a more stable and profitable commodity.

Tawau Hills Park, a 28,000-hectare reserve of lowland rainforest forming an important catchment area for the town, is located about an hour's drive north. Unfortunately, there is no public transport to the park, and the road, passing through cocoa and oil palm estates, is not marked. The Park, well maintained by Sabah Parks, has a small waterfall with several pools suitable for swimming, a small hot spring and a number of trails through the forest.

You are promised the chance to "see a chocolate tree" if you take a tour organized by Tawau's Hotel Emas. This begins with a visit to a **cocoa plantation**, then goes on to a processing factory, you can see the dried, fermented seeds transformed into cocoa powder, cocoa butter and chocolate.

TOMMY CHANG

If you wander the main highstreet of **Semporna**, where every second man seems to be wearing the white cap proclaiming him a *haji*, a Muslim who has made the pilgrimage to Mecca, its surprising to learn that Semporna, where the British once set up a trading post, was initially settled by Chinese traders. Semporna flourished, despite with attacks and looting in the early days.

The main attraction of Semporna, just 1 1/2 hours by road from Tawau, is a "floating" restaurant offering live crabs, lobsters and grouper, scooped out of huge netted enclosures in the sea when you order; there's also a wide range of other seafood. Built on stilts over the shallow bay to one side of Semporna's jetty, the **Ocean Tourism Centre** consists of the Dragon Inn, offering several rooms and chalets tastefully constructed of timber and thatch, as well as the Pearl City Restaurant.

Crystal waters and coconut groves

The scattering of lovely islands off Semporna are poised for protection and limited tourism development with their gazetting as a marine park approved in 1992. Although Sabah Parks have established an office in Semporna, it will be some time before these islands are formally established as a park and accommodation constructed.

In the meantime, it is possible to hire a fishing boat in Semporna to visit **Pulau Sibuan**, popularly known as Battleship Island. The crystal waters, white sandy beaches and coconut groves make this island the stuff of dreams, although sadly most of the corals have been destroyed by dynamite fishing.

Further afield, the islands of **Pulau Bohey Dulang** and nearby **Gaya,** with their almost vertical outcrops, are actually the rim of a long extinct volcano. The variety of corals around Bohey Dulang is exceptional. Unfortunately, it is not yet possible to visit Bohey Dulang as it is leased to a Japanese company which runs a successful pearl farm.

Diving in a dream world

Arguably the most spectacular island in all of Malaysia — and certainly the only oceanic one, not connected to the continental shelf — the glories of **Pulau Sipadan** are reserved for those who are able to don scuba gear and explore its underwater magic. Visited by nothing more than nesting sea turtles, migrating birds and the occasional fisherman until a decade ago, Sipadan rises up a sheer 600 m

from the floor of the Celebes Sea, mushrooming out to form a 12-hectare island.

In the early 1980s, intrepid divers making their way via Semporna (an hour or so away by fast boat), camped on Sipadan and spent days exploring its wonders. Sipadan is almost too rich and beautiful to be believed with its dazzlingly colorful hard and soft corals blossoming like flowers; its undersea caverns which provide evidence that they were once above sea level; literally dozens of marine turtles swimming fearlessly by; shoals of barracuda; schools of basking white-tip sharks; fat moray eels and a giddying number of vividly coloured tropical fish. Even Jacques Cousteau, who's seen a dive spot or two over the past fifty years, proclaimed Sipadan "an untouched piece of art" and a "jewel".

The first dive company to set up shop on Sipadan was Borneo Divers, who began in 1989 with a few simple thatched huts but have since expanded considerably. As the word spread, other dive operators set up and there are now three basic but comfortable resorts on the island, as well as a jetty running out over the reef to where the jade-green water changes color abruptly to deepest indigo, marking the vertical drop-off.

Opposite and above left: *Tiny Pulau Sipadan attracts divers from around the world.*
Above right: *Semporna's stilt villages are home to the once-nomadic Bajau Laut.*

Concerned about the negative impact of increasing numbers of visitors on this highly fragile ecosystem, the Sabah government has drawn up plans for making Sipadan a marine park and regulating activities there. Unfortunately, a border dispute with Indonesia (which claims Sipadan and nearby Ligatan islands should be part of Kalimantan), has delayed the implementation of such plans.

Divers who knew Sipadan before it was developed talk of a reduction in underwater visibility, yet for the moment, the marine life remains among the richest that can be experienced anywhere in the world.

The island is also an important nesting site for Nicobar pigeons, as well as 46 other species of bird. The turtle population — one of the unique features of Sipadan — is under threat owing to egg collection by a family claiming rights granted by the Sultan of Sulu a century ago, and by more development than such a small island can support. The only chance for Sipadan's long-term preservation is to ban all human habitation on the island, something unlikely to happen in the near future.

For the moment, however, Sipadan remains an island of astonishing beauty. To see it at its best, avoid weekends and peak holiday periods, when day trippers and snorkelers join the groups of divers intent on discovering Sipadan's exquisite underwater environment.

Beware of pirates

Kunak, just over an hour by mini-bus through endless oil palm plantations from Semporna, has little to merit a pause, apart from some excellent and ridiculously inexpensive seafood sold in restaurants in the old wooden shophouses on the right of the road. Try Vui Kee which has that rarity, an English menu, on the wall and serves excellent Teochew-style steamed fish. Although there are several beautiful islands off Kunak, such

as Pulau Adal (three hours away), and the closer Silumpit, locals will advise you not to risk hiring a boat to go there because of the very real risk of pirate attack.

Madai Caves, their edible birds' nests harvested for centuries by the Ida'an people, are located in a limestone outcrop just 13 km from Kunak. Getting right to Madai Caves by public transport can be a bit inconvenient; if you can't persuade the mini-bus to make a diversion for you, it's a rather hot two-km walk from the highway. (You should have no

difficulty in picking up another mini-bus heading for Lahad Datu or Semporna on the highway before late afternoon.) Madai's limestone massif has some 25 cave chambers, one of which has a small river running through it.

Although less accessible than the Gomantong Caves near Sandakan, Madai Caves are more interesting and well worth exploring in company of a local guide, who will probably also point out the remains of ancient coffins found here.

The legend of the golden deer

The Ida'an, coastal people converted to Islam during the 15th century, have jealously guarded their rights to the collection of the valuable edible birds' nests, and have documents recording these rights for more than twenty generations. Each patch of cave is, to this day, under private ownership. According to Ida'an beliefs, the caves were discovered by a local hero, Apoi, who was led here by a golden deer which he tried, but failed, to kill.

The Madai Caves are still subject to many superstitions and traditional practices, and government officials politely request permission before entering the caves. The Wildlife Department advises (but cannot enforce) harvesting periods to ensure the continued existence of the swiftlets, so the Ida'ans will not "kill the bird that makes the golden nest".

To protect the nests from theft, guards sleep within the caves day and night throughout the year. A village of crazily jumbled wooden houses clusters at the base of the caves, with other shacks jostling each other for space right at the mouth of a couple of caves. During the harvesting season, the village is transformed into a hive of activity with as many as 500 workers involved in the dangerous task of scraping the nests from the walls and roofs of the caves. Phone the Wildlife Department in Lahad Datu, (089) 84416, to check on the harvesting season, generally in May, September and December.

Madai Waterfall, obliging close to the main road, slides over a rocky lip to fall around 20 meters into a wide pool below. Unfortunately, logging upstream has turned the once-clear waters to a murky brown.

Visitors to **Lahad Datu** will find it a small but busy town in a stage of transition as its stilt villages gradually give way to reclamation, and old open-air markets are supplemented by a gleaming, blue-tiled edifice on the waterfront. The main reason for coming to Lahad Datu, which has an airport, is to travel on into the **Danum Valley Conservation Area**, within an immense forest concession belonging to a subsidiary of the Sabah Foundation.

Studying the rainforest

Experiencing the virgin tropical rainforest, with its complex interaction of plants, insects, birds and mammals, is often a lot more difficult than one might expect in most of Borneo today. Experiencing it in comfort is an even more elusive dream, but one that can be realized at the Danum Valley Field Centre. Located within the huge Sabah Foundation forest concession southwest of Lahad Datu, the 438-sq-km Danum Valley Conservation Area was set aside for research and education in 1981, and the field centre opened in 1986.

While tourism is not one of the priorities of the Field Centre, it is possible for interested visitors to visit Danum Valley. The international-standard Borneo Rainforest Lodge is due to open at the end of 1993, but in the meantime, visitors can stay in the comfortable resthouse or hostel and explore some of the 50 km of trails leading through the forest, go on a night drive searching for the many nocturnal creatures, bird-watch from the observation towers and even frolic quite unscientifically in the Segama River.

All of Sabah's mammals are known to exist within the Conservation Area, although don't expect to see them in profusion — the rainforest is a very different environment to the open savannahs of Africa or of southern Nepal. Conscious of its role in education as well as research (and there are always several on-going projects carried out by foreign as well as Malaysian scientists), the Field Centre has several self-guided trails with explanatory notes, as well as guides to help reveal the mysteries of the rainforest.

The buildings of the Field Centre are located right on the Segama River, which is spanned by a suspension bridge, the perfect viewing platform for watching the giant flying squirrels at dusk as they launch off from their favorite tree to glide for up to 300 m across the river.

Around 240 species of bird, including all of Sabah's hornbills, are found in Danum Valley. The Field Center's star is a solemn Buffy Fish Owl, which invariably astonishes visitors with its fearlessness, until they learn that he was reared here.

Apart from the profusion of plant and animal life in Danum Valley, there are also several rocky overhangs where burial jars and other items have been unearthed, traces of habitation by the Orang Sungei centuries ago.

— *Wendy Hutton*

Opposite, left: *A cleverly camouflaged lizard.* **Opposite, right:** *Even fungi can be surprisingly beautiful.* **Below:** *Ida'an birds' nesters have been harvesting Madai Caves for more than 20 generations.*

ALBERT TEO

PART IV

Southwest Sarawak

In the early days, what little was known about Borneo was not encouraging. The coast was regularly swept by pirate fleets from Sulu and other parts of the southern Philippines. Local pirates, or natives bent upon a spot of inter-tribal warfare, issued from any of the bigger rivers at the drop of a hat. The island itself was inhabited by fierce headhunters, men with tails, and cannibals, for all one knew. It was such a pity those gold and diamond deposits were so inaccessible...

Englishman James Brooke must have heard just such stories in Singapore in 1839, but he agreed to take a letter to the ruler of Sarawak anyway. He was a young man invalided out of the East India Company, owner of a small inheritance and sizeable "yacht", on his way to see the world.

An English oriental potentate

Brooke found the Brunei Viceroy of Sarawak and settled at his one-boat capital of Kuching. The Viceroy was a pleasant gentleman, languidly engaged in putting down "a little trouble" among his local subjects. Would the visitor be interested to lend a hand? In return for certain privileges, like the governorship of a rather troublesome little province?

This, in very broad outline, is what happened. Brooke's imagination was fired by the idea of becoming an oriental potentate. He saw much that was wrong in Sarawak, and he intended to put it right. A few Brunei and local Malays resented Brooke's interference with their hereditary perquisites, like fleecing the Dayaks. The pirates were a perennial problem, complicated by the fact that Iban tribes weren't averse to joining Malay-led maritime looting expeditions.

Brooke's energetic efforts at "pacification" involved the Royal Navy, and soon he had the Society for the Protection of Aborigines down on him. In 1857 he lost his house and goods, and nearly his life, to a rebellion of Chinese goldminers. But Brooke rule sur-vived. The gold and diamonds proved rather more scanty than supposed in Singapore; profitable agriculture pre-supposed a pool of labor which simply didn't exist.

James was succeeded in 1868 by his nephew. Charles Brooke wasn't the Byronic hero his uncle had been but he was an able administrator. The official chronicle entry for 1871 reads: "Sarawak Budget Balanced for the First Time."

What's in a name?

Sarawak, or Serawak in old Malay, means antimony, a mineral used as medicine and dyestuff. Small quantities of it were mined in the catchment of the Sarawak and adjoining rivers. One river thus gave its name to the whole state, expanding eastwards as the White Rajahs deftly moved the survey pegs at the expense of their nominal overlord, the Sultan of Brunei.

In the days before roads, practically all settlements in Borneo were built on the waterways. A small stream joining the main river provided drinking water, and the township's name: Sungai Mata Kuching has lent its name to Kuching. Mata Kuching ("cat's eye") refers to a fruit of the lychee family; the hill at the confluence is Bukit Mata Kuching ("cat's eye hill") because the trees were abundant there.

Cute stories about The Town Called Cat abound. Rajah James is supposed to have asked a Malay: "What's that?", pointing to the township, but the simple native saw a cat by the waterfront and answered: "*Itu kuching.*" (It's a cat). In Sarawak Malay, however, "cat" is *pusa*, and the town was known as Kuchin (possibly *kochin*, "harbor" in Chinese) long

Overleaf: *His back covered with tattoos, an Iban acts as lookout in a boat heading upriver.*
Opposite: *An Iban shaman slashes with his mandau to destroy any evil spirits lurking in the longhouse. Photos by Jill Gocher.*

before James Brooke set eyes on it.

On another level, however, the changing of road and town names is a party game played with gusto by those who have nothing more urgent to do. Within the last two decades the country town Simanggang has become "Sri Aman Binatang "Bintangor," Nonok "Asajaya," Tanjung Mani "Tanjung Manis," Muara Tuang "Kota Samarahan," Pendam "Sadong Jaya" and 10th Mile "Kota Pedawan." There are no plans at present to change Kuching to "Anjing" (dog), but watch this space.

The infrequent traveler is the real loser; he who was here ten years ago and wants to travel on his own again. A tourist on his way to Skrang who asks for the Simanggang bus may be directed to the Semongok one. With good intention: Semongok, 21 km out of town, is the Wildlife Rehabilitation Centre, a place much frequented by fair-haired strangers with hazy pronunciation.

Defining the Dayak

Borneo is inhabited by Chinese, Malays and Dayaks. Question: What is a Dayak? Answer: That depends on who's speaking. Not a Dayak, anyway. "Dayak" gained currency among Dutch and British explorers in the 19th century. They heard it from the trusty guides engaged at the coast.

Locally the term *dayak* has connotations of "inland people." So does Bidayuh, the erstwhile "Land Dayaks" who inhabit the longhouses nearest to Kuching. Retreating from aggressive neighbors, the Bidayuh built their homes in the hills of the upper Sadong, Sarawak and Kayan rivers. The common characteristics of this fragmented group are hill rice farming, a men's meeting house or "headhouse," an egalitarian society, and the ingenious use of bamboo for anything and everything.

The men's house is built separately from the Bidayuh longhouse. In the past it served as the sleeping place for bachelors, visitors, and the occasional sulking husband. In case of an attack, able-bodied young men swarmed out from the headhouse to fend off the foe. Here the community's head trophies were suspended above the central hearth. Here meetings and ceremonies were held, important visitors officially welcomed.

Melanau or Malay?

The Melanau are now found mostly in the Rajang delta and further east, although they previously must have lived along the coast;

some coastal people who consider themselves "Malay" are likely to be Melanau who have embraced Islam. Until recently times the trend was for a Muslim convert to "become Malay."

Living between the tides, the Melanau are fearless fishermen who venture to sea daily in mere cockleshells. The Melanau resemble Orang Ulu in that their society used to be strongly stratified. The lower classes owed the aristocrats obedience and unpaid labor.

Pathways

To the south and southeast of Sarawak, a watershed of steep hills and mountains forms the boundary between the state and Indonesian Borneo (Kalimantan). The coastal plains consist of alluvium swept down over the thousands of years. Most of the coastline and the estuaries are swampy, with settlements generally found upriver. Far to the northeast of the Kuching, the watershed of the Rajang is hilly, although few mountains are over 1,500 meters high.

Whoever described Borneo as a "trackless wilderness" and its nomadic tribesmen as "lost" was merely describing himself. The wilderness has been crossed from coast to coast for centuries, by traders, jungle-produce collectors, warriors and migrants.

Great rivers were Borneo's main traffic arteries until the middle of this century. All of them rise in the island's central knot of mountains, fall over the rim of the high plateau and then wind their way through the alluvial plains to the coast. Rapids in the middle course were an effective barrier to large-scale travel and trade, and still are. The interior developed separately, a "*World Within*" (see Further Reading).

"Free creatures of the forest"

The fringe of Borneo has been known to seafarers and traders since time immemorial. Local chieftains set themselves up in the river mouths. Some of these settlements evolved into mighty kingdoms, like Brunei which once claimed tribute from most of present-day Sabah and Sarawak. A coastal chieftain's rule over the interior tribes was tenuous to say the least. On the whole he left them well enough alone, unless mutual arrangements were made for warfare and piracy. No river-mouth princeling ever tried to enforce obedience from upriver "subjects." When a Kayan headman from the Baram heard that Brunei had generously donated his tribe to the Rajah of Sarawak, he pointed out scornfully that he and his people were "free creatures of the forest, none of the Sultan's poultry yard."

For traveling in the old days, the basic division was between the sail and the paddle. The main rivers could be ascended as far as the first rapids in sailing ships, above that a dozen pairs of strong arms were needed. As river currents are so strong, ships headed up river only on a rising tide.

Campsite etiquette

But even the gorges of the mountain massifs are not trackless terrain. The path is marked into day marches. At the end of each there is a camp site, roughly levelled. Remains of the last wayfarers' hut still stand, a stack of firewood is ready. Some of the travelers set to lighting a fire for boiling the rice pot, others make quick repairs to the hut. Before departure the next morning, it is imperative that a fresh supply of wood be stacked for the next group of travelers.

The Bidayuh of Southwest Sarawak walk, for days if necessary; some of them manage boats only awkwardly. Here too the etiquette of the pathway is observed: shelters and firewood supplies are maintained at convenient halting spots. At watersheds and river crossings, a special sign reminds traveling parties to make a brief halt: a bamboo water pipe is found in the branches of a tree or between two rocks, for travelers to take a few puffs before carefully putting it back in its dry place for the next smoker.

Of roads and rivers

As the 20th century creeps towards its end, so roads creep forward, around and into Borneo. The 4-wheel drive vehicle is still recommended for serious travel, but a reasonably sturdy car will take a family from Kuching to Sibu, from Miri to Bintulu, and up several feeder roads. New longhouses and villages spring up along the roads, some hastily built with little thought about hygiene and water supply. The main roads bypass existing bazaars (village trading posts) as much as possible, but a ferry crossing attracts sellers of drinks, snacks and local produce who have a captive clientele in the drivers waiting for their turn.

The road is supplementing the river, not replacing it. River boats have come a long way from the chugging steamers of the 1950s. Locally built express boats, named *Concorde* and *Hoover*, *Happiness* and *Heineken*, are air-conditioned capsules with sealed windows which whiz along at great speed. One of the most popular express routes is Kuching-Sarikei-Sibu; the traveler can now choose between air (40 minutes), road (6 hours) and sea/river (4 hours).

— *Heidi Munan*

Below: "Mr Brooke's Bungalow" *shows the modest home of Sarawak's first rajah.*

IBAN

A Lively and Mobile People

The Iban, at 30% of the population are, by far the largest indigenous group in Sarawak, They comprise one half of the total number of persons engaged in agriculture (largely dry-rice cultivation and small holdings of rubber and pepper). They are found throughout Sarawak, especially in lowlands, living mostly in longhouses along streams and river banks.

The Iban are also sometimes incorrectly called Sea Dayaks; this is because in the 1840s, when the Ibans were first contacted by Europeans, some of them were found in the company of Malay pirates. In order to describe them differently from the Biyayuh, whom the Europeans called Land Dayaks because they were found living in the interior hills, the Iban were called Sea Dayaks.

Life is rice and rice is life

Hill rice cultivation, the core of Iban culture, dominates the annual social and economic life cycle of the Iban in the longhouse. Rice cultivation is associated with all kinds of rituals, folklore, and beliefs. As shifting cultivation of rice requires large areas of land, in the past the Iban became land hungry and therefore aggressive and expansionist, developing martial values and skills. The Iban social organization, including the *bilek*-family and longhouse system, were geared towards making them mobile, individualistic and aggressive, a combination which helped them achieve common goals.

A community under one roof

The Iban are skilled iron workers, making sharp *parangs* or machete, and large war canoes. The women weave beautifully designed cotton blankets by the *ikat* method (that is, tying bunches of colored threads to form intricate designs). Iban women also wear elaborate costumes during festivities.

Iban material culture developed along simple and practical lines, centered around the requirements of hill rice farming, war and ritual activities. Old Chinese jars, brassware, gongs, beads, head-trophies and brass cannon were, and often still are, highly valued; each family in a longhouse possessing a number of these items.

The longhouse: a village community living under one roof, is the heart of Iban life. It probably originated as a means of collective

defense. A longhouse is usually situated near the banks of a river, and on average contains 14 "doors" or apartments (*bilek*) in which families live. Normally, a family consists of six people, containing three generations: the couple, their children and their grandparents. Most longhouse families are related, but there is no common property. Each family has its own farmland, family apartment and room, and is responsible for the maintenance, from the private areas to the passageway outside the room (the *ruai,*) and the drying platform outside.

Communicating with the spirits

The unshakable conviction that all beings possess a separable soul is the foundation of Iban belief system. Their pantheon includes intricate cults relating to rice-cultivation, healing, the dead and headhunting. The soul of the Iban is a means of communicating with the unknown powers through dreams and other ethereal encounters, when the gods appear before the fortunate ones.

After dreams, the second important means of communication with the spirit world is through ritual festivals or *gawai*. The celebration of all *gawai* involves a general pattern of rites. First, sacrificial offerings (*piring*) are made; secondly, there is a cleansing ceremony (*biau*) which involves invocation and waving of cockerels; and thirdly, the most important part of the festival, the prolonged chanting of a sacred texts (*timang* or *pengap*) by ritual experts or bards (*lemambang*).

Gawai are of varying scope and significance. They can be classified into four main classes: rituals connected with cultivation of rice; rituals connected with health and longevity; those concerning the acquisition of wealth and, finally, *gawai* connected with headhunting and prestige.

Leaving the longhouse

Nowadays, many Iban have left their rural longhouses and farms to work in Sarawak towns or in neighboring Brunei, or even overseas. When this happened in the past, it could have been attributed to the Iban custom of *bejalai*, where men — especially unmarried men — leave their villages to undertake any journeys that give them material profit and social prestige.

This has now turned into an exodus of not just available manpower, but whole families. More often than not, longhouses are half-deserted, and visitors to these famed, hospitable people are greeted by the old folk and children; the only ones left behind to provide some semblance of longhouse living. Some Iban now believe that longhouse life, with its economic dependence on cash crops, is no longer viable. Economic pressure has already caused many Iban to reluctantly leave the comfort of their longhouses to earn wages in urban centers.

The taste of urban living

This trend will persist until the price of commodities rises, when it could then be economically viable for them to return. But it is not certain that families will ever return to their longhouses, or at least to the kind of life they were used to. Having tasted urban living, it would be difficult for them to readjust to rural life, especially the children who generally prefer to be educated in towns and enjoy other aspects of modern living.

What seems to be the trend is not only that more Iban are beginning to be urbanized, but are also beginning to develop skills in various jobs, such as carpentry, plastering, other building skills, and working in the petroleum industry.

— *Peter M. Kedit*

Opposite: *The hornbill or kenyalang is sacred to the Iban, who believe it is a messenger from the spirit world.* **Below:** *A typical Iban man returns from a day at his farm.*

JILL GOCHER

HORNBILL

Sacred Bird of the Iban

One of the most striking birds in the world, the huge hornbill, has been adopted as Sarawak's national emblem, although it is found throughout Borneo. The hornbill's most dramatic feature is its long "double-decker" bill, consisting of a deep beak with a projection known as a casque on top. Hornbills are renowned not only for their distinctive calls but for the loud "whooshing" noise they make as they fly, rather like a low-flying plane.

Eight species of hornbill are found in Borneo, basically blackish or dark brown in color, with white markings on the tail. They have a mixed diet, feeding on fruits as well as insects, lizards, small birds and even small mammals. They are among the most important agents of seed dispersal for rainforest trees and lianas, especially those with large, oily or astringent fruits not favored by smaller

MORTON STRANGE

birds or by monkeys and apes.

All hornbills have an unusual method of nesting. The female enters a spacious hole in a large tree, then imprisons herself by blocking up the entrance with droppings, along with clay and wood added by the male. A narrow slit is left, through which the male and other related hornbills feed the female while she lays her egg(s) and later tends her young. When the youngster is ready to fly away, she knocks down the mud wall.

At least one hornbill species occurs in most of the accessible forests in Sabah, Sarawak and Brunei. Probably the best chance of seeing several species in the wild during a short visit to Sarawak is in Gunung Mulu National Park, while the lower Kinabatangan area and Danum Valley are recommended for visitors to Sabah.

Sarawak's state emblem

Perhaps the best-known of all the species, and the one which is Sarawak's state emblem, is the black-and-white rhinoceros hornbill. The bill is yellow, with bright red coloring on the casque. This hornbill plays an important role in the culture of the Ibans of Sarawak, being regarded as a bird of omen.

The helmeted hornbill has an extraordinary tail, about 60 centimeters in length. Its casque, unlike that of other species, is heavy and solid. In the past, this casque was one of Borneo's most valuable trade items, for the Chinese carved it like ivory. This bird makes a series of "poops" which become faster and merge into a maniacal cackle.

The wreathed hornbill, common in the hill ranges of eastern Sabah is distinguished by a bright yellow patch on its throat and a call like the yelp of a small dog. Similar to this hornbill but smaller, with a white throat pouch and red casque, is the rare wrinkled hornbill, a mysterious bird rarely seen away from remote coastal forests.

The dark grey-brown bushy-crested hornbill is perhaps the least attractive but most common of all the species in the hill ranges. The handsome black hornbill occurs only in the lowlands, occasionally startling the newcomer with sounds which bring to mind a retching pig. The closely-related pied hornbill lives in forests along large rivers. Finally, the white-crowned hornbill is the most bizarre of Borneo species, with a white "hat" of feathers and the habit of skulking in dense vegetation so that it cannot be seen as it utters its subdued, syncopated "mm-papa's."

— *Junaidi Payne*

PUA-KUMBU

Weavers of Spell-binding Iban textiles

One of the most surprising discoveries for a visitor to an Iban longhouse is the magnificent *pua-kumbu*, a woven treasure whose name literally means "blanket." No such mundane function as wrapping someone during sleep ever befalls the *pua-kumbu*, for these are ritual textiles used in religious ceremonies and festivals associated with birth, death, healing or "soul searching," and war or, in the old days, head-hunting.

Traditionally, the woven cloths are a status symbol in the longhouse community, equal to the value of old ceramic jars or brass cannons. Among Iban women, the ability to weave skillfully, create designs and to mix the vegetable dye earns the woman a high status in her community, similar to that which head-hunting once gave the men.

The making of the *pua-kumbu* is a complex process that begins with the soaking of the cotton yarn in a mordant bath imparting the potency to the yarn to absorb the blood-red colour. A simple rectangular frame is prepared, and the cotton yarn, arranged in groups of thread, is stretched over it. Using strands of the dried leaves coated with bees' wax, the weaver then wraps and ties (*ikat*) the warp threads to form the patterns and designs of the *pua-kumbu*. Being tied-up, these threads will resist the brown/red colour dye when the entire lot is taken off the frame and dipped in the dye-bath, retaining the original beige colour of the cotton.

Once dry, the warp threads are put back onto the frame and the areas which the weaver desires to retain the brown/red colour are wrapped and tied. With a second dye-bath of indigo blue, the design process of the weaving is completed. The top end of the warp threads are then stretched out over a fixed rod (warp beam) between two poles of the weaver's room. The lower end of the threads are held down by another rod (breast beam). A back-strap made of bark is attached to this breast beam. By strapping herself to the breast beam, the weaver is able to keep the entire warp taut. The actual process of weaving and beating in the weft threads is relatively simple compared to the design and composition on the warp threads. No sketches are done beforehand — everything is conceived in the weaver's mind.

Divine inspiration

Traditionally, designs are spiritually inspired. The weaving goddess who ordains weavers also reveals new patterns to them. Thus, the imagery of the *pua-kumbu* evolves around Iban animistic beliefs, the spiritual realm and the world around them (trees, animals, insects, jungle life and so on). Designs are therefore vested with meaning and energy. Important ritual weavings, *pua-mali*, are woven by a select group of master-weavers.

Pua-kumbu designs and their place in traditional Iban culture have held researchers and scholars spell-bound for decades, while their undeniable beauty and complexity fascinate even the novice. Iban textile art is without doubt among the finest warp-*ikat* weaving found anywhere in the world.

— *Edric Ong*

Opposite: *Although there are eight varieties of hornbill, it is the striking rhinoceros species that is Sarawak's state emblem.* **Below:** *The most skilful women weavers earned a status similar to headhunters among the Ibans.*

JILL GOCHER

KUCHING

The Charms of a Town Called Cat

Kuching is a town of immediate appeal. New arrivals may be momentarily disappointed because tourism posters had promised them thatch roofs, beads and feathers, but the town's charm soon takes over. The old buildings along the river could have been designed for picture postcards. Darkling crooked lanes in the Old Town enchant all but lorry drivers. Rustic river ferries make talk of a second bridge rank heresy.

The good citizens of Kuching are inclined to agree, on the whole, that their town is under special protection. Literally so — Sabah's main settlements were reduced to rubble in 1941 and again in 1945. Miri found the consecutive attentions of the Japanese and the Australian armed forces devastating. The few bombs dropped on Kuching only set fire to a fuel store instead of hitting their presumed target, Fort Margherita.

Straight across the river from the Fort stands the main temple, **Tua Pek Kong.** Its situation on a rocky outcrop at the confluence of two rivers, facing distant hills, commanded the best possible *feng shui* (geomantic influence), but the waterfront improvements of 1928 put the creek into pipes. The temple's view of distant hills was partly obscured by the Chinese Court (built by Rajah Charles Vyner on purpose, so some Chinese grouched at the time, to depress their community's excessive good luck) and by the new Secretariat. Traffic, instead of water, now washes around the shrine's foundations. But judging by the steady stream of devotees and the clouds of incense that billow forth on feast days, it may be inferred that there's still quite a lot of *feng shui* left.

The temple stands at the east end of the old town, the Malay mosque at the west — also in an auspicious position by Chinese standards. The new **Kuching Mosque** is of Moorish-style design with many gold cupolas. In the early days, when Kuching consisted of three dozen huts, the Malay *kampung* clustered around the house of prayer. In this village lived the Abangs of Kuching, high-ranking Malays led by their Datus. The main thoroughfare was called "Datus Road" as it led from Datu to Datu. (It is now called Jalan Datuk Abijah Abol.)

Today, the *kampung* spreads out along a loop of the river, as far as the old and new

bridges at Satok. (Satok suspension bridge was built in 1926 to carry the pipes which bring water from Mt. Matang to Kuching.)

From mansions to humbler houses

A few old houses in the *kampung* are beautifully kept, in particular No 504 and 507 at the bend of **Jalan Datuk Ajibah Abol**. The well-to-do Abangs had their residences built by carpenters and carvers specially imported from Java. Humbler houses share many features with these mansions, in particular the floor-level windows, guarded by carved railings, which admit a cooling breeze on people who sit, work and sleep on mats on the floor.

All of Kuching can easily be viewed in a morning's stroll. Make that a leisurely stroll, broken by cool drinks at a marble-topped table in a coffee shop— visitors who get nagging headaches in the tropics may be suffering from mild dehydration.

The old town is built mostly in the southern Chinese style, testimony to the Hokkien and Teochew immigrants who made their homes here in the last century. The main traffic lane was the river and tidal inlets, still indicated by the strange layout of the older roads: Main Bazaar and Gambier Road fronted the busy waterway, while the parallel India Street and Carpenter Street represent the town's early expansion.

Brooke's Kuching started with a Residence, a Fort and a Church, all within hollering distance of each other. The **Astana**, built by Rajah Charles in 1870, is now the official residence of Sarawak's Governor and thus closed to the public. But it can be photographed in its graceful setting from the Pangkalan Batu ("stone jetty") next to the original fort site.

White Rajahs and rebellion

That fort was burnt down by rebellious gold-miners in 1857 (defended by wardens, prisoners and a lunatic!), but the **Square Tower** stands in its place. The *tambang* ferry jetty lies behind this convenient landmark, next to the old Sarawak Steamship Company *godown* (warehouse), now the **Sarawak Tourist Information Centre**.

The riverside along Main Bazaar was undergoing a drastic beautification in 1992-3, with a landscaped area replacing many of the old *godowns* which once lined the river.

Across the road from the Square Tower is another cherished symbol of Brooke rule, the **Court House**. Constructed in 1874 to replace what residents referred to as a "barn," it housed all government offices at the time. Rajah Charles could sit over breakfast on the verandah of his residence and

Opposite: Fort Margherita, named after the second rajah's wife, dominates the river bank opposite the Old Town. Most of Kuching's colonial buildings remain intact.

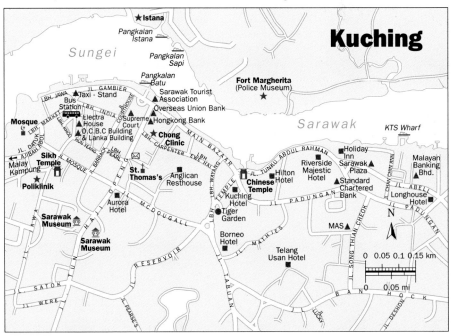

check on the punctuality (or otherwise) of the civil servants, gold watch on the table, spyglass to his one good eye.

The building now houses the "High Court in Borneo," and is open to the public. The Court Chamber has a remarkable ceiling painted in traditional motifs by a group of native artists. Visitors are reminded to dress decently and preserve respectful demeanor if they drop in while the court is in session. Landwards from the Court stand the **Round Tower**, the pseudo-Greek **Post Office**, and a fantastic plaster confection known as The Pavilion.

For a late breakfast of the best *siow bee* pork dumplings in town, try **Fook Hoi** coffee shop just opposite the Post Office. Its remarkable name made the establishment an immediate hit with Commonwealth troops during Confrontation in the sixties.

On a little hillock behind these temporalities stands **St.Thomas Cathedral**, Sarawak's first church. The Cathedral Compound, a lovely old park, is open to the public. Kuching's oldest building, **Bishop's House** (1849), is not. The former boarding house of the girls' school is now run by the Anglican Mission as an economical travelers' hostel. **St.Thomas School** (1886) with its twin turrets is another Brooke-era building Kuching is proud of, but all pales before Sarawak Museum.

The **Sarawak Museum**, which celebrated its centenary in 1991, is justly famous for housing a comprehensive and well kept Borneo collection started by Rajah Charles. It is spread over two buildings, the Old (a remarkably stately edifice) housing the ethnographic and natural history sections, the New, archaeology and a matchless set of antique ceramics. The Museum is open seven days a week, from 9 am to 6 pm.

Joggers, cows and blunderbusses

The **Reservoir Park** in the hills beyond the Museum holds what used to be Kuching's main water supply. A winding road leads from that popular dawn-jogging venue towards the Chinese temple; this used to be the course of the river, Sungei Mata Kuching. The shophouses a long **Tabuan Road** here, with massive woodwork and heavy roofs of China tiles, are probably the oldest in Kuching. They were spared when a fire devastated most of Main Bazaar in 1884.

A second bridge is planned, but it will be built several miles upriver. It certainly won't affect the little ferry boats (*tambang*) plying the river. The most popular jetty is **Pangkalan Batu,** which lies behind the Square Tower, where passengers embark for Pangkalan Sapi ("cow jetty," as the opposite landing point is called because the Rajah's dairy cows grazed near the Astana).

The best way to visit **Fort Margherita** is by boat. From Pangkalan Sapi it is but a short walk up Fort Hill. The Fort is inside the Police School so visitors are asked to produce some identification. Named after the second Rajah's lady, the Fort was completed in 1879. It served mostly constabulary purposes and is now a **Police Museum** stocked with old uniforms, brass cannon, blunderbusses and gruesome pirate swords. Executions used to be carried out in the fort yard. Visitors with a taste for the macabre can inspect Death Row, the gallows, and realistic wall paintings depicting various other creative termination methods used in Sarawak over the decades.

Kuching's eclectic architecture

Until the 1920s, Kuching town stretched from Mosque to Temple. A steep path led up to a few select residences on Bukit Mata Kuching, including that of the Borneo Company Manager. After a road had been built around the front of the temple, Padungan became part of town. The shophouses of **Padungan** were built in the 1920s and 30's, financed by the rubber boom. This road is wide, straight, tree-lined. False gables adorn houses, some topped by ornamental stone balustrades or birds. Behind this elegant thoroughfare, between the shops and the river, Kuching's first industrial quarter sprang up between the wars. Shady Padungan Road is ideal for a morning or late afternoon stroll.

There's a bonus offered: walk to the end and you'll see the **Great Cat of Kuching,** paw raised in benediction, bottom turned somewhat disdainfully towards the town, alas! The Great Cat, a magnificent piece of vintage kitsch, is a labor of love by self-taught artist, Yong Kee Yet, who has been making plaster creatures for each year of the Chinese zodiac, including: a monkey, a tiger, a snake, an ox. These statues are displayed each New Year at the front gate of his home where they attracted much attention. People bring along children dressed in their best New Year outfits to be photographed with the auspicious creatures. The Great Cat was unveiled in 1988 to celebrate Kuching's elevation from municipality to city status. It is still a popular backdrop for family photos.

More of Kuching can be seen by **bus**. The

bus stops bear the numbers of the lines which serve them but the blue-and-white (or grey) town buses have numbers only, not names. White-and-colored buses serve the wider Kuching area. Green-and-yellow and red-and-yellow are up-country buses, most of them with names like "Bau," and "Serian," as well as numbers. When in doubt, ask. Getting into an up-country bus by mistake could involve a very long trip.

Handmade souvenirs of Sarawak

To visit Kuching's famous **potteries**, however, you need to get into an up-country bus for the first eight km of its journey. Just tell the driver you want to be dropped at the potteries, or *kilang pasu*. The return trip starts from across the road. The original kilns stood by the river's edge, at Tanah Puteh ("white earth" i.e. clay beds); now they are a little out of town. These potteries once produced utility ware: tall water jars, curry and casserole pots, pickling basins, medicine teapots.

Most switched to the tourist market in the 1980s, colorfully decorated vases and small dishes that fit into even the most overflowing suitcase. But don't let the size of a really nice urn discourage you—the potteries are well equipped to pack and ship large items for their customers. Just be prepared for a longish wait. The Chinese owner of a pottery may be Henghua or Foochow, but nearly all of Sarawak's working potters are Teochew.

The craft has long descended from father to son, or at least nephew. A few modernzations have crept in: the ground-level kick-wheel is still used, but is now mechanically driven. A pug-mill takes over the work of foot-kneading fresh clay. Some potteries have started to cast intricate pieces in molds, though purists frown on such frivolity.

The master potter at **Ng Hua Seng Pottery** (on the right side of the road if traveling from town) is one of the best craftsmen. Don't expect small talk or smiles for the camera from Ng Hua Ann (smiling isn't exactly his line anyway), just admire his skilled hands, and click away. The more with-it potteries fire their wares with gas, but some still use the tunnel or "dragon" kiln. The kiln is loaded, the door bricked up, the fire started. The gods' kind assistance is solicited by fragrant joss sticks above the firing pit. Even seasoned potters still get a thrill out of knocking away the bricks after the kiln has cooled, getting that first glance at the success (or otherwise) of a week's work after the firing. Each pottery has a shop, but it's quite in order for visitors to stroll around the working area. Just be sure you don't get in the way.

— *Heidi Munan*

Below: *Typical Kuching scene, with Chinese shophouses lining the street and the Moorish Kuching Mosque in the background.*

TRIPS FROM KUCHING

From Potted Culture to Pitcher Plants

The area of Kuching and its neighboring Divisions is well served with roads and amenities. Interesting excursions can be undertaken by public bus or boat without the trouble of guides, porters, maps and compasses —or search parties.

The area of **Santubong/Damai,** around the mouth of the Sarawak River, is being developed into a major tourism area. Besides good tourist hotels and a golf course, the **Damai Cultural Village** is a main attraction there. This village concentrates Sarawak's 124,000 square kilometers into a mere 6 hectares. Typical houses represent the major racial groups: Iban, Malay, Bidayuh, Melanau, Chinese, Orang Ulu and Penan. Costumed guides introduce visitors to each house and explain its salient features.

Dance performances called "Cultural Shows" are given at regular hours. A terrace restaurant and a souvenir shop complete the outfit. Touristy? Yes, and meant to be. Here the past is preserved, the Sarawak many a visitor had dreamt of: quaintly rugged homes without TV or plumbing, colorfully dressed natives in beads and feathers. In contrast, the satin, sequins and fringe used for "modern traditional" costumes are more than a litle garish, but for an easily accessible summary of times past Damai Cultural Village is hard to beat.

Like a miniature Matterhor, **Santubong** mountain looms majestically over the west mouth of the Sarawak River. A sizeable trading town stood on the site of Santubong village roughly 1,000 years ago, with Chinese and Indian traders bartering textiles, ceramics and beads for jungle produce, kingfisher feathers and edible birds' nests.

On the tidal swamp of Sungei Jaong is a mysterious set of decorated boulders the most prominent, *Batu Gambar,* is decorated with a spread-eagled human figure. To see these puzzling stones (for no one can explain who made them or for what purpose), turn off the road from Kuching just before the 6 km sign, where there is a small reed mat hut; 30 m on from this, between a couple of boulders, a footpath leads from the road to the left. Follow it through farmlands, some rubber gardens and secondary jungle, a distance of about 2 km to where the boulders lie brooding in the forest.

Southwest Sarawak

Semongok or **Semongoh** (both spellings may be found on maps) is a wildlife rehabilitation centre 20 km south of Kuching. Orangutan which were kept illegally as pets are liberated here, and if necessary taught "jungle skills" by (human) wardens. The center is half an hour's walk, some of it uphill, from the main road; good shoes and a reasonable standard of fitness are recommended. There is a motor road down to the center's office, but tour buses aren't allowed on it. Only genuine emergencies (excluding blistered heels or shortage of breath) may be evacuated by jeep, the rest of us have got to hoof it back the way we came.

Semongok is due to become a research center in the near future, when it will be closed to the public. At present it is open during office hours, 8 am - 12.30 pm, and 2 pm - 4.15 pm. The animals are fed between 8 and 9 am, a good time to visit because orang-utan prefer to spend their time high in the treetops. A new wildlife park will be opened in due time at the foot of Mt. Matang, near a series of waterfalls and small rapids which are a popular picnic spot for Kuching folk. A **crocodile farm** with an attempt at a very small private zoo is situated a few miles from Semongok. This is reached by the Serian bus; ask to be put off at Jong's Crocodile Farm.

Serian Kuching Road is the first leg of Sarawak's No.1 trunk road, slated eventually to link up with Sabah. **Serian**, 64 km from Kuching, boasts a set of small waterfalls and rapids at **Ranchan Pools**, located about 5 km from the township. It is also the staging point for trips onward to Sarawak's only **tea plantation** at Mayang.

Bidayuh longhouses

The road to Tebedu and thence **Pontianak** in West Kalimantan branches off the highway 1.5 km before Serian. The **Bidayuh longhouses** in Kuching area lie on roads off the same highway, before Serian: Penrissen Road leads to **Benuk**, Padawan Road to **Gayu** and **Annah Rais**, Mongkos Road to **Mentu Tapu**. Be prepared for a shaky ride in each case.

The Bidayuh, who have suffered in the past from more aggressive groups of peoples in Sarawak, and were frequently raided or had their children stolen as slaves, have historical reason to be shy of strangers. This is not to say they are hostile towards visitors— far from it— merely that they are somewhat wary of them. And no-one likes being made feel like inhabitants of a zoo; imagine if you had foreigners coming and staring at you as you went about your daily business.

The Bidayuh longhouses best prepared for tourists are **Anna Rais** and **Benuk**. Both charge a small admission fee to help maintain the traditional longhouse (the modern trend is towards single-family houses) and toilet facilities for visitors. As most accessible Bidayuh longhouses are within a day-trip of

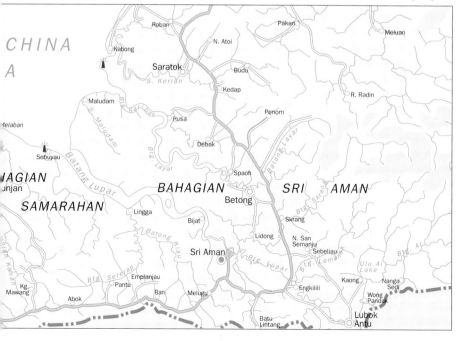

Kuching, it is not common for people to stay overnight. There is accommodation available in the Community Hall at Kg Abang; people who go in for serious hill trekking may choose to spend the night there.

Searching for pitcher plants

Bako National Park is the national park nearest to Kuching, accessible by a road, car ferry and boat trip in one long day. To get anything like the feel of Bako, however, an overnight stay is recommended. Bako's trails can take from 2 hours to 2 days. The best time to walk the well-marked paths is early morning. The park is also ideal for lolling by the sea and strolling in the sand. Nature provides original artwork in cliffs and rock plates washed by wind and water, filed into fantastic sculptures by the elements and streaked by colors and textures.

In Bako as well as in other national parks, one common question is: "But where's the wildlife?" The wildlife is there but it is, as the name suggests, wild. Large groups of visitors stomping through the undergrowth frighten the animals. The best times for wildlife watching are dusk or dawn when many of the forest creatures come out to feed. Find a vantage point, spray yourself with mosquito repellent and just sit still. They'll come. At the Park Headquarters, it is not unusual to see a wild boar or two rooting between the guest bungalows in quest of tidbits, or walking to the

waterfront in search of clams.

Plants are unable to run away when visitors approach, but they bloom in unexpected places. Many "jungle flowers" are inconspicuous green inflorescences, not gaudy blooms. On top of the low hill on **Lintang Trail** there is the strange landscape of **Padang Batu** ("rock plain"), an area the size of a football field covered in rock plates. Sparse shrubs grow in the cracks, the famous pitcher plants among them. Pitcher plants grow near the ground, often obscured by leaves, and even seasoned botanists have been known to walk right past them.

One very visible Bako wildlife is the *kra* or macaque monkey which has become very tame. Keep rucksacks well buckled if they contain food, don't leave small items lying around unattended, unless you fancy retrieving your camera from a coconut palm. These delightful apes will get into bungalows if doors or windows are left open; rumor has it that they also know how to undo the catch of food safe doors.

Bako is a lovely place for lolling by the sea and strolling in the sand. The well-marked hiking routes should only be attempted by reasonably fit folk in good footwear. (Pick up a brochure from the Tourist Association or National Parks before going; this contains detailed information on all the trails.)

Gold mines and beaches

Bau, once the gold mine of Sarawak in a literal sense, lies about 64 km land from Kuching. Some gold is still mined there. The road from Bau to **Lundu** and the beach town of **Sematan** (27 km from Lundu) is in the process of being upgraded, which means some sections are good, some indifferent and some awful.

The bone-rattling drive to Sematan is undertaken by rugged individualists who consider the five-star beach resorts in the Damai delta too "soft." There's a simple hotel in

Lundu and a few beach bungalows of the rough-and-ready kind at **Pandan** (the nicest beach of all, with surf) and at Sematan, but the fishing is good, the crabs are meaty, and there's no major river to silt and pollute the beaches. During the jelly-fish season (May-June) you can watch that wobbly wonder being prepared for the market in "instant factories" on the beach. Lundu has an open market with food stalls that serve meals, both Lundu and Sematan have coffee shops where simple meals can be ordered.

Walking to Kalimantan

The boundary between Indonesian and Malaysian Borneo follows the watershed, more or less. Several old trading routes lead south, from Sarawak into Sambas and the Kapuas basin. Only one of these is an official border-crossing, the one at **Tebedu** (Entekong); the others are open to legitimate barter trade but not foreign tourists. Before going to Pontianak overland (or by air), visit the Indonesian consulate in Kuching to acquire a visa.

The mountains and coastal plains of Southwest Sarawak are criss-crossed by paths, but they are used only by people with a good reason for getting to out-of-the-way places. Visiting relatives is among these, as are hunting and "jungle collecting," a vague term that includes the poaching of birds' nests and turtle eggs. A few hot springs and rapids or waterfalls attract picnickers from town, but these good folk get lazier year by year. If there's more than a couple of minutes' walking involved, not even a gently steaming forest pool will entice them. None of the natural attractions is spectacular enough in itself to get them out of their air-conditioned cars.

Mt. Penrissen, on the border between Malaysia and Indonesia, might just be an exception. This peak of 1,330 meters is worth a couple of days' exertion, but it mustn't be attempted without guides. The journey starts

with a road trip to the end of Pedawan Road; the night has to be spent either at the longhouse Annah Rais or at one of the guest rooms in the Community Hall at Kg Abang. Contact William Tanyuh Nub in Kuching (082-410858) for details. Don't expect to find accommodation arranged or guide and porters standing at the ready the minute you arrive. A guide can usually be found at the longhouse, at Kg Abang, or through the Penghulu (Headman) at Kg Pedawan, but he isn't professional; he is a farmer doing the occasional traveler a favor.

The trip to the mountain is entirely on foot, steeply uphill and down dale right up to the mossy trickle that marks the source of Sarawak River. Camp is made under an overhanging rock at the foot of Mt. Penrissen's summit; to reach the peak itself, a vertical cliff has to be scaled with bamboo ladders. Depending on the state these are in (the last expedition may have used them a few years ago) several hours may have to be spent repairing ladders. Good hikers will make the Penrissen trek in two days from Kg Pedawan.

— *Heidi Munan*

Opposite, left: *The sharp-eyed visitor can spot Bako's pitcher plants.* **Opposite, right:** *The car ferry taking vehicles to nearby Bako Park.* **Above, left:** *Plank walks enable visitors to explore Bako's mangrove swamps without getting their feet wet.*

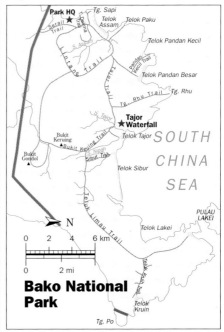

Bako National Park

VISITING LONGHOUSES

Communal Living Along the Rivers

A longhouse is a village under one roof, an association of households who have inherited this lifestyle from their ancestors and have chosen to stick to it. Visitors should remember that a longhouse is a collection of private homes. Guests are tolerated and usually welcome, unless they act as if they own the place or forget they're visiting a home, not a museum or zoo.

The major rivers nearest Kuching — the Skrang, Lemanak and the upper reaches of the Batang Ai — as well as the more remote Rajang River longhouses, are mostly inhabited by the Iban. As you move further up the Rajang and into the Balui above Belaga, you'll encounter different peoples known collectively as Orang Ulu.

Sri Aman (previously known as Simanggang), which can be reached by bus from Kuching, serves as a staging point for trips to the Skrang, Lemank and Ulu Ai. If you have to wait for a boat, keep an eye on the river. It has a spectacular tidal bore (*bena*) which comes roaring upstream about two hours after high tide; during king tides it is nearly 2 m high. Loungers on the waterfront (where the buses leave from) usually know when it is expected.

It is possible to go on by bus from Sri Aman to **Skrang** village or **Sebeliau** (about 1 1/2 hours). Solo travelers may be able to "hitchhike" to a longhouse with a party of Ibans who like the look of him if they wait around the Skrang village jetty. In most cases part of the trip to a Skrang longhouse still has to be made by boat. One popular destination is Rumah Bansing at Nanga Murat. The Skrang is the most popular river and the first to experience organized groups of tourists as long as 20 years ago.

To explore longhouses along the Lemanak river and Ulu Ai, take the Lubuk Antu bus. If your destination is **Lemanak**, ask to get off at Rumah Bareng in Sebeliau, just beyond the bridge; there are longhouses both upriver and downriver from here. If you ask nicely, you may be able to stay the night at Rumah Bareng and continue your search the following day.

To get to **Ulu Ai**, go to Lubok Antu bazaar by bus, then look for the (infrequent) bus for "the hydro;" this is the dam and its lake, built to generate electricity. From this point, you

JILL GOCHER

have to go by boat. Brandah Anak Aloh, owner of the floating shop at the landing stage, can usually tell when the next one is due and where it's heading. Delok is a popular destination; another is Rumah Penghulu Tedong at Engkari, which usually welcomes tourists.

Longhouse etiquette

After alighting at the longhouse jetty, visitors call out and wait for somebody in the house to respond. If there has been a death, a special festival or ceremony, a whole house may be *pantang* (taboo), and therefore not able to receive visitors. Permission granted, visitors scramble up the notched log that serves as staircase. They cross the outer platform and enter into the inner verandah. They make their way to the rooms of the *tuai rumah* (longhouse elder) and announce their presence. Footwear must be removed before stepping on mats if you didn't take it off when entering the verandah. Visitors are usually served a cool drink, the elder or in his absence some of the older men will chat with them, and eventually inquire into the purpose of the visit.

This is the time when solo travellers ask politely if they could spend the night in this house; group tours from an agency have these arrangements made and will deposit travelers' bags in their host's rooms. After drinks and small talk, visitors ask if they may look at the longhouse. This request is seldom refused, it being understood that the guests will confine themselves to the outer and inner verandah or the immediate surroundings of the house. They do not go to the farms, or enter into family rooms without being specifically invited by the owner.

It's acceptable to photograph the public areas of the house, including the head trophies suspended over small fireplaces in the verandah, but do not snap people without their permission.

Traditionally, visiting men sleep on the verandah and women inside the rooms, but if they are total strangers to the longhouse folk they may prefer to stay together on the verandah. A mosquito net is essential for a night in the longhouse. Visitors are usually invited inside the room to eat, and straight after the meal, they troop outside again for an evening lounge and chat .

Visitors should offer presents to their hosts at this point. Even if you're on a group tour, where you're assured the gifts are "taken care of," it would be much appreciated if you brought items such as tinned fish or

meat. The guest who plans to stay several days should bring his hostess a blouse, a nice *batik* or something useful for the kitchen. Children's books are much appreciated (they should be in Malay), as are imported magazines with lots of pictures.

In the evening, there may be a little dancing, and the women often offer handicrafts for sale. This "bazaar" can be an embarrassment in the more frequented longhouses, especially if two dozen women spread out their wares for three or four visitors who couldn't possibly buy something from each.

Privacy, propriety and prices

Some tour operators have built comfortable guests houses with all facilities near the longhouse so that a modicum of privacy is preserved for both visitor and visited. Where there are no toilets, remember that the river serves as water supply to longhouses. Wander into the secondary jungle surrounding the longhouse and find a nice dense bush.

Nudism and even a revealing swimsuit is considered very uncouth in Borneo. When swimming or bathing, covering yourself with a *sarong* is the best idea.

No longhouse is obliged to accommodate visitors. The longhouse hospitality of the past worked so well because it was never over strained. Hosts became guests in their turn. Longhouses on the main "tourist routes" charge travelers a fee (M$5-$20) for board and lodging. The cost of travelling to longhouses comes as a shock to many Sarawak visitors. Tourist agencies charge between M$200-400 per person, depending on whether the visit will be one day, overnight or two nights.

— *Heidi Munan*

Opposite: *A longhouse kitchen in the private family quarters or* bilek. *Visitors should ask permission before entering this area.* **Above:** *Getting there is, as they say, half the fun!*

THE RAJANG

Sarawak's Greatest River

The incessant screeching of express boat sirens starts the day early in the towns along the mighty Rajang River. From the misty darkness of 6 am, boats herald their imminent departure amidst a flurry of activity. Passengers crowd into narrow streamlined craft, throwing down their assorted bags and mysterious string-tied cardboard cartons to reserve their place in the ongoing scramble for seats. .

Outside, the curved white roof is piled high with more luggage. Cartons, containing newly purchased goods from the "city" or, if upriver, fresh jungle fruit and vegetables, live chickens and giant river fish, are stowed securely. The controlled chaos continues at regular intervals through the day, until the last boat departs, usually by mid-afternoon, to arrive at its destination before nightfall.

Malaysia's longest river and one of Sarawak's main arteries, the 563-km Rajang (in true Sarawak style, also spelled Rejang) is one of several water highways that were once the only means of access from the coast. This river system is joined by a vast network of tributaries, dissecting Sarawak's jungled and mountainous interior from headwaters starting close to the Indonesian border. The Linau, Murum and Kajang tributaries join the upper reaches of the Balui, which becomes the Rajang. At Belaga, the Batang Belaga adds to the flow, while further downstream, the Sut, Gaat, Majau, and Mujong rivers join the Baleh, entering the Rajang near Kapit.

In the early days, river travel was arduous and even a short distance meant days of hard paddling. Ascending the notorious Pelagus Rapids above Kapit could take a week of heavy labor, dragging the solid wooden boats over rocks and battling strong currents. The advent of the outboard engine brought new mobility, while today's high-powered express boats have revolutionized river travel; journeys which once took weeks now take a few hours.

The river is busy with a continual stream of traffic: express boats, chugging motor launches or *tongkangs* operated by Chinese traders and tugs towing rafts of logs, often hundreds of meters long, to be taken down to Sibu and eventually shipped overseas.

Groups of Iban and Kayan once staged memorable battles on the Rajang as they

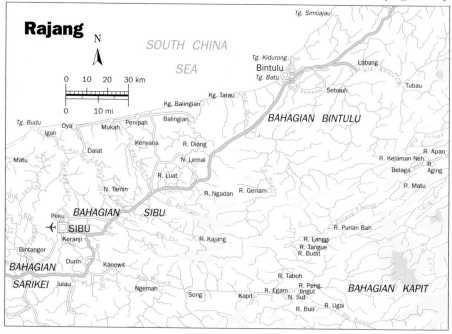

fought over arable farmland, with the acquisition of heads a happy by-product, bringing spiritual power to the owners. As the Ibans made their way upriver, fierce Kayan and Kenyah raiding parties did their best to stop them, resulting in constant skirmishes.

The battle known as the Great Kayan Expedition, waged in 1863, is still referred to upriver as the "Great War" as if it happened yesterday. Led by Charles Brooke, a party of 12,000 Iban in over 300 war canoes made their way upriver past the Pelagus Rapids to avenge the murder of two of Brooke's men at Kanowit fort. An uneasy peace was eventually made, with all parties later feasting together at Kanowit.

Later, in 1875, a wooden fort at Kapit was built to maintain peace by preventing the Ibans moving upriver and the Kayans and other Orang Ulu people moving down.

Peoples of the Rajang

While the Iban occupy the lower reaches of the Rajang and lower tributaries, the Orang Ulu people inhabit the remote areas upriver, still adhering to traditional boundaries. Spreading from the Upper Rajang across to the Baram Basin, the Kayan originated in Indonesian Kalimantan. The Balui and its numerous tributaries support many groups known collectively as Orang Ulu: the Kenyah, Kajaman, Kajang, Ukit, Belawan, Lahanan and the semi-nomadic Punan and Penan.

The Kayan and Kenyah are quite different to the egalitarian Iban, coming from highly structured societies whose aristocratic leaders once kept slaves. They are considered to be the most artistic of all the tribal groups. Their graceful and elegant dances are heavily stylized, while the haunting melodic music of the wooden *sape* (a simple string instrument, but difficult to master) has been largely adopted by others.

Essential equipment

Kayan handicrafts are beautifully made, even those used in everyday life. Woven rattan mats, baskets and decorative *parang* (machete) are the essential equipment of every longhouse dweller and superb wood carvings decorate longhouses and burial tombs. Beadwork makes up much of the traditional costume in the form of hats, headdresses, skirts and bags, and often embellishes the superb baby carriers. Even the large shady hats used when working in the fields will usually display some superb example of beadwork on the crown.

Kayan tattoos are among the most intricate. Aristocratic women were once tattooed from fingertip to forearm and from foot to thigh with superb but enigmatic designs which took years to complete. Today, only the

Below: *Longhouses are now built of modern materials, yet hospitality remains traditional.*

JILL GOCHER

older generations still wear tattoos.

A river adventure

A journey up the Rajang is filled with the promise of adventure. Most upriver journeys begin at Sibu's busy ferry wharf, reached by express boat or by plane from Kuching, or by bus or plane from Bintulu or Miri. **Sibu is** a fast growing town, the supply centre for the entire Rajang. Apart from the bustling night market, with an array of tantalizing cooked food (including particularly good roasted chicken, duck and pork), snacks and cakes, the main point of interest for the traveler is the multi-storied **Chinese pagoda** attached to the riverside Taoist temple. Climb up to the top levels for a dramatic view over the Rajang, and if the temple supervisor is not too busy, ask him to explain a little about the various deities depicted on the walls.

If you're traveling overland to Niah Caves or Mulu National Park, Sibu is the place to pick up a bus. It's also the gateway to the interior, with dozens of streamlined express boats, waiting to make their way along the Rajang, lining the river.

The express boat upriver to Kapit passes the small settlement of **Kanowit,** with the next village, sleepy little **Song**, halfway to Kapit. Just beyond Song, the Katibas River — which feeds into the Rajang — is Iban territory, lined with agreeable looking longhouses and the odd timber camp.

Exploring the **Katibas** presents no problem. Two longboat "taxis" depart from Song and head upriver each morning, stopping at longhouses along the way. Katibas Ibans are friendly and welcoming, and because tourist traffic scarcely exists in Song, prices are far more realistic than in Kapit.

Kapit - fast food and upriver permits

Fort Sylvia still stands, high on the banks above the river at Kapit, its wooden walls recording the height of record floods when the river rose up to 18 m above its normal level. The wooden bazaar, rows of simple but solid shophouses which once nestled between patches of jungle, has given way to blocks of functional concrete shophouses amidst broad expanses of bare red earth.

Kapit is the big city or the last outpost — depending where you are coming from — a place to find a pizza, chocolate-topped ice cream, fried chicken, air-conditioning and communication with the outside world. Hotel rooms have real baths with hot water — an unspeakable luxury after days of bathing in the river (or in a dark shed with a tin of cold water). Kapit is also a place to get permits for upriver travel, to buy large-scale maps and generally enjoy the sensation of being "in the interior."

Open-fronted shops overflow with jeans, cheap bright clothes, provisions, ammunition and other necessities. The town is fast

JILL GOCHER

becoming a mini-metropolis, with new roads, mushrooming public buildings, hotels and shops proclaiming Sarawak's developing prosperity. But the recent development and timber wealth can't erase the frontier mood of this lively town.

Below Kapit's high riverbanks, longboats tie up to the mooring logs beside the Shell fuel barge, slightly upriver from the express boat jetty. Their owners, balancing precariously on slippery logs, make their way ashore, bringing goods to sell or trade, while others make ready for their return, loading their boats with longhouse provisions.

Visiting a longhouse

Most Kuching-based tour operators take visitors to longhouses relatively close to Kuching, along the Skrang, Lemanak or Batang Ai. Visiting longhouses in the Rajang area can be done alone or with a guide that you find in the nearest town. Going without a guide requires good luck and a measure of audacity. Guides will sometimes help you to understand customs, explaining aspects of longhouse life, but they may also form a barrier to the people you want to meet. Some travelers seem able to set off upriver and find nice places to stay unassisted. Others with guides tell of being ripped off or being taken to dreadful places alive with mangy dogs and undernourished children.

Longhouse tales and experiences vary with every individual. If you want something more than a two-day/one-night organized adventure, with time to talk and interact with the people and see something of the life, be prepared to work at it. A familiarity with Bahasa Malaysia helps enormously. You must also be prepared to give as well as to take; many longhouse people have horror stories of visitors who come to their place, sit down, expect to be fed and entertained without contributing anything, and then leave.

Even one night in a longhouse provides an unforgettable experience, a glimpse into the communal lifestyle of the Iban or Orang Ulu. Anyone expecting to find people living in loin cloths and feather headdresses in the style of even 20 years ago will be sadly disappointed. Although old skulls can be found in the odd longhouses, they have lost their spiritual power, lying dusty and forgotten in the rafters. Life in Sarawak is changing fast and even remote areas are not immune to change as logging trails open up vast tracts of once impenetrable jungle, and youths leave home to work in timber camps or move to town. But for many, longhouse life still has a magic which modern life cannot hope to emulate.

River folk are renowned for their remark-

Opposite: *An Iban proudly displays his fighting cock on the longhouse drying platform.* **Below:** *Glutinous rice roasted in a bamboo tube makes an impromptu meal.*

able hospitality and it is a tradition for river travellers to stop overnight at a longhouse before moving on the next day. Visitors can enjoy the same hospitality by observing a few simple niceties. The first step is to find the *Tuai Rumah* (chief) and ask permission to stay. It is important to take along presents and some food to contribute to your keep. Not every longhouse is rich and folks appreciate the gesture.

Even if you don't smoke yourself, others enjoy a puff and cigarettes make a welcome present. Beyond Belaga, the preferred tobacco is the chewing type from Belaga bazaar. Whiskey or any cheap alcohol is always popular , except if you are staying in a "dry" Orang Ulu community.

There is little point in recommending individual longhouses, as this could cause an unwelcome glut of visitors in a particular area. Experiences are as personal as the individual, whether you take a guide or strike out on your own. There are interesting longhouses to visit all along the Rajang, although as the waters of the Rajang are so muddy, a tributary is generally preferable. Start from Song, Kapit, Belaga or Tubau.

Up the Baleh towards Kalimantan

There are numerous longhouses around Kapit, both on the Rajang and the network of tributaries that flow into it. Several are modern, accessible by land, only five minutes drive from town. The nearby **Baleh River**, with more logging camps than its 24 longhouses, is lined with interesting communities along its banks and makes a good place to start exploring. An express boat reaches several hours upriver to the Putai lumber camp, then the river continues almost to the Indonesian border. A Kenyah longhouse established by a group of Indonesian Kenyahs is about a day's travel further up the Baleh.

Some of the tributaries of the Baleh are reported to be still wild, with traditional longhouse communities living there. With no logging in their catchment areas, the rivers are clear and green, brimming with fish, and the surrounding forests still support game.

The magic of nights sitting in long dark verandas (*ruai*) filled with small pools of light from flickering oil lamps is being replaced by the brighter reality of generators and fluorescent light. But nights are usually fun and entertainment is varied. One night after dinner, as we sat down to a lesson in the subtleties of Kayan dance, the door creaked open to reveal the beginnings of an endless parade of "sick" Kayans. Foreign medicine enjoys a high status amongst these folk and it seemed that every inhabitant of the longhouse suffered from some minor malady.

We dug out our meagre pharmaceutical supplies to render skilled treatment, only to discover that not just any medicine will do. When one of the women was informed that

the oil I was offering her was from Belaga and not an exotic foreign destination, she swiftly forgot her disability and left in a huff amidst much hilarity from the audience.

On another night we were sitting in the *ruai* of a remote longhouse newly converted to Christianity. Half the gathering converged at one end of the *ruai* attending the evening Christian ritual, singing hymns and praying devoutly. The rest occupied the lower end and, ignoring the religious fervor, brought out the rice wine (*tuak*) and drank with the

visitors. Even old women drink with enthusiasm, if they are fortunate enough to get a drink passed to them.

Raging rapids to the last outpost

Further upriver, all boat traffic must pass through the perilous three-km Pelagus Rapids, the most dangerous part of the river. It takes a highly skilled driver to steer a course through the mountainous waves and ferocious whirlpools, dodging between bare rocks and hurtling logs as the river bed rapidly gains altitude. The rapids are only navigable during optimum conditions, when the river is high. During dry spells, express boats stop running and only the trusty *tongkangs* and timber barges head upstream.

Belaga is truly the last outpost on the Rajang. The path from the solid timber wharf leads up to the few remaining wooden shophouses, remnants of the old bazaar. Beyond the morning market is the commercial centre, where rows of concrete shophouses are filled with an array of canned provisions, giant packs of sweets, chewing tobacco from China, trade goods, ammunition and handicrafts brought from surrounding longhouses.

The faces in the street show the diversity of the upriver people. Kayan and Kenyah with their fantastic tattoos and elongated ear lobes wander through the bazaar, sitting and chatting, gazing about at life in town. Upstairs from the open-fronted cafes and shophouses

are several small Chinese hotels. Standing on top of the thickly jungled hill across the river is a magnificent Kayan *salong* or burial tomb, the first of many that adorn the river banks and hills upriver.

Many longhouses are accessible from Belaga, by taking the upriver express boat. Longhouse people are accustomed to having the odd foreign guest drop by and are generally hospitable.

Upriver from Belaga

Beyond Belaga are more timber camps and longhouses of the Orang Ulu. On leaving the last town behind, the natural rhythm of life in the interior takes over. Longhouses of the Orang Ulu appear, with their fantastic, highly stylized decorations of swirling faces. Along the banks, you can glimpse *salong,* the elaborately carved and curling burial houses of Kayan chiefs. Even though most Kayan people now adhere to Christianity, the compelling "tree of life" designs are incorporated into the new religion.

The second last express boat stop is **Long Murum**, also known as Uma Bawang. This sprawling well-built Kayan longhouse has been visited by Prime Ministers and other VIPs. The *Tuai Rumah* is the Penghulu or Chief of the Lower Balui, who exerts control over twelve surrounding longhouses.

The last stop for the express boat (when the Balui River is high) is **Long Linah**, a modern Kayan longhouse opposite a timber camp. To go further upstream from here requires hitching a lift with a longboat or chartering one at great expense.

A few hours further upstream is the traditional **Long Lahanan** longhouse, inhabited

Opposite: *Souvenirs of the headhunting past can often be seen in the rafters.* **Above, left:** *Watch out for finely carved Kayan burial huts in the upper reaches of the Rajang.* **Above right:** *Orang Ulu girls.*

by the Lahanan, another Orang Ulu group. Beyond this is **Rumah Ukit** — the one Ukit longhouse of a people who were. until recently, nomads. Their exceptionally young chief is less than thirty and takes his role seriously. Further still upstream, the remote **Long Jawi** is now also accessible by a logging trail from the Baleh River as is the Penan **Long Pusau**, one of the last longhouses on the Balui.

Bintulu to Belaga

A diverting alternative to a two-way journey along the Rajang is the overland journey from Bintulu to Belaga or vice versa. During the dry season, when the express boats aren't running, it's possibly the only way to get to Belaga if you're not prepared to fly. Starting from Bintulu, the Tubau express boat heads up Batang Kemana, passing Iban longhouses and the inevitable logging camps on the way.

Tubau bazaar is a trading post in the old style. Cavernous timber shophouses face across the single street, with covered wooden walkways give a feeling of stepping into a set from a Western movie without the horses. Tubau pace is slow.

Outside the bazaar, the river is a scene of constant activity as longboats ferry passengers between nearby timber camps. Chinese *tongkangs* unload provisions from Bintulu, while women do their laundry and bathe their children in the river. The busy corner restaurant is the center of activity. The girls serve

up steaming dishes of whatever is currently available: *babi hutan* (wild pig), venison, fresh-water prawns, seafood fresh from Bintulu or an array of jungle vegetables which make a delicious change from fried *mee* or rice with canned pork.

Owing to the danger of accidents with heavily laden trucks, some timber companies will not allow their drivers to take passengers, although others are happy to do so. We managed to hitch a ride from Tubau to **Long Metik**, upriver from Belaga, later taking the express boat down to Belaga bazaar. Alternatively, it is possible to get a ride on transport between Tubau and Belaga.

After arriving at Long Metik, we visited the nearby longhouse. Standing at the foot of the stairs wondering what to do next, we were rescued from our quandary seconds later when one of the more senior inhabitants invited us upstairs. Moments later, *Tuai Rumah* Amato Ato appeared and invited us to stay in his family quarters (*bilek*).

Long Metik is 'dry'; after converting to Christianity, the chief banned alcohol much to the dismay of some. The Kajaman inhabitants are friendly and welcoming to visitors, although their English is somewhat limited. Inevitably, the longhouse during daylight hours is fairly empty. Every able-bodied person who hasn't gone to work for "the Company" is out in the fields, clearing land, planting or harvesting *padi*. Only the very young and old stay at home.

Modern Sarawak and northwards

Few visitors do more than pass through Bintulu, once a sleepy fishing village of Melanau people and still famous for its *blacan* (dried shrimp paste) made in **Kg Jepak** across the Kemena river from the old bazaar. The fast-growing industrial area of Bintulu. together with its modern port, is north of the old town.

Still further north is **Similajau National Park**, which is currently reached by boat from Bintulu. Roads being built to what is reputed to be the nicest beach in Sarawak, and a range of accommodation, will no doubt make this park worth visiting. Contact National Parks in Kuching to check on the status of facilities.

— *Jill Gocher/Wendy Hutton*

Opposite: *Orang Ulu woman in the upper Rajang.* **Left:** *Clear waters can only be found in areas undisturbed by logging activities.Photos by Jill Gocher.*

PART V

Northeast Sarawak

The Baram River, which begins in the mountainous interior close to the Kalimantan border, has for generations been one of the major highways of northeast Sarawak. Its silt-laden waters the color of *kopi susu* (local milky coffee), the Baram disgorges into the South China Sea at Kuala Baram, just north of Miri. This town gives its name to a district which includes the impressive and archaeologically important Niah Caves, the surprisingly diverse Lambir Hills National Park, and one of Sarawak's most remarkable attractions, Gunung Mulu National Park.

All of what is now northeast Sarawak was under the sovereignty of the Brunei sultanate during the 19th century. After a series of revolts, the coast from just north of Bintulu up to the mouth of the Baram, together with the land upriver, was handed over to Rajah Brooke in 1883.

Moving the survey pegs

One by one, other regions were either given or leased to Sarawak: the Trusan River and tributaries near Lawas in 1885; Limbang area in 1890, and the fertile but sparsely populated Lawas region in 1905. With the continued northward expansion of Sarawak's borders, even British North Borneo (Sabah) was briefly considered as a possible addition to Sarawak. Charles Brooke, whose rule in Sarawak was highly paternalistic, strongly criticized the British North Borneo Company as "an association of European capitalists whose every motive in native eyes is the acquiring of wealth and the disregard of native religion, customs and happiness." He obviously believed these "natives" would be better off under his care.

A series of protests by well meaning but perhaps partially informed Western environmentalists has focused upon this region of Sarawak in recent years, in an attempt to draw world attention to excessive exploitation of the forest and what some consider to be the abuse of native rights. The only immediate result of these actions has been limits imposed on the work of serious scientific researchers and on the movement of travelers.

Sarawak's immigration authorities, like those anywhere in the world, did not take kindly to the flouting of immigration laws by the Swiss, Bruno Manser, who lived for six years among the Penan, organizing timber blockades. No-one would deny the alarming rate of logging in recent years, yet even before such protests, the Forestry Department acknowledged the need for more rigid enforcement of regulations; unfortunately, the sheer size of Sarawak and a shortage of manpower make this a difficult matter.

Positive developments include a proposed Penan "biosphere" region, offering those who wish to maintain a semi-nomadic lifestyle an alternative to settled villages. Other developments such as a "permaculture" project teaching the Penan to grow food crops without fertilizers and pesticides are already underway, an indication of the Sarawak government's concern.

Until 15 years ago, it was still possible to discover traditional lifestyles in longhouses in the upper reaches of the Baram River. The logging industry has irrevocably changed both the environment and the relatively untouched ways of the Orang Ulu. However, if you don't come in search of the past but prepared to discover a wealth of natural treasures in the National Parks, and to enjoy the continued hospitality of Sarawak's peoples, you won't be disappointed.

— *Wendy Hutton*

Overleaf: *Longboats at Long Pala, on the edge of Gunung Mulu National Park, where most tourist lodges are located. Photo by Jill Gocher.* **Opposite:** *A young Kayan in ceremonial dress. Photo by Jock Montgomery.*

ORANG ULU

Aristocrats and Forest Nomads

The origin of the term Orang Ulu is unclear. Some say it began when the people of the interior were asked "Who are you?" and they replied "*Kami Orang Ulu*," or "we are the people of the interior or upriver," meaning upriver from the Brooke forts.

The Orang Ulu are not a distinct ethnic group but a conglomerate of groups: Kenyah, Kayan, Lun Bawang, Penan, Bisaya, Kelabit, Kajang, Tagal, Tabun, Ukit, Bukitan, Lisum, Tatu, Sa'ban and Sihan. They live farther upriver than the Malay, Iban, Chinese and Melanau, in northeastern Sarawak. However, there is a coastal group of Penan in the Niah area, while the Bisaya live in coastal areas near Brunei Bay.

The Kayan and Kenyah, both with a socially stratified culture (unlike most of Borneo peoples) form the largest Orang Ulu group. Although culturally distinct, especially linguistically, the Kayan and Kenyah have come to be closely associated since they live side by side in the Balui, Baram and Keman rivers and their tributaries. Both groups came to Sarawak from the Apo Kayan in Kalimantan to Sarawak.

The Kayan language is uniform, with minor regional differences. The Kenyah, however, speak a number of dialects, some of which are not mutually understandable since this group is comprised of a number of sub-groups: Sebop, Seping, Kiput, Badang and Berawan.

The Kayan and Kenyah are gifted craftsmen whose arts and crafts have influenced those of other Dayak people. They excel in carving, boat building, bead work, ironwork and weaving mats and baskets. They reside in longhouses raised almost a meter above the ground. Each longhouse contains individual apartments (*amin*) and a common verandah. The nobles usually occupy the central part of the longhouse. Their apartments are identifiable since they are normally much larger than the apartments belonging to the non-ruling nobles or the commoners.

The Kayan and Kenyah, like most Orang Ulu groups, practice their traditional religion through omens, taboos and prohibitions. In theory, omens could be good or bad but in reality, most omens were bad; if a man saw a bird or animal of evil omen, or had a bad dream, he would abandon his current project

KAL MULLER

or stop work for a short time.

People converted to Christianity—Roman Catholicism or Borneo Evangelican Mission (BEM)—to free themselves from taboos, omens and prohibitions. Those who did not want to become Christian but nevertheless wanted to free themselves from such restrictions became followers of a new Kayan religion, Bungan, which includes ideas from Christianity combined with the traditional Kayan religion.

People of the highlands

The Lun Bawang and the Kelabit are often thought of as one people by outsiders because they speak almost the same language. They consider the Kerayan-Kelabit highlands in the interior of Borneo as their place of origin. They practice a form of wet-rice cultivation and are one of the few groups in Borneo which make salt from salt springs, as well as raising water buffalo and cattle for cash income.

The Lun Bawang in the past lived in long-houses similar to those built by other Dayak groups, although the Kelabits continue to live in longhouses. The traditional beliefs of the Lun Bawang and the Kelabit are similar to other Orang Ulu groups, but now most of them are practicing members of the Borneo Evangelical Mission.

The Tabun of Limbang river, the Treng of Tutoh and the Sa'ban of upper Baram are similar culturally and linguistically to the Lun Bawang and the Kelabit. The Tagal, of which there are a few hundred in the Lawas District, have a lifestyle similar to the Lun Bawang, since the two groups live side by side. Most Tagal live in Sabah, where they are called Murut.

The Penan (known as Punan in Kalimantan) live in the most remote areas of the Limbang, Belaga and Baram districts. Traditionally, the Penan were a nomadic people, subsisting on wild sago and game.

Although most have now settled, the forest remains an important source of food and material for handicrafts and buildings. The Penan weave excellent quality rattan mats and baskets and are also good at blacksmithing and making blowpipes; these articles are made for domestic use and for sale.

Three other groups, the Ukit, Bukitan and Sihan, were formerly a nomadic people like the Penan. There is one Ukit longhouse in upper Balui river, and several Bukitan communities in Kapit and Tatau Districts. The

Sihan reside in two small villages near Belaga Bazaar.

The Bisaya live along the lower Limbang river near Brunei Bay, in single-family dwellings built close together. The Bisaya grow wet rice in swampy valley floors and, like other Orang Ulu groups, practice swidden agriculture. They also raise water buffalo which are important not only as symbols of wealth, but also as beasts of burden. Buffalo meat is considered the proper meat to serve at ritual meals. Traditionally, the Bisaya believed in many gods and spirits which could be either malign or benign, and they carried out numerous rituals to appease the spirits. Most have now converted to Christianity.

The Kajang, one of the earliest people to inhabit the upper Rajang river, are comprised of four sub-groups: Kejaman, Lahanan, Punan Ba and Sekapan. Punan Ba are also found in the Tatau and Bintulu districts. Traditionally, sago was their staple food, but they now practice swidden agriculture. Linguistically, the various subdialects of the Kajang are quite close to the Melanau.

— *Ann Armstrong-Langub*

Opposite: *This Kelabit man combines the past and the present in his best outfit.* **Above, left:** *Vivid designs decorate the wall of a Kenyah longhouse.* **Right:** *Nomadic Penan children in their jungle camp.*

NIAH ARCHAEOLOGY

Uncovering the Secrets of Borneo's Past

Niah Cave is the best known, most extensively excavated and most expansive archaeological site in Malaysian Borneo. Several archaeological sites are scattered throughout the cave network, the two best known and most accessible being the West Mouth and the Kain Hitam (or Painted) Cave.

A visitor arriving at the caves via the plank walk passes first through the Traders' Cave, then enters the actual cave network through the West Mouth.The site is actually in two parts. The so-called habitation area, where the oldest finds were discovered, and which has been far more deeply excavated, is just outside the cave mouth under the shelter of an overhanging rock wall.

The cemetery stretches along the wall which runs into the cave on the left hand side. The outer area contained stratified deposits with stone artifacts of a range of

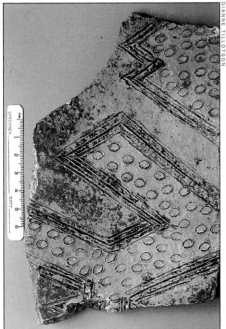

technological types. In the lowest levels were flake stone tools, including simple flakes, choppers and pebble tools, representing a Palaeolithic technology. In the higher levels were polished stone tools of both round and quadrangular cross-section, as well as sandstone pounders and mortars. Other cultural remains included bone points, shell scrapers and various shell ornaments.

While the outer area was designated as a habitation area, some human remains were found here. The most famous was the skull found in a very deep level, and provisionally dated by association with charcoal layers to around 40,000 years old. In the late 1950s, when the skull was excavated, this was considered an exceptionally early date for modern humans in this part of the world. More recent discoveries from Australia have made the possibility of such a date less unlikely.

Human remains buried in flexed position, and some dismembered or incomplete burials were also found in this area of the site. These were assumed to pre-date the neolithic and early metal age burials in the cemetery.

Differing styles of burial

The cemetery area was densely packed with human remains representing a range of different burial techniques. Sometimes these had overlapped or interfered with each other, so that is was difficult to disentangle associations between human remains and artifacts. Grave goods were few, but there was a certain amount of associated pottery, with a few glass and metal items testifying to the use of the cemetery into the metal era.

Many burials were simple inhumations with the body in extended posture; some were placed in simple log coffins, others in bamboo wrappers. There were remains of mats or textiles used to wrap the bodies. Two large coffins contained the remains of several individuals.

There were also secondary burials, where the bones of the dead had been collected and given some form of extra treatment before being deposited in the cemetery. Some of these bones has been burned, others simply sprinkled with haematite before being redeposited in the site in large earthenware urns, in wooden coffins or in less durable containers. In many parts of Borneo, until recent times, people carried out secondary treatment of the bones of the dead, accompanied by elaborate funerary ceremonial and infused with complex beliefs. The burials from Niah Cave suggest that such concepts about death were developing in the era before metal was introduced to the island.

Distinctive pottery

Handmade earthenware was found in the cemetery, with impressed marks made with a carved paddle, a paddle or stick wound with string, or with matting. Some sherds were decorated with designs made with the edges of shells. The most distinctive form of pottery found in Niah Cave was the three-color ware, painted in red and black and incised with elaborate geometric designs; some pieces were very large, suggesting that they may have been used for the burial urns. There was evidence that this pottery was made within the cave itself. The other form of distinctive Niah pottery was the double spouted vessel. These plain but finely made vessels have two spouts pointing in opposite directions.

Cave paintings and grave goods

The Kain Hitam or Painted Cave dates from much later than the West Mouth cemetery. In this cemetery the remains of the dead were placed in a series of boat-shaped coffins with carved animal heads, set up on frames in a row along the floor of a long narrow shelter. When they were discovered, the supports had collapsed and the coffins fallen over, spilling their contents. The presence of Chinese stoneware among the grave goods indicated a date after around 1,000 AD.

It takes some time for the eye to distinguish the hematite wall paintings that give the cave its name, as they are quite small and extend in a long narrow frieze from a dark back corner of the cave along the wall behind the area where the coffins were arranged. Many of the paintings represent boats filled with human figures. The boats seem to be undertaking an arduous journey across the cave wall through lurking hazards. Mythologies about water journeys for the dead abound in Borneo and are represented by the boat shaped from of coffins, still used in modern times.

Other anthropomorphic figures also appear, some in a spread-eagled posture found in recent central Borneo art forms, such as carving and beadwork. The natural rocky outcrops of the cave protect larger anthropomorphic figures, and net-like designs whose meaning is unclear.

Various caves and crevices in the Subis mountain complex were used for human burial until around 1,400 AD and it seems possible that the whole mountain may have been a significant ritual and mythological site.

— *Dianne Tillotson*

Opposite: *A potsherd of unusual three-color ware, which may have been made within the cave itself, was excavated at Niah.* **Below:** *Wall painting in the Kain Hitam Cave, showing spread-eagled figures and canoes.*

DIANNE TILLOTSON

Northeast Sarawak

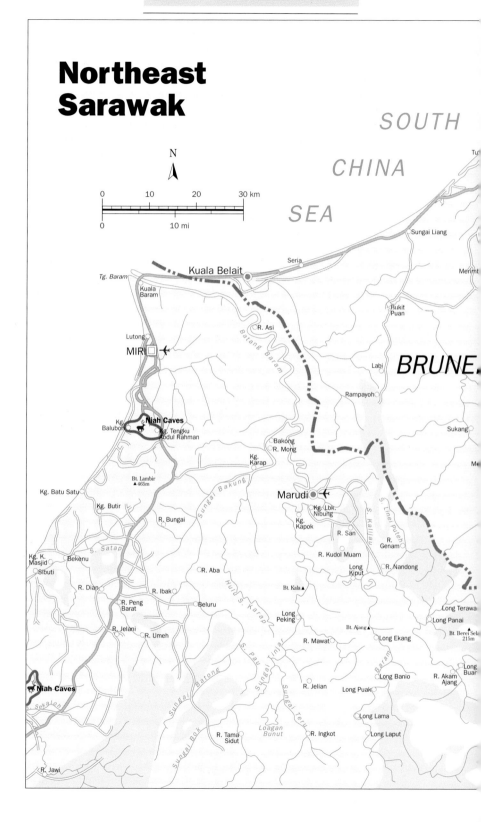

N

0   10   20   30 km

0   10 mi

SOUTH

CHINA

SEA

Sungai Liang

Tu

Merimt

Seria

Kuala Belait

Tg. Baram

Kuala Baram

R. Asi

Bukit Puan

Lutong

MIRI

Labi

BRUNE.

Batang Baram

Rampayoh

Kg. Balubo

Niah Caves

Kg. Tengku Abdul Rahman

Sukang

M

Bakong

R. Mong

Kg. Karap

Sungai Bakung

Marudi

S. katiau

S. Linei Puteh

Bt. Lambir
▲ 465m

Kg. Batu Satu

Kg. Butir

R. Bungai

Kg. Lbk. Nibung

Kg. Kapok

R. San

R. Genam

R. Kudol Muam

S. Satap

Kg. K. Masjid

Bekenu

R. Aba

Long Kiput

R. Nandong

Sibuti

R. Dian

Hulu S. Karap

R. Ibak

Beluru

Bt. Kala ▲

Long Terawa

Long Panai

R. Peng Barat

Long Peking

Bt. Ajang ▲

Long Ekang

Bt. Berei Sela
215m

R. Jelani

R. Umeh

S. Pau

Sungai Tinjar

R. Mawat

Baram

Long Banio

R. Akam Ajang

Long Buar

Niah Caves

Sungai Batong

Sungai Terk

R. Jelian

Long Puak

Long Lama

S. Sekaloh

Sungai Rok

Loagan Bunut

R. Tama Sidut

R. Ingkot

Long Laput

R. Jawi

MIRI DISTRICT

Niah Caves and Surprising Lambir Hills

If you stand in the old heart of Miri town, you can just see the steel tracings of an oil derrick, the Grand Old Lady, sitting on top of Canada Hill. This oil well, which began pumping in 1910, was the *raison d'etre* of Miri, a busy riverside-town which has gone from strength to strength on the back of this valuable commodity. The "black gold" from Sarawak's offshore wells, as well as oil pumped from nearby Brunei, is refined at the huge Lutong refinery.

Miri, temporary home to thousands of Shell company expatriates over the years, now sees hundreds of tourists flocking in, heading for Gunung Mulu National Park and the Niah Caves. Although Miri has pleasant pockets, especially around the river-front markets and Taman Selera Beach, visitors generally pause just long enough to organize their tour operator and permits for Mulu, or to voyage down to Niah Caves National Park.

Many people — whom one suspects have gone no further than the first three waterfalls 15 minutes inside the park — dismiss Lambir Hills as merely a playground for Miri residents at weekends. The Park, only 30 minutes by bus or taxi from Miri, is surprisingly rewarding if you take the trouble to continue along the well-marked trail to the 40-m tree tower, where you get an excellent view of the forest canopy and can also spot birds in the early morning.

The world's most diverse forest?

Walk on deeper in the forest and you'll find Lambir Hills, with both dipterocarp and heath forests, has some of the most interesting vegetation in Borneo. Scientists are currently engaged in taxonomic studies to confirm that Lambir's dipterocarp forest has the greatest number of species of any forest on earth.

As you wander the steep ridges of Lambir Hills — preferably in the fresh early morning — watch out for the unusual number of beautiful palms, rare tree ferns, pitcher plants and orchids, as well as other typical dipterocarp and heath forest species. The Pantu and Tengkorong waterfalls are about 1 and 2 hours away respectively, a delicious reward at the end of a very hilly (and invariably hot) hike. Before visiting, pick up the informative brochure on Lambir Hills at the Miri Office of National Parks and Wildlife.

JILL GOCHER

ALAIN COMPOST

Visiting Niah Caves is an exhilarating experience. Unlike Mulu Caves, you are free to roam at will, unhampered by timetables and guides. Niah is worth at least a day or two, giving you time to enjoy both the caves and surrounding forest, particularly in the evenings when busloads of day-visitors have left and the Park is peaceful once more.

Immense and unmissable

Located 109 km from Miri (almost half way to Bintulu), the Park Headquarters are 13 km off the highway. Niah National Park consists of 3,140 hectares of lowland forest surrounding a limestone massif dominated by 394 m Gunung Sibus and its cave complex.

There are three main caves in the Niah complex. Walk through the Trader's Cave, containing bamboo structures used by traders during the nesting season, to the Great Cave: one of the largest caves in the world, its yawning entrance (West Mouth) is over 244 m wide and 61 m high. Beyond, right through the heart of the Great Cave, is the Painted Cave, with its hidden treasures.

Niah has been under protection of the Sarawak Museum since 1958, when archaeologists discovered a skull initially believed to be 40,000 years old. The Painted Cave, once used as a burial chamber, still has relics of ancient wooden coffins and rock paintings of red haematite, the only such paintings ever discovered in Borneo.

A risky but lucrative occupation

Ironwood plankwalks lead right from the park entrance to the caves, freeing the eyes to enjoy the forest rather than continually checking for leeches and protruding tree roots. Those who take it slowly and quietly may catch a glimpse of monkeys, hornbills, Rajah Brooke's Birdwing butterflies, bulbuls, flying lizards and tree squirrels.

Within the inky darkness of Niah's Great Cave, disembodied voices can be heard above the high-pitched squeaking of myriad bats. Flickering oil lamps illuminate the makeshift canvas and plastic shelters of the various bands of bird's nest collectors safe-guarding their territory. Long spindly bamboo poles hang from the cave roof 50m above. Seemingly match-thin, they support the weight of the men who risk their life to explore the roof crevices for the edible nests built by several varieties of swiftlet.

Previously, territorial wars were waged by different groups intent on staking claims

DUNCAN MACSWAIN

within the caves. For some years, the local Ibans and Malays competed with Indonesian Bugis, until the intruders were defeated. Now an uneasy peace reigns with the territory amicably divided among the victors. Even during the off-season, skeleton crews guard the site in anticipation of the coming season. The caves produce several grades of nest, including the most highly prized "white" variety, worth around US$500 per kilo.

Birds' nests are not the only valuable product within Niah. Every day, tonnes of guano are deposited by the millions of bats living within the caves. Less valuable than the nests, guano provides a decent (and far safer) income for the men who carry enormous sacks of the fertile brown powder down to the Chinese trader opposite the Park depot.

A walk to the caves just before sunset to witness the nightly bat exodus is an unforgettable experience. As the swiftlets return after a day's foraging for food in the forest, clouds of bats fly out, in a dramatic changeover of shifts. The bats keep to the high path while the swiftlets fly beneath, with never a collision between them.

— *Jill Gocher/Wendy Hutton*

Opposite: *The West Mouth of Great Cave.*
Above, left and right: *Lambir Hills contains what is possibly the world's most diverse dipterocarp forest, with an astonishing variety of plant, animal and insect life.*

HEADHUNTERS' TRAIL

Following in the Steps of Headhunters

Most visitors to Gunung Mulu National Park arrive by boat or by air, but there's a more interesting way which follows part of the route used by Kayan headhunters in the 19th century. This involves either starting at Limbang on the coast and traveling in to Mulu "via the back door," or if you prefer, leaving Mulu via Camp 5.

Following the headhunters' trail involves riding canoes along rivers, sleeping in a longhouse and a few hours' trekking. From a physical point of view, it is not difficult, but the logistics could be complicated, you therefore either need lots of time and the ability to speak Malay; or a tour operator who knows the ropes and can make all the necessary arrangements, including food supplies. As the trip requires canoe chartering over fair distances, it's not cheap for individual travelers but with the cost split among a group, the price is reasonable.

Kayans on the warpath

During the first half of the 19th century, great war parties of up to 3,000 Kayan came down from the upper Baram River and its tributaries to hunt for human trophies. It was no easy journey for the warriors and their war canoes, some up to 18 meters long. They descended the Baram to the Tutoh branch and ascended the Melinau River to the western Mulu Range.

At the Melinau Gorge (near today's Camp 5 in Gunung Mulu National Park), where no waterway followed the warpath, the Kayans built a 3 km road for hauling their canoes to the Terikan (formerly Trunan) River. The road, now completely disappeared, was 4 meters wide and surfaced with slender tree trunks laid across and secured about a meter apart to make the canoe drag possible.

All the members of the fleet joined forces to power one boat at a time to the Terikan River, and on a further 50 km of the Medalam river until they arrived at Limbang, where they sought their gruesome trophies among the Murut longhouses and hapless Chinese pepper farmers.

Starting in Lawas

Lawas is a small but bustling center of communications and commerce, populated mainly by Lun Dayeh and Chinese. Regular flights run form here to Kota Kinabalu and Long Pa Sia in Sabah, to Ba'Kelalan in Sarawak's Bario Highlands, and to Limbang and Miri. Buses make the trip from Lawas to Kota Kinabalu in 4 hours, while express boats roar regularly to Labuan and to Limbang.

Several new shopping complexes were recently built to supplement the existing ones, they also have hotels and open restaurants where beer flows to a steady stream of *ringgit*. coins. Near the Lawas River, a large market features stalls selling many kinds of vegetables and colorful fruits. Saturdays are the busiest day of the week, when clothes sellers from Sabah arrive *en masse*.

The jobs created by logging contribute a great deal to the prosperity of Lawas. There is plenty of evidence of the industry on the way to Lawas from the Bario Highlands as well as during the two-hour express boat ride between Lawas and Limbang.

Most passengers traveling from Lawas choose the air-conditioned interior of the express boat for its main attraction: wrestling videos. You might prefer to opt for the front of the boat (the back is too noisy and receives all the fumes); get there early and stake out some space before baggage heaps up.

In the middle of Brunei

Limbang is a bigger version of Lawas, located on a river which flows through a section of Sarawak squeezed between the two halves of Brunei. The beer is colder than in Lawas, the women dress more elegantly and the Malay element is more in evidence, though still in a minority.

Located a little upriver from Brunei Bay, Limbang, like Lawas, was for centuries a trading center for the rich produce of the interior. Archaeological finds unearthed at Limbang give evidence of an ancient Hindu-influenced civilization, with a stone bull, elephant and gold jewelery among the items discovered.

To save a lot of boring river travel, you can take a 45-minute minibus ride to Kuala (Nanga) Medamit, upstream on the Limbang River. From there, an hour's longboat ride up the Limbang takes you through minor rapids, where you may have to push your craft through the shallows. You then follow a tributary, the Medalam, to an Iban longhouse at Mentakung.

The Iban presence in this area is relatively recent, going back perhaps 50 years when they started migrating to the Limbang River and its tributaries from Southwest Sarawak due to a shortage of land. In the case of Mentakung, a couple of Ibans scouted the area and obtained permission to move the inhabitants of their longhouse from a man named Bala Lasong, a Lun Bawang who had property rights over the area. Bala Lasong, who subsequently married one of his Iban protegées, took the post of longhouse chief.

An uninspiring longhouse

The 23-door longhouse at Mentakung perches its two storeys on two-meter high stilts. The mud underneath serves as a pig-sty and three decrepit TV antennae sprout from the tin roof. Less than overwhelmed by the architecture, I thought that since I was stuck here anyway, I would just spend the night and be on my way early the next day.

Then I noticed that many of the older men sported extensive tattooing. One white-haired Iban had his throat, chest, back and one leg covered with traditional tattoos while on one forearm there was some tattooed writing which I could not make out. Another chap sported a definitely non-traditional tattoo of a man and wife on his chest, along with the usual Iban motifs on his shoulders and back. Things were looking up a bit. Then over supper, our host and longhouse chief casually mentioned that shortly they would try to kill a ghost. Would we like to watch? The longhouse at Mentakung was suddenly becoming a lot more interesting.

After supper, we sauntered down the longhouse verandah to where the action was to take place. The ritual centered around a family whose members had been frequently sick. A short while back, one of the older women dreamed that it was a particular ghost that was responsible for the illnesses. It had to be killed in a ritual called *nolang*, which is seldom performed; this was only the third time since the longhouse was established at its present location, over twenty years ago.

Iban ghost-busters

The affected family sat in a tight bunch, circled completely and hidden from view by suspended sleeping mats draped with woven Iban cloths. Four "ghost-busters" were sitting around, waiting to get to work. All electric generators in the longhouse went out one by one and we sat in the flickering light of oil lamps. A drum was beaten for a few seconds, then there was a bit of chanting by the four-

Below: *An Iban community has established a longhouse along the route once followed by parties of Kayans in search of human skulls.*

KAL MULLER

man team who then got up and started off by circling the mat-enclosed family. One carried a drawn *parang* machete, another a squealing piglet. All other inhabitants of the longhouse sat in nervous silence, occasionally whispering a comment to their neighbors.

The reverential hush was broken by a squawking hen which jumped up on the high partition separating the longhouse commons area from the outside walkway. The hen thoroughly scared me and, I suspect, not a few of the other spectators. It was definitely not a

good move for the chicken. A young man grabbed it by the head and handed it to one of the ghost-busters.

After striding around the still hidden family, the team of four walked out of one end of the longhouse. Soon we could hear one of them shouting. An Iban sitting next to me whispered in Malay that the ghost was being invited to partake of a delicious meal set aside for him in the affected family's kitchen. The men returned inside and checked out the kitchen, *parang* ready to chop up one nasty ghost. But the food was untouched.

The procedure was repeated several times but the ghost was not about to be lured in so easily. Once when the four men were outside, we heard a strange noise, like a low roar. My neighbor whispered to me that the ghost had arrived. But he never came in for his meal, surviving to bother the people of Mentakung another day.

New names from a chicken

But they were not beaten yet. The next morning, all members of the ghost-tormented family changed their names in another ritual so that if the ghost returned, it would not recognize anyone, keeping the folks safe from mischief. It was the hapless hen of the previous evening who picked the new names — and had its last meal in the process.

The chicken was offered various plates of rice representing different new names. When

it pecked most vigorously, the corresponding name was given to one of the affected family until everyone, including babies, had acquired a new identity. A few grains of rice were placed on the heads of each "new" person, along with water dripped from a string of old beads, little metallic bells and shells. Afterwards, the hen was taken outside and its head cut off, unceremoniously and with no words of thanks.

Realpolitik in the longhouse

By the time the ritual was over, it was too late in the day to go to work and prepare the land for rice planting. Some men busied themselves making fish traps out of bamboo slats tied together with strips of rattan or some other jungle vine. Others sat around in small groups, chatting about this and that. I was invited into several of these groups. One bunch asked me to explain about America and Saddam Hussein. They told me that Muslims they had met in Brunei and Sarawak were anti-American and very pro-Hussein because he was a Muslim. What did I say to that? I wriggled out of it by trying to tell the folks about money, oil and realpolitik.

Another discussion group centered around the present government education system where English — considered necessary for a good job — was no longer taught. Only a few of the parents bothered sending their children to the local school, half an hour's walk away. They wished the old colonial English school system would return: I kept my mouth shut on that one.

I asked if any old head-hunting trophies had been kept. After a bit of hemming and hawing, it was admitted that two skulls were still kept in the longhouse. Could I see and photograph them? The owner of the skulls, whose grandfather had chopped off the two heads, readily agreed. I followed him back to his kitchen where he produced two blackened skulls. Answering my query, he said that the skulls were still fed, once a year, during a *Gawai* (harvest ceremony), so that their spiritual power would remain and aid the longhouse of Mentakung.

I was amazed to find much of the traditional culture remaining here so close to so-called "civilization." This is perhaps due to the fact that fundamentalist Protestants — who demand a clean break from the past — have concentrated their efforts on the most remote regions of Sarawak. They had been kept out of the interior during the Brooke period by the official policy of "no missionaries or lawyers," enabling the indigenous inhabitants to maintain their traditional way of life. That changed drastically after World War II, when the British took over Sarawak as a Crown Colony and left the missionaries free to convert away.

Rivers, rapids and swarms of leeches

From Mentakung, it's a four-hour outboard-powered longboat ride to Kuala Terikan and the beginning of a trail into Gunung Mulu National Park. There are a few mild rapids on the way plus lots of shallow spots (in the dry season) requiring getting out and pushing the longboat; our two-man team handled the craft superbly. On the way, we saw bright blue kingfishers, parrots and a flight of white-tailed hornbills as well as logging works, with bulldozers clearing a road to the riverside.

After about three hours, numerous large rocks began to appear in the river, some sculpted by the water into incipient works by Henry Moore. Half an hour after our park permits had been checked at Mentawai, we were dropped off at the beginning of the trail on the Terikan River, just off the Medalam.

This trail, which is just over 11 km and took us a bit over three hours to cover, leads to Camp 5 in the park. All of it was through primary rainforest with some muddy stretches and a moderate leech population. There was no way to get lost: the park service had painted many of the trees with a red and white band. The trail generally followed the course of the Terikan River, past Lobang Cina (Chinaman's Hole — one was supposed to have died there) and a large, curiously shaped stone, Batu Rikan, next to where we crossed this river.

Batu Rikan was covered with a thick tangle of vegetation and we had neither the *parang* nor the energy for exploration. In 1856, Spencer St. John wrote that "the river disappears in a rocky eminence, its sharp edges concealed by... luxurious vegetation...

There was an arched cavern into which we pushed our boats... looking down into the clear water, we saw two huge holes below — the passages whence the river came. We went round to the southern side of the rock, and there we found the river purling along to this lofty wood-crowned mass of limestone, and then entered a spacious hall it was lost, descending, as it were, to the passages before mentioned. There were various chambers with water floors, to the surface of which fine fish arose occasionally. This place is called Batu Rikan. We stayed there a night during which it rained [making it impossible to cross the river]. We kept on the right bank until we reached the spot where the whole river issued from the face of the precipice; it was a fine sight, this body of water running impetuously from this natural tunnel."

All along the trail, creeks were spanned by logs with no handrails for the faint-hearted. These required balancing acts just barely within our sphere of competence. A downpour near the end of the trail soaked us thoroughly and brought out swarms of leeches. Gunung Mulu National Park's Camp 5 was indeed a welcome sight.

— Kal Muller

Opposite, left: *An Iban holding up an ancient trophy.* **Opposite, right:** *Kuala Medamit on the Limbang.* **Below:** *This Iban baby's name is changed to confuse a troublesome ghost.*

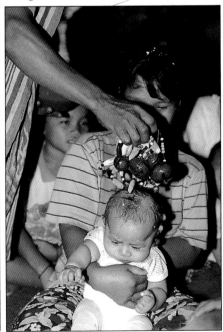

KAL MULLER

GUNUNG MULU

Sarawak's Last Great Wilderness

As the ancient white limestone cliffs of Mulu turn to gold in the setting sun, the first hesitant bats appear, fluttering about the entrance of Deer Cave before spiraling upwards to head off into the Borneo jungle on their nightly forage for food, a journey which could take them as far as Brunei. Gradually the numbers increase until a steady stream of the creatures ascends like a serpentine trail of smoke, the beating of wings softly audible 50 m below. This nightly exodus from Deer Cave is just one of Mulu's natural wonders that fills visitors with awe.

Unless you fly to Gunung Mulu National Park, the second stage of your journey from Miri ends when your express boat from Kuala Baram stops at **Marudi**, the main supply centre or "bazaar" for the Baram region. Marudi has the feel of a frontier town, its shops stocking everything from outboard engines to plastic pails, chain saws to handicrafts. Wander upriver from the bazaar to the hillock where the government offices occupy the solidly built Fort Hose, constructed in 1901; its ironwood tiles and brass cannon out the back are items that Charles Hose, the first Resident of the Baram District, would recognize. Beyond the fort, the old colonial resthouse overlooking the river is now dwarfed by the huge new Civic Centre.

A century of exploration

Within the boundaries of Mulu, Sarawak's largest national park, all the major species of Borneo's inland vegetation can be seen, as well as several endemic species found nowhere else. The 600-700 cm of annual rainfall contribute to the lushness and immense diversity of the rainforest.

Mulu has attracted explorers for over a century, the first of note being Spenser St. John, who failed in his attempts in 1856 and again in 1858 to conquer the summit of Gunung Mulu but recorded some vivid descriptions of the area in his *Life in the Forests of the Far East*.

In 1932, during a six-month expedition with fellow Oxbridge undergraduates, Edward Shackleton (later made famous by his exploits at the South Pole) became the first European to reach the summit of Gunung Mulu.

Geologist Dr G. E. Wilford first surveyed

Deer Cave and a section of Cave of the Winds in 1961, leading to the gazetting of the area in 1974 as Gunung Mulu National Park. Three subsequent expeditions have been made to the Mulu. In 1977-8, the British Royal Geographical Society combined with with the Sarawak Government to mount the first major scientific exploration of Mulu, with all aspects of the ecology studied.

Over 100 km of caves and passages were explored, giving for the first time an idea of the true vastness of Mulu. Subsequent expeditions in 1980 and 1984 surveyed another 150 km of passages, yet it is estimated that only 20-30% of the total caves have so far been surveyed and documented.

The world's largest cave passage, Deer Cave, could hold London's St Paul's Cathedral five times over, while the world's largest natural cave chamber, the Sarawak Chamber, is estimated to be capable of holding an incredible 40 Boeing 747s or 16 football fields. It has earned a place in the *Guinnesss Book of World Records* as the world's largest cave chamber, while Clearwater Cave at 75 km is the longest cave in Southeast Asia.

In the beginning

Mulu began life as a shallow coastal basin where coral reefs grew on beds of sandstone and shale. Over millions of years, the corals were compressed to form the limestone that constitutes the massif. Around 3 to 5 million years ago, during a massive geological upheaval, lifting and folding resulted in the formation of the limestone and sandstone mountains that comprise Mulu today. Permeated with complex networks of caves and passages on numerous levels, Mulu Caves are the result of constant erosion.

Opened to visitors in 1985, Gunung Mulu National Park has developed rapidly from a remote wilderness to a fast-growing tourist destination. Much has been done to improve the accessibility and facilities such as plankwalks which aid walkers' progress and protect the forest floor and caves from the effect of too many footsteps.

Exploring the caves

So far, only four of the 25 caves and passages so far discovered in Mulu are open to the public: Deer Cave, Clearwater Cave, Lang's Cave and the Cave of the Winds. Guided adventure caving to a number of caves is available for those who enjoy wading through icy cold mountain streams and bat guano in pitch darkness.

The most visited of all the caves, **Deer Cave** was once inhabited by deer which have long since vanished. A 3-km plankwalk starting from Park HQ passes through a peat swamp forest where several species of orchid can be seen by those who walk slowly enough to look. Your guide may also point out, just away from the plankwalk, an ancient Penan burial cave still containing several well-weathered skulls, or an *ipoh* tree, from which the Penan collect poisonous sap for their blowpipe dart tips.

From the echo-filled cave entrance, a concrete path leads through mountains of bat guano, a tonne of which is replenished by the bats each day. This unsavoury mass is constantly moving, alive with several species of cockroaches, earwigs and other creatures.

The path continues through the mountain to the **Garden of Eden** — a hidden valley filled with ancient vegetation that has existed undisturbed since time immemorial.

The **bat observatory** allows tourists to come close to nature as they sit with a cold drink in hand, idly observing the late-afternoon exodus of the bats.

Situated off a small walkway close to Deer Cave, **Lang's Cave** is perhaps the most

Overleaf: *Gunung Mulu is superb for adventure caving. Photo by Jerry Wooldridge.*
Below: *Enjoying the waters of Clearwater Cave.*
Above: *Bats leaving for their nightly forage.*

attractive of the show caves. Strategically placed lights illuminate the more spectacular stalactite and stalagmite formations.

Clearwater Cave is located on a small tributary off the Melinau River about half an hour by longboat from Park HQ. At times when the river is low, everyone has to get out and help pull the boat. The water flowing out from the cave is green and clear, with small and highly protected fish playing in its shallows. This is a perfect spot for a cool swim. During periods of heavy rain, 150,000 tonnes of water rush from the cave entrance each hour, carrying away rock and limestone particles which continue the erosion process that has been occurring for several million years.

Brilliantly colored butterflies flit through the shade beneath the trees, making it a perfect spot for a picnic, if one can get away from the hoards which descend on this idyllic spot each day.

Along a path leading up from the Melinau River is the entrance to the King's Room of the **Cave of the Winds**, so named because of the constant draught that blows through its chambers. Walkways and lighting enable visitors to enjoy a pleasing display of stalactites and stalagmites.

Although not accessible to the casual tourist, the **Sarawak Chamber** can be visited by more adventurous groups which undertake the 4-hour walk from the nearest river before reaching the tiny entrance and slipping through into the vast depths of darkness. According to the calculations of engineers and scientists, the vast void of Sarawak Chambers simply should not exist — limestone is just not strong enough to support such an immense roof span. Nature triumphing over man's science perhaps.

The Pinnacles and Fire Mountain

"Sharp axes below, pointed needles above, such is the mountain of Mulu," reported Spenser St. John in 1856, quoting the old Malay description of the **Pinnacles**. The unofficial logo of the Park, the 50-m high Pinnacles on the side of Gunung Api (Fire Mountain), are one of the Park's most spectacular sights and well worth an excursion. The climb is so arduous that Gunung Api was first scaled only in 1978, but those who undertake it are in for a memorable experience.

The first base to head for is Camp 5, involving a 2-hour boat ride up the wild Melinau River, with the occasional scramble to pull the boat over rocky, shallow rapids. After landing at Kuala Berar, you begin the five-km trek through lowland forest to Camp 5. While climbers sit enjoying the idyllic surroundings, comparing leech bites or gazing across to the still unconquered Mount Benarat (1585 m), the guides set about making tea and preparing the evening meal.

To the less than perfectly fit, climbing to the Pinnacles can seem like be something

akin to conquering Mount Everest. Although only a short trail of less than 3 km, the formidably steep Gunung Api provides a real challenge. The lowland track quickly gives way to the face of the mountain where the track disappears among tree roots and slippery limestone debris. Take only bare essentials and a large bottle of water for this climb.

The time it takes to reach the top depends totally on your level of fitness. The ultra-fit guides could probably run the entire way in an hour, but less fit amateurs take from 3 to 6 hours. Limbs can scarcely believe the constant demands made on them, and slim tree trunks begin to look like good friends as they lend their strength to straining muscles hauling up meter-high steps.

Around an altitude of 850 m, the lowland dipterocarp forest gives way to the enchanted realm of the the mossy forest, an ethereal and silent world where dripping mosses festoon all plant life in a myriad nuances of green. Sheltering in protected corners, insectivorous picher plants feed on a diet of insects and ants, digesting them in highly specialized enzymic juices. High above, singular species of orchids add touches of rare beauty and, when in season, rhododendrons lend bursts of color to the all-encompassing green.

Into an ethereal world

It is just after reaching the mossy forest that the steepest part of the climb begins. A series of shiny gleaming aluminum ladders have been strategically placed over the worst of the gaping voids between the limestone points, leading to the vantage point and a small flat space surrounded by comforting rocks, which looks right down on the Pinnacles.

Gunung Api has eroded on the exterior, resulting in the formation of these spectacular grey limestone pinnacles, razor-sharp points protruding up to 50 m above the surrounding vegetation. Standing on top of the world, one can gaze at the marvelous silver-grey needles rising above the surrounding forest, as swirling mists alternately reveal and conceal this wonder. Although some climbers stay overnight, it is more usual to eat lunch (or breakfast for the early birds), and return to Camp 5, while those in a hurry go all the way to the Park HQ in what must be a very full day.

On to Gunung Mulu

The summit of Mulu was first reached by an expedition led by Lord Shackleton in 1932, although the Gunung Mulu trail was previously discovered by Tama Nilong, a rhinoceros hunter. He followed a trail which led by the cliffs to the southwest ridge of Mulu, from where Shackleton later reached the summit.

This is the same trail followed today by those fit or adventurous enough to attempt the climb to Mulu's summit (2326 m). Although the path is now clear, much of the three day climb involves steep grades, requiring a high level of physical strength.

— *Jill Gocher*

Opposite: *The Pinnacles, aptly named "Pointed Needles" by the Malays.* **Above:** *Attention to detail will reveal such remarkable plants as these vivid fungi.* **Below:** *Ladders help climbers up the steepest stretches of limestone from where they can gaze down on the Pinnacles.*

BARIO HIGHLANDS

Trekking in a World Much Changed

High on an often misty plateau in the center of northern Borneo, the Kelabit people lived for generations in almost total isolation, developing the most sophisticated system of irrigated rice cultivation in all of Borneo. They also erected megaliths and carved designs into rounded boulders until as late as the 1950s. The ancient way of life has, however, been lost with the widespread adoption of fundamentalist Christianity.

For the traveler, the main attractions of this large uplands area — generally referred to as the Bario (or Bareo) Highlands — are the primary jungle and the friendly people, many of whom still live in longhouses. Don't expect much in the way of traditional customs: for better or worse, they have vanished.

The Bario Highlands are part of a large plateau which is shared with the Indonesian province of East Kalimantan. On the Mal-aysian side of the border, at just over 1,000 m altitude, Bario is the best known and biggest of the three highland villages which have regular air services. The other two are Long Lellang, to the south and on the western side of the Tama Abu mountain range, and Ba Kelalan to the north, past Mt Murud.

Trekking is the only way to get around. There are some easy jaunts of 1 to 4 hours from the landing strips to longhouses and Penan villages, where you can stay overnight or return to (relative) comfort the same day.

Trips for the tougher trekker

For those in good physical condition (and not unduly bothered by leeches) the highlands offer several long treks. From Long Lellang, it's 5 to 6 days to reach Bario via Pa Tik, a Penan settlement and the only village along the way. Or, also from Long Lellang, it's a 7 to 12-day trek to Bario via several Penan villages, along with Long Peluan and Ramudu, both Kelabit longhouses. A guest book comment on this trek illustrates the hardships: "...an exhausting eleven days, 3,000 leech bites, almost swept away by rivers..." Not for the fainthearted or out of shape.

Between Bario and Ba Kelalan, it's either a relatively easy 2 days via Indonesian villages in Kalimantan (including some stages by motorcycle) or a bit tougher but more interesting two to four days via Pa Lungan and Pa Rupai. From this trail, it is possible to make

KAL MULLER

side trips of several days to climb Batu Lawi or Mt. Murud.

Bario then and now

For those who have read Tom Harrisson's *World Within,* (see Further Reading) Bario is bound to be disappointing. In fact, today's Bario is in a different place, a couple of kilometers from the old site, now called Bario Asal. Next to the landing strip, a small cluster of buildings represents the "downtown" area, with lodgings, stores, a couple of coffee-and-snacks restaurants, and a concrete complex for 30 shops nearing completion in late 1992.

The remaining buildings are made of wooden planks with tin roofs and of no redeeming architectural value. There are usually several motorcycles and, when there's a plane, a couple of trucks hanging around. To the west, a dirt road of sorts heads towards several *kampung*, villages, most with a longhouse, each in varying degrees of modernity. While many Kelabits live in these longhouses, many have opted for individual dwellings.

Whereas in the 1950s Bario declared having only 16 able-bodied men, the population of the area referred to as Bario had, by the 1960s, swelled to a total of 1,500. The current population is about 1,300, by far the greatest concentration of Kelabits, whose total number barely surpasses 3,000. But even this low figure is said to be almost double that of a generation ago.

The good old days

Tom Harrisson, an Englishman who was to become curator of the Sarawak Museum, parachuted into Bario in 1945, at the head of a team to organize native resistance to the Japanese prior to the Allies' landing on the coasts of Borneo. He found the Kelabits a most tradition-minded group who spoke practically no Malay and had very seldom been visited by Europeans.

Although the Kelabit were not averse to the occasional spot of head-hunting, they never practiced it on the scale of the Iban or Kayan. Unlike most other inland people, the Kelabit concentrated their energies on rice cultivation, having perfected an elaborate system of irrigation and producing regular yearly surpluses of this staple. Along with iodine-rich salt from natural springs, the ample rice insured that the Kelabits could maintain their self-sufficiency and independence.

This linguistic group also organized elarate *irau* (funerary rituals) which, for wealthy aristocrats, entailed the erection of stone monuments. During every ritual observance (any pretext would do), a part of the surplus rice was converted into an alcoholic drink called *borak*. Great drunken times were had by one and all, until the missionaries arrived in force after World War II.

Harrisson wrote that by 1958 "Tattooing, long hair, flashy beads, leopards' teeth, bored ears, exposed breasts, loin cloths, slit skirts, bone hairpins, leg bangles: all this and much else are OUT. The cycle of *irau* funerary and exchange festivities in now centered on Easter and Christmas, as Christian observances... there is less and less that is strange in them still to visit."

Of course, none of Borneo is what it was 50 years ago. It's not so easy nowadays (but then again it never was) to parachute into a tribe practically untouched by the modern world. But those with lowered expectations can still see a few of the outward manifestations of the old culture and feel the continuing warmth and hospitality of the Kelabits.

A modern wedding

During a recent wedding in Bario, in one of the outlying longhouses, I witnessed a mixture of the old and the new. A total of 14 pigs

Opposite: *Tayun, a Kelabit from Bario, was a handsome young bachelor in 1945, when Tom Harrisson arrived by parachute; he later featured in Harrisson's* World Within.

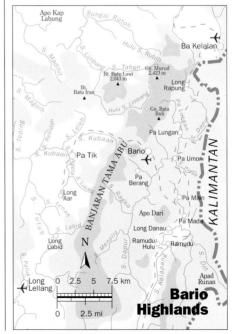

KAL MULLER

(cost: M$10,000) were slaughtered for the feast. Inside the longhouse, a dozen men spiked chunks of pork on wooden skewers and most impressive quantities of meat piled up for the feast. Nowadays, it is during weddings that men can build up status (and acquire pig-debts) judged by the quantity of pork available for the guests.

In the late afternoon, everyone bathed and dressed to the hilt to greet the guests who started arriving at dusk; they kept on arriving until about 600 men, women and children spread themselves on the floor of the longhouse. The center of the communal area was decorated with balloons and paper streamers converged on a red banner proclaiming the names of the couple: Donna and John. The groom, looking nervous, his best man, his father and several elders were all dressed up in suits and ties, but were barefoot as required by longhouse etiquette.

Hymns instead of Borak

The show started with an hour of guitar-enhanced hymn singing, led by a young woman with microphone connected to a powerful amplifying system. While the folks were busy singing, one could unobtrusively check out some of the more interesting faces: strong featured elderly men and women with great, shiny brass ornaments dangling from shoulder-length earlobes. Several elders sported "upside-down bowl" haircuts with long strands in the back neatly tied up in a bun. Most of these men still showed the effects of eyebrow plucking in their youth, formerly a sign of beauty. At least these faces would have warmed Tom Harrisson's heart, although hymn-singing was definitely not his cup of *borak*.

The bride appeared, dressed in white, veiled and on her father's arm. She took her place next to the groom and the wedding proceeded quickly, to the pop of flashes on assorted mini-cameras and the whirr of a video-recorder.

With the couple safely wed, elders in neckties got up to give them advice on how to behave in life. As these speeches dragged on, the guests were served tea, milk and crackers to take the edge off budding appetites. In due time, at the end of the formal proceedings, the feast began. Each guest, including children, received a leaf-wrapped packet of solid paste made from boiled rice, and a skewer of pork, with alternating chunks of meat and fat. As no salt is used in cooking, the guests each had their own supplies, carefully wrapped.

After the meal, taped traditional music emerged from the loud speakers. It seems that no one present owned or could play the *sape*, a string instrument formerly used by the Kenyah and the Kayan as well as the Kelabit. The young men prefer the guitar, but *sape* music is de rigeur for traditional dance.

Right from the start, several elders volunteered to dance, performing slow, graceful motions quite similar to the movements of a bird. This bird-dance is a pan-Dayak one which perhaps originated with the Kenyah and is widespread in Kalimantan. After the ageing pros had finished their dance numbers, members of the audience were invited to perform similar solo numbers. A young man had the job of picking the next (reluctant) dancer by placing a hat decorated with hornbill feathers on the head of the victim.

Problems of booze

All alcoholic beverages, notably the traditional rice brew, *borak*, were conspicuously absent from the wedding and kept the atmosphere from straying into gaiety. Alcohol is most severely frowned upon by the church and its sale prohibited in Bareo. Smoking is also strongly discouraged: young men sauntered in the narrow walkway just outside the longhouse, grabbing a quick if not very furtive smoke while trying to chat up the girls who were hurrying by, giggling.

It is obvious that Satan is at work and the grip of the church is slipping on a portion of the younger generation. In the words of a visiting retired Australian missionary, the Bario elders are "as a church, terribly concerned about the younger generation" and offer frequent prayers so that the young ones will return to the path of the Lord.

Evangelization of Bario

The shift away from the "worship of evil spirits" diffused into Kelabit-land and Bario from what was then Dutch East Indies. According to oral church history, the Kelabits had become nominal Christians even before World War II, thanks to American-administered fundamentalism centered in Long Bawan in what is now East Kalimantan.

From the Sarawak side, two Australian missionaries made it to the Bario Highlands in 1939, after canoeing up the Limbang River and its tributaries, then trekking across sawtooth mountains. The Reverend Alan Belcher first arrived at the Kelabit village of Long Lellang after five arduous weeks' travel from the coast in late 1946, then trekked with his wife to Bario in early 1947 to help spread the word of the Gospel.

When Mrs Belcher returned with several male members of the evangelical team, she quickly found out about a dismaying aspect of Kelabit longhouse hospitality: young girls taking the initiative to sleep with unattached male guests, even Bible-toting ones. In order to "protect" the men of her team, Mrs Belcher had to spread her sleeping mat by their feet and intercept any young lady trying to sneak over her. Satan was foiled again.

During the 1950s, the Kelabits underwent mass conversions and abandoned all that was objectionable to the missionaries. Families started paying 10% of their rice and any other income to the church, but while this tithe was universal for a while, only about half of the families follow the practice today.

A shakedown stroll

Before taking any long treks your body might not be ready for, try the three-hour stroll to **Pa Berang**. It's almost all level, with the path relatively well kept up, so even during the rainy season after an all-night downpour you can easily cover the distance. Pa Berang has no unusual buildings, but it's the closest Penan village to Bario.

While the trail is an easy one, there's one crossing to test your mettle. A couple of hours out of Bario, a big log across the Dapur River marks the entrance to Penan territory, as well as this jaunt's most difficult equilibrium test. Some Westerners breeze

Opposite: Pork is prepared for a longhouse wedding, though rice wine is no longer part of the feast. **Below:** *Trekkers must cope with logs like this one over the Dapur River.*

KAL MULLER

right over, upright. Others straddle it and ignominiously inch their way across. It takes just a bit of courage to try it standing up, with help from the guide's rock-steady hand.

The dry rice fields of the Penan start across the river. In the eyes of many Kelabit farmers, it's the Penans' ability to grow rice which makes them either "good" or "lazy." The inhabitants of Pa Berang are the "good" kind, those who have given up the semi-nomadic life and settled down, adopting Christianity with a vengeance.

Family units with cold showers

The village of Pa Berang consists of a small longhouse and several family-sized units, all of sawn planks, on 1.5-m tall stilts and with tin roofs. Three bath houses afford a measure of privacy for a (very) cold shower; there is even an enclosed squat-over-the-hole toilet. The gentle, hospitable Penan who live here spend much of their time singing hymns and praying when not working in their rice fields or hunting and gathering.

Early afternoon often finds the village deserted, except perhaps for an elderly lady or two and a few infants under their care. Smiles and a bit of goodwill could overcome language problems and will probably result in an invitation to enter the longhouse.

The Penan generally look somewhat different to the other peoples of Borneo: much lighter skinned and with more marked Mongol features. The chief of Pa Berang, Tama Simun, is tall and of massive thighs. Along with a couple of the elders, he wears his hair long in the back with an upside-down bowl haircut on the front and sides.

Pa Berang was settled in 1979, when the neighboring Kelabit gave the Penan land for their village and fields. At one time there were about thirty families living here, but many have moved to Long Lamai, another Penan village which has a school. The parents of Pa Berang send their children to Bario for their education.

Realistic expectations

After trekking to Pa Berang, you will know if you want more of the same, but over much more difficult terrain. A path leads out of Pa Berang and reaches **Ramadu** in some seven hours. From there, it's three hours to the longhouse at **Long Danau** and another seven to return to Bario.

The trek from Bario to **Ba Kelalan** leads through primary jungle after starting in open country. The enjoyment of this jaunt will depend on several factors: physical condition, amount of time available and the weather, which also has a bearing on the numbers and ferocity of the trailside leech population. But basically, it's a matter of expectations.

Primary rainforest fires up the imagination, invoking swarms of exotic animals, bright birds, slithering snakes and ferocious felines. You see none of the above. In fact, only leeches are (almost) guaranteed, along with spiders, butterflies and ants. With lots of luck, you could see gibbon monkeys, but don't count on it.

The vegetation is punctuated by the occasional huge tree, one of the dipterocarp family whose trunks shoot straight up before branching. They tower over sparse undergrowth which struggles from thin layers of soil towards the sunlight. There's an occasional creek. The range of visibility is limited; one can usually see further underwater than in the rainforest.

If you combine none-too-great scenery with aching legs, bootfuls of leeches and hurrying to stick to a tight schedule, you have a sure recipe for an awful time. As another traveler wrote in a guest book: "Call this fun? Great trip but it's much better now that it's finished." Still, many consider the jungle trek a unique, magnificent experience. Just be aware of what you are getting yourself into.

The time required for this trek depends on physical condition and finances. From landing strip to landing strip, its an easy 10 hours for a Kelabit. Double that for the average mortal. A lot depends on how much you have to carry, or if you can afford a porter (highly recommended).

A trail for hardcore jungle-lovers

This trail breaks up into four stages: Bario - Pa Lungan - Long Rapung - Pa Rupai - Ba Kelalan. The first and last segments are easy: good road or path, mostly level. The second and third chunks are on narrow jungle trails, leeches awaiting: this is the jungle experience you came for.

Stage one, from **Bario to Pa Lungan**, takes 2 1/2 to 4 hours. For the first hour or so, it's a wide road for trucks, shadeless and hot when the sun is out. The road ends at the village of Pa Ukat but the path from there is still tiptop: a meter or two wide, with drainage ditches, good enough for motorcycles except after a heavy rain. The open country offers pitcher plants and, with luck, a squawking gathering of a dozen black-and-white hornbills. A large trailside boulder features carved, low-relief human faces, megalithic funerary art from the pre World War II era.

The village of Pa Lungan consists of detached family units around a large rectangular fenced field for pigs and water buffalo. Supper here could consist of wild boar and mouse deer, along with the usual rice and whatever else you brought along.

Elusive Mount Murud

Luck might reveal Mt. Murud (2,622 m/7946 ft), but it is often hidden by mist. This is the area's highest landmark, but once you enter the jungle, there are no openings to see the mountain. Shortly after leaving Pa Lungan, the trail climbs a mini-mountain, a steep slope rising some 200-250 m. No problems here as you are still fresh from a good night's sleep. However, a trekker coming from the other direction, already tired, said that after the "killer mountain [he was] ready for the oxygen tent and the orthopedic ward at the Sarawak General Hospital."

About 4 hours out of Pa Lungan, clusters of huge bamboo announce the abandoned village of **Long Rapung**. It lies in a bend of the Dapur River which starts at Mt Murud and flows through the Bario highlands to end up as the longest of the great Baram River's headwaters. A small, low shelter at Long Rapung protects overnighters, with unlimited drinking and bathing water a few meters away. If time permits, we suggest spending a night here, taking time to stroll around (with your guide or you might get lost) into the jungle just for a leisurely look without having to continuously power ahead under a knapsack.

Alternatively you can keep on truckin' out of Long Rapung, feeling already a bit tired but wanting to stick to schedule (often a mistake). The next chunk of trail takes 4-5 hours to **Pa Rupai**, often with scads of leeches. Somewhere along the way, the path crosses into Indonesia, obvious by the bright red discarded packs of Gudang Garam shining in the brown mud and sparse green foliage. A long downward slope heralds the journey's end, with irrigated rice fields at the bottom and, at last, Pa Rupai. Here one might enjoy porcupine meat, the usually excellent rice, as well as papaya, mangoes and bananas.

The last stage of the trek, an easy 2 hours, first passes by the villages of Long Medang, from where it is possible to motorcycle to the town of Long Nawan and fly to Tarakan, if you have a visa for Indonesia. The trail to Ba Kelalan curves out of Long Medang and climbs a short but steep hill whose top marks the Malaysian border.

Once the hill is behind, it's a flat pitch going through water-buffalo pastures and skirting irrigated rice fields until you reach the army post outside just outside **Ba Kalelan.** A quick passport check and you're free: civilization beckons. A neat little town, clustered to one side of the landing strip, a small hotel (Green Valley Inn), stores, coffee shops (but no booze, yet).

On towards a beer

We suggest flying out of Ba Kalelan. But you can also leave overland by first trekking a couple of hours where four-wheel drives await at the head of a recent logging road, just beyond **Buduk Aru**, the site of a Bible College. Over the logging road, it takes 4 speedy hours to Lawas with clouds of dust caking passengers — unless you are lucky enough to sit in the cab with the driver. The scenery is definitely not worth the misery. What you see are huge logs piled up roadside and trucks hauling huge loads of timber at snail pace. Flying costs a little more than the dusty ride, but it does enable you to get at a well-deserved cold beer that much faster.

— *Kal Muller*

Below: *Returning from a day in the* padi *fields. The Kelabits developed the most sophisticated irrigation system in all of Borneo.*

KAL MULLER

PART VI

Introducing Brunei

Four centuries ago, Brunei ruled much of Borneo and the southern islands of the Philippines. Today, Brunei Darussalam (Abode of Peace) is still a Malay Islamic Monarchy but has been reduced to 5,765 sq km on the northwestern coast of Borneo. Bruneians spend little time regretting this decline in regional hegemony as they enjoy the immediate benefits of a wealthy petroleum-based economy thanks to the discovery of vast reserves of oil and natural gas is 1928. Bruneians have a high per-capita income (US$19,000), free health care, free education, interest-free car and housing loans, generous pensions, and no income tax.

Malays comprise 68% of Brunei's population of 260,000. Ethnic Chinese are the largest minority at 18% but may appear more numerous because of the influx of Chinese from Malaysia and Singapore to work in the commercial sector. Dusuns, Ibans and Punans living in the interior make up only 5% of the total population, while the remaining 10% of the population consists of expatriates

Unlike their sea-faring ancestors who traded internationally, Bruneians today tend to be inward looking. Social and political life revolves around the Sultan, Islam and family. The Religious Affairs Department was established in 1954 to guide Bruneians in making Islam a way of life. More recently, a government decree know locally as M.I.B. (Malayu Islam Beraja, or Malay Islamic Monarchy) promulgates the unifying role of the Sultan in nurturing and strengthening the Bruneian Malay culture following Islamic values. The sale of liquor was banned in January 1991, but non-Muslims are permitted to import alcohol for personal consumption. A more conservative dress code is also now in effect.

The Sultan of Brunei, His Majesty Paduka Seri Baginda Sultan Haji Hassanal Bolkiah Mu'izzadin Waddaulah, Sultan and Yang Di-Pertuan, is also the Prime Minister and Defense Minister. One brother is the Minister of Foreign Affairs and another is the Minister of Finance. Eight other ministers and a special advisor assist the Sultan in governing Brunei.

Bruneians have rebelled only once against the royal prerogative in recent history. This was in 1962, when the Sultan was urged by the British to join the Federation of Malaysia. The rebellion was put down within a week, and Brunei made the decision to stand alone, becoming fully independent of British protection in 1984.

For centuries, the center of power and government in Brunei was embodied in Kampung Air, the Water Village in the Brunei River. In one generation, however, Bandar Seri Begawan, the capital of modern Brunei, has developed from a small river-front town to an urban sprawl that extends over several kilometers.

Because of its petroleum wealth, Brunei has not exploited its forests or other natural resouces to any great extent and 80% of Brunei is still covered by forest and provides a secure sanctuary for its wildlife.

Brunei-Muara, the most highly developed district, is home to 60% of the population. Belait District is second in population size (24%) and includes Seria, a town built on reclaimed peat swamp; most residents in Seria are connected with the oil industry. Kuala Belait is the administrative center for Belait District and the point of departure for Miri, in Sarawak. Tutong District, with 12% of the population, is agricutural, with many traditional Malay *kampung* in the interior. Temburong, which has no road links with the rest of the country, is the least populous district with only 4% of the population.

— *M.M. Ng*

Overleaf: *The Omar Ali Saifuddin Mosque, overlooking the stilt houses of Kampung Air.*
Opposite: *The vast banquet hall of the Istana Nurul Iman. Both photos by R. Ian Lloyd.*

BRASSWARE

Superbly Wrought Heirlooms

The name of Brunei and the craft of brass manufacture are inextricably intertwined. The sultanate was a celebrated center for the production of often ornate brassware from the 16th century onwards.

Sadly, the great age of brass is over. Like other indigenous cottage industries, brass production in Brunei began to decline in the 19th century because of competition from European imported goods and changes in local societies and lifestyles.

It is likely that brassmaking developed in Brunei well before European contact. As an important trading center, Brunei had commercial links across the Indian Ocean to the Middle East and northwards to China; it also received visitors from many other parts of Southeast Asia. It is not surprising that Brunei Malay brass production shows similarities in techniques, forms and decorations with aspects of Middle Eastern, Indian and Chinese traditions.

As one might expect in a cosmopolitan port, certain quarters of the town specialized in different activities, some of which were under royal patronage and served the needs of the court. Even today, various parts of the famous "water village" are remembered for their association with particular crafts and guild organisations. There were three main brass-working communities: Kg Ujung Bukit, Sungei Kedayan and Kg Burong Pingai.

Brunei craftsmen commonly used the lost-wax or cire -perdue method of manufacture, in which molten metal replaces the melted wax inside a specially fashioned clay mould. They produced beautiful betel-nut sets, caskets, salvers, lamps, jars and perfume sprinklers for the wealthy, including, of course, the royal family, as well as a range of ordinary objects such as cooking pots, bowls, water and rice containers, pedestal trays and deep-rimmed gongs. The most famous items were the Brunei cannon and kettles.

Widespread items of trade

In the past, brass was traded along the coasts of Borneo and up and down its main rivers. Traditionally, it served as a means to store weath and as a unit of currency. Fines and bride prices were often calculated in terms of weights and types of brassware, and brass goods were kept as heirlooms by Malays and Dyaks. Of course, some items had everyday uses such as the storage vessels, containers and cooking pots. Gongs, too, were used to provide musical accompaniment in dance and ceremony and, in the headhunting and piratical past, to sound warnings of an imminent attack. Cannon were used as weapons of war.

Brass also fulfilled social and cultural functions. Prominently displayed, it bore witness to the prestige and rank of its owner. Given as special gifts, it established or helped sustain political alliances. The Brunei sultan, for example, often honoured senior administrators and regional chiefs by endowing them with titles and presenting them with cannon. Conversely, the sultan's supporters would periodically offer gongs or cannon as a form of tribute to demonstrate their continued loyalty to their master.

As treasured heirlooms, certain brass objects — especially the fine jars and cannon — acquired magical properties; some were considered as gifts from the gods or spirits. There is much local folklore which tells of famous heroes enduring perilous journeys

COURTESY BRUNEI MUSEUM

into unknown lands in search of brassware. Brass goods such as gongs were commonly used, and to some extent still are, in ceremonies to ensure fertility, longevity, physical well-being and spiritual strength.

Richly ornate embellishments

Brunei styles in brassware are distinguished from other Malay repertoires by their decorative ornateness. Brass cannon were often embellished with dragon (*naga*) designs, or miniatures of crocodiles, snakes and other creatures affixed to the barrel. Sometimes the whole gun would be fashioned in the form of a dragon or crocodile. The flared mouth of the creature, often displaying sharp teeth, served as the muzzle; the body of the creature comprised the barrel, usually decorated with reptilian scales, and the curved tail became the rear handle of the gun. These "dragon cannon" exhibit very strong Chinese influences. However, many cannon display the sober austerity of Muslim craftsmen who, true to their religion, satisfied their artistic needs by decorating guns with foliated or floral motifs, commonly stylised lotus designs, or with Koranic inscriptions.

Given their importance both as a weapon and as a symbol of a man's social position, it is perhaps not surprising to learn that particular sultans and some prominent Malay and Dayak leaders became associated with famous named cannon. Sultan Bolkiah, an early and most revered sultan of Brunei, was reputed to possess a cannon called Si-Gantar Alam, which when fired was likened to the sound of thunder.

Kettles still used in rituals

The most distinctly ornate of Brunei brassware are the kettles, sometimes weighing as much as 30kg. They are still sometimes used as water containers in Malay ceremonies such as weddings to serve water for drinking and for washing and purifying the hands and feet. Some kettles are engraved or embossed with the Islamic lotus or fig-leaf decorations or Arabic calligraphy. But more commonly they have Chinese-style animal and human forms. Perfect miniatures of lizards, frogs, crabs, fish, dragons, crocodiles, serpents, dogs, birds, lions and human figures seated on horses or being devoured by dragons are fixed to the outside of the kettles.

Some of these decorative motifs have symbolic meanings, and in the ancient religions of the Indonesian archipelago such creatures as lizards, crocodiles, snakes, dragons and dogs usually had a strong connection with beliefs about fertility. Some were also associated with indigenous cosmologies, which differentiated an Upperworld, symbolically connected to birds and inhabited by beneficent spirits and deities, from an Underworld which contained baleful and potentially harmful forces.

However, what is most striking about Brunei brassware is that these distinctive ornate decorated objects such as cannon and kettles are quite different from the austere beauty and exquisite shapes of the tall, elegant lamps, the large lotus bowls decorated with stylised lotus petals, and the small incense vessels. The aesthetic appeal of these items derives from the skill and care with which the overall form has been crafted, and not from dazzling and complex combinations of symbolic elements.

Unfortunately the traditional splendor and variety of Brunei brassware is no longer part of a living tradition. Examples can now only be seen in the collections of the local museums, in Chinese antique and curio shops and in some Malay and Dayak houses where they are still treasured as heirlooms.

— *Victor T. King*

Opposite: *This ornate kettle with miniature animals is a fine example Brunei craftsmanship.*
Below: *Brunei gongs are cherished heirlooms throughout Borneo.*

EXPLORING BRUNEI

Stilt Villages and Royal Opulence

Brunei, although a pleasant place to live, is a difficult place to be a tourist. Determination, fitness, stamina, and a better-than-shoestring budget are prerequisites for anyone visiting the sultanate. Travelers can see Brunei's attractions if they are prepared to take taxis (there is little public transport) and walk greater distances than usual, should transport for the return trip fail to materialize.

Unless otherwise indicated, most destinations worth visiting are within Bandar Seri Begawan (BSB). Distances from the taxi stand in front of the multi-storey car park on Jalan Cator are shown in parentheses for attractions not within easy walking distance.

Water village on centuries-old site

Chinese writings from as early as the 6th century may have mentioned the **Water Village** (Kampung Air), but it was the 16th-century European accounts that revealed the vibrancy, power and wealth of the old capital of imperial Brunei. Kampung Air is not a single village but consists of about 40 wards, each with its own headman. The government is encouraging residents of Kampung Air to apply for houses in resettlement schemes on land, to reduce population pressure on what has become — for Brunei — a sub-standard residential area.

To get a first hand look at what remains of the "old Brunei," hop on a water taxi from any of the landing points along Jalan Residency and ask for *Kampung Air* Saba; you will be dropped off directly across the way at any one of four wards sharing this name. Residents usually don't mind courteous visitors using their walkways and having a look around. The trip over will be short but exciting because of so many speeding water taxis on near collision courses.

Tambing wharf, near the corner of Jalan Pretty and Jalan Roberts, sells seafood which comes directly from the boats of local fisherman, unlike that sold elsewhere in BSB.

Many local residents still prefer to shop in the *tamu* or open market along Jalan Kianggeh, across from the Brunei Hotel, because of the freshness of the produce and the range of jungle fruits available, plus the nostalgic festive atmosphere of an old-style market day on Friday and Sunday mornings.

Devoted to culture and history

The **Brunei Arts and Handicrafts Training Centre**, in Jalan Residency, was established to revive disappearing traditional crafts. A wide range of goods produced by the Centre's students and instructors are on sale. The Centre has also started to market baskets and mats made by traditional groups living in the interior. Open daily.

The Sultan's private collection of Islamic Art is the centerpiece of the **Brunei Museum**, in Jalan Kota Batu (4.5 km). There is a world-class array of illuminated manuscripts of the Koran, ceramics, metalwork, glass, jewellery, coins, rugs and more. The neighbouring gallery prepared by Brunei Shell explains the geological and industrial processes that contribute to Brunei's wealth. The Natural History gallery displays some of the wildlife that occurs in Brunei (except the orang-utan). Archaeological finds and traditional Malay cultural practices are also highlighted in their respective galleries. Open daily except on Mondays.

A short walk down the hill from the Brunei Museum, the **Malay Technology Museum** (5.5 km) highlights traditional house-building techniques, methods of fishing, boat-making and metal-working. Open everyday except Tuesday.

The old Churchill Museum (the current sultan's father was a great fan of this statesman) was replaced in late 1992 by the **Royal Regalia Exhibition Hall**, full of items commemorating the 25 years of Sultan Hassanal Bolkiah's rule. An imposing gold-domed building with intricate mosaics opposite the Youth Centre in Jalan Kianggeh, the **Royal Ceremonial Hall** is where traditional ceremonies are normally held. Yet another monument associated with royalty is the **mausoleum** in Jalan Kota Batu, marking the tomb of the fifth Sultan of Brunei, Sultan Bolkiah.

A surprising wealth of wildlife

Bukit Patoi, Temburong (15 km from Bangar on the road to Labu) is located within the Peradayan Forest Reserve. A well constructed 1.6 km trail goes through dipterocarp forest to heath forest.

There cannot be another place in Southeast Asia where it is possible to hear the call of the rare Malaysia Honeyguide bird (*Indicator archipelagicus*) with the Muslim call to prayers as accompaniment. **Bukit Saeh** can be reached by taking a water taxi to Kg Sungai Kebun; walk away from town towards Kg Lumapas for about 2.5 km. Ask passers-by for help in finding the entrance if the track is overgrown. The track leading to the summit (220m) follows a stream that flows over formations of sandstone; it is possi-

ble to get a spectacular view of Bandar from the summit.

Speeding through the mangrove

Brunei has some of the most interesting mangrove in North Borneo. The easiest way to see it is to hop on a boat to **Temburong**. The "flying coffin" races along the streams amid the mangrove, past unbroken stands of *nipah* palm and the stilt-rooted mangrove tree *Rhizophora acuminate*. The attentive and lucky observer may also catch a glimpse of proboscis monkeys along the banks.

Persiaran Damuan, a well-manicured park along the river bank on Jalan Tutong (7 km), provides a distant but unobstructed view of the **Istana Nurul Iman**. It's a popular spot for joggers and strolling families; a modest restaurant serves seafood in the evening. The native mangrove vegetation lining the river bank and the exotic shrubbery planted on higher ground attracts over 40 species of birds. Sharp-eyed evening observers may catch a glimpse of proboscis monkeys settling for the night in the mangrove vegetation across the river.

A hut perched high on the hillside across from the waterfall in **Tasek Lama**, provides good views of forest birds such as barbets, bee-eaters and leafbirds in an area surprisingly close to the town center.

You can't miss the **Omar Ali Saifuddin Mosque**. On a clear night the illuminated gold dome of this impressive mosque right in the center of town can be seen from the summit of Gunung Pagon, Brunei's highest mountain, about 80 km away. The replica of a 16th century royal barge in the lagoon adjoining the mosque is used for Koran-reading competitions. Visitors to the mosque should dress modestly and remove their shoes before entering. Do not touch the Koran or pass in front of someone praying. Closed to all non-Muslim visitors on Thursday. On Friday open from 4.30 pm-5.30 pm; Saturday through Wednesday from 8 am-12 noon, 1 pm-3.30 pm, and 4.30 pm to 5.30 pm. Brunei's **new mosque** can be seen from the highway leading to the airport.

The world's largest palace

The Sultan is reputed to be the wealthiest man on earth and fittingly lives in the largest palace in the world. The **Istana Nurul Iman**, on Jalan Tutong (4.5 km) has 1,788 rooms and is where the First Queen resides and the Sultan carries out his duties as Prime Minister. The Istana is opened to the public only on the second, third and fourth days of Hari Raya, the holiday that marks the end of Ramadan, the Muslim fasting month. The official residence of the Second Queen, the **Istana Nurul Izzah**, in Jerudong, (about 25 km from Bandar Seri Begawan) is relatively modest in scale.

The royal stables at **Jerudong Park** house about 650 polo ponies plus a range of sports facilities, beach houses and mini-palaces. The facilities are not opened to the general public but it is possible for visitors to drive by some of them.

— *M. M. Ng*

Above, left: *Bruneians enjoy a high income and interest-free government loans for the purchase of cars.* **Above right:** *Polo, the Sultan's favorite sport, is played at the private Jerudong Park.*

West Sabah Practicalities

KOTA KINABALU

GETTING THERE

Kota Kinabalu can be reached by air (see p. 191 for details); by ferry from Brunei via Labuan, or by mini-bus from Lawas in northern Sarawak. The airport is just 7 km from the city; as there is no bus service, take a taxi which will cost between M$8-M$12. The Sabah Tourism Promotion Corporation maintains an information center at the airport.

AIRLINE OFFICES: British Airways, Harrison & Crossfield, Jln Haji Saman, tel: (088) 215011. **Cathay Pacific**, Kompleks Kuasa, tel: (088) 54733/54758. **MAS**, Kompleks Karamunsing, tel: (088) 51455 **Royal Brunei**, Kompleks Kuasa Tel: (088) 242193/242194. **Singapore Airlines,** Kompleks Kuasat, tel: (088) 55444/55449. **Thai Airways International**, Kompleks Kuasa, tel: (088) 232896.

GETTING AROUND KK

Buses run from the center of town to the beach at Tanjung Aru and other suburban destinations. There is also a network of minibuses plying local routes. **Taxis**, generally painted white, can be taken from ranks located near major shopping areas or hailed in the street. They are usually air-conditioned and have meters; although official rates are M$1.40 for the first km, with M$1 for each subsequent km, most drivers prefer to negotiate the fare in advance. From downtown to the Museum should be around M$5; to Tanjung Aru, M$8. To call a taxi, phone (088) 52113, (088) 56346, (088) 52188 or (088) 52669. For **car hire** details, see "Getting Around Sabah."

ACCOMMODATION

Hotels in Sabah are often more expensive than their counterparts in Sarawak. Tourist-class hotels impose service charge (10%) and government tax (5%) for both rooms and food. Prices given are net unless otherwise indicated. (AC = air-conditioned.)

Luxury (over M$200)

Shangrila's Tanjung Aru Resort, Jalan Aru, Tanjung Aru. Tel: (088) 58711/225800. Fax:

(088) 217155. 254 rooms and suites, plus another 165 due to open mid-1993. From M$340 S, M$370 D + 15%. Sabah's premier luxury hotel located less than 10 minutes from downtown, with free bus service to city. Beautiful garden setting with swimming pool, tennis courts, fitness center, playground, and marina offering wide range of water sports plus transport to nearby islands. Best Western food in town in coffee shop and Pepino Italian restaurant.

Hyatt Kinabalu Hotel, Jln Datuk Salleh Sulong. Tel: (088) 219888. Fax: (088) 225972. 350 rooms and suites, from M$240 + 15%. Conveniently located in the heart of town. Swimming pool, restaurants, business and health centers, travel services, full room facilities. Chinese and Continental restaurants; delicatessen with excellent bread, pastries and pizza, perfect for picnics on the islands.

Moderate (M$100-M$199)

Hotel Capital, 23 Jln Haji Saman. Tel: (088) 231999. Fax: (088) 237222. 107 rooms. M$125 S, M$135 D. Long established hotel in center of town. Full room facilities, very popular restaurant and coffee shop.

Palace Hotel, 1 Jln Tanki, Karamunsing. Tel: (088) 211911. Fax: (088) 211600. 160 rooms. from M$143. Pleasant hotel with full room facilities, restaurants, business center, travel services and swimming pool. Five minutes from downtown.

Hotel Jesselton, 69 Gaya Street. Tel: (088) 55633. Fax: (088) 225985. 27 rooms. M$140. Charming older hotel in center of town.

Hotel Shangri-La, Bandaran Berjaya. Tel: (088) 212800. Fax: (088) 212078. 126 rooms. M$120-M$380. Full room facilities, 24-hr coffee shop and Chinese restaurant.

Inexpensive (under M$100)

Ang's Hotel, Jln Tun Adbul Razak. Tel: (088) 234999. Fax: (088) 217867. From M$48.30 S, M$56.35 D. One of KK's oldest hotels, recently renovated; right in center of town; AC, TV, attached bathroom, phone.

Cecilia's B & B, 413 Jln Saga, Likas. Tel: (088)35733. Fax: (088)424998. 6 double rooms; in a residential area 5-10 minutes from downtown KK.

Hotel Rakyat, Lot 3, Block 1 Sinsuran Shopping Complex. Tel: (088)211100. 9 rooms. M$30 S with fan and shared bathroom. M$37 D fan and shared bathroom. M$45 D bathroom and AC. One of the better budget hotels in the downtown area.

Seaside Travellers Inn, Km 20 Kota

Kinabalu/Papar Rd, Kinarut. Tel: (088) 750313/750479. Fax: (088) 223399. Accommodates 35 in S & D rooms plus 1 dormitory. M$20-M$60. Relax on the water's edge in homely surroundings, 20-30 minutes by frequent mini-bus from KK. Dining room, TV and barbecue area. Ideal for families.

Sukan Sports Complex Hostel, Likas. Tel: (088) 52174/221721. M$15.75 S in separate men's and women's hostels, M$42 deluxe double room with AC. Excellent value; 10 minutes from center of town.

DINING

Kota Kinabalu has an excellent array of fresh seafood, also temperate-climate vegetables direct from the slopes of Mount Kinabalu plus interesting tropical produce. Malaysian favorites (Chinese, Malay and Indian) as well as Western cuisine, Thai, Japanese, Korean and American-style fast food readily available. (Prices given are average cost per head, without drinks.)

Seafood

Excellent seafood can be enjoyed in almost every restaurant, although some specialize. A number of simple fan-cooled coffee shop restaurants feature barbecued seafood at night. Local favorites include seasoned fish, prawns or ray, wrapped in banana leaf and grilled over charcoal.

100% Seafood Restaurant, Jln Aru, Tanjung Aru Beach. Tel: (088) 238313. A tempting market-style display of fresh seafood and vegetables enables you to select your favorites and request them cooked in whatever style you want. No menu, unfortunately, but you can ask for advice on the best way to treat your scallops, crab claws, grouper etc. Free transport from Hyatt and Tanjung Aru Resort hotels. Around M$20 per person.

Port View Seafood Restaurant, Jln Haji Saman. Tel: (088) 22153. Open only in the evenings, this very casual and popular open-fronted restaurant chalks up the daily specials on a blackboard. Delicious *asam pedas* fish curry, good shellfish, with live fish kept in a tank making the ultimate steamed fish. M$10-$12.

Windbell Seafood Restaurant, 20 Jln Selangor, Tanjung Aru Beach. Tel: (088) 222305, or (088) 812305. Live seafood in tanks, as well as other very good Chinese dishes, including steamboat (a type of fondue with a wide range of ingredients you cook at the table). Modestly priced therefore usually crowded, so be sure to book. Free transport to your hotel provided. M$10-M$15.

Chuan Hin, Jln Kolam (next to Cottage Pub), Luyang. Tel: (088) 235960. Simple suburban coffee shop with perhaps the best banana-leaf barbecued seafood in KK sold during the evening; don't miss the delicious ray. The banana-leaf wrapped beef and fried Chinese *woh teh* dumplings are also excellent. M$8-M$10.

Chinese food

All the restaurants recommended for seafood also offer good Chinese cuisine, although neither Port View nor 100% Seafood serve pork. Some of the best Chinese food is found in unpretentious suburban restaurants. The following, more conveniently located restaurants are recommended:

Nan Xing Restaurant, Jln Pantai. Tel: (088) 212900. Popular long-established restaurant, well known for its morning *dim sum* and good Cantonese food. M$10-M$15.

Phoenix Court, Hyatt Kinabalu Hotel, Jln Haji Saman. Tel: (088) 221234. Cantonese and Szechuan favorites, *dim sum* available for lunch. Conveniently located downtown; good service. M$15-M$18.

Malay/Indonesian

Sri Kapitol Restaurant and Coffee Shop, Hotel Capital, Tel: (088) 231999 Jln Haji Saman. Arguably the best Malay food in town, with highly regarded sour fish curry (*ikan asam pedas*), coconut beef curry (*rendang*), mild chicken curry (*ayam korma*). Chinese dishes (including good yam basket filled with chicken and vegetables) also available. The 1st floor restaurant has a wider selection and costs around M$15-M$18; the ground floor coffee shop meals are around M$8.

The stalls above the **Central Market**, especially those at the far corner overlooking the sea, offer a wide range of inexpensive food, including the Buginese *coto/soto Makassar*, a spicy beef soup from southern Sulawesi. A plate of rice with several dollops of meat, fish and vegetable (*nasi campur*) will cost around M$3. Closes early evening.

Sri Rahmat, Segama Complex. Delicious Malay food in casual but spotless restaurant right in the heart of town. Has separate airconditioned room which makes it ideal for lunch. Select from a wide array of ready cooked spicy dishes. About M$5. Closes 9 pm.

Sri Sempeleng, Jln Sembulan. An open eating shop with Malay and Indonesian favorites. Packed with government clerks from nearby offices throughout the day. Reputedly the best spicy chicken noodle soup (*soto ayam*) in town:

bony but delicious. M$3-$5.

Indian

Shiraz Restaurant, Sedco Square, Kampung Air. Tel: (088) 225088 Only northern Indian restaurant in town; nothing fantastic but has good vegetable dishes and *tandoori* chicken. The oven-baked breads (*naan*) are disappointing; stick with the saffron rice. M$15-M$18.
Restoran Bilal, Segama Shopping Complex. Basic open-fronted eating shop in convenient location. Good southern Indian curries, flaky pancakes (*roti canai*); M$5.
Kedai Makan Mars. In Sinsuron Shopping Complex, near Hotel Rakyat. Open-fronted southern Indian restaurant with *roti canai*, *murtabak* and — although not listed on the menu — good rice-flour pancakes (*dosai*) served with delicious fresh coconut chutney. A selection of tasty vegetable dishes makes this a good spot for vegetarians. There is also the usual spicy meat, fish and poultry. M$2-M$5.

Western Food

The best Western food in town is at the **Tanjung Aru Resort coffee shop**, including lavish luncheon buffet and food from different regions each evening. Tel:(088) 58711/ 225800. M$15-$35. Their outdoor **Garden Restaurant** is a romantic spot to dine on a tropical evening. **Pepino's** Italian restaurant in the same hotel scores highly in terms of ambience and service, the food varying from adequate to very good. Stick with the hors d'oeuvre and pasta and you can't go wrong. Expensive wines. At least M$50 for food alone.
Semporna Grill at the Hyatt, (088) 221234, features American steaks as well as Continental dishes. M$30-M$40. Their coffee shop has a good buffet lunch.

A Bit of Everything

A wide range of inexpensive **local dishes** (around M$3-$5) together with **Western fast foods** (Pizza Hut, Kentucky Fried Chicken) can be found in the airconditioned basement of **Centrepoint** shopping center. There are also a number of local foodstalls on the 3rd floor of Yaohan department store within Centrepoint, while pasta, ice creams and local dishes are available at Caprilano, in the atrium of Centrepoint.

First floor of **Wisma Merdeka**, at the back of the building overlooking the sea, you can get some of KK's best local food, especially in **Chomp Chomp Park**: there's delicious Singapura Nasi Ayam (chicken rice); excellent desserts such as *bubor cha cha* (coconut milk with everything) or *pulot hitam* (black rice pudding), and lovely sour Penang noodle soup (Penang *Asam Laksa*). Near Chomp Chomp Park, the small **Kinabalu Cafeteria** often has Kadazan specialities such as *hinava* (raw fish) and *sambal bambangan* (local mango pickle) as part of its mixed rice (*nasi campur*) range.

Popular at lunchtime for its local favorites as well as several Western dishes, the air-conditioned **Wishbone Cafe**, in Hotel Jesselton in Jln Gaya is pricier at around M$8-M$10, but cool and convenient.

Expensive but good Thai/Chinese food is served at **Jaw's Restaurant**, 4th fl, Gaya Center, Jln Haji Saman. The best Japanese restaurant is **Azuma**, on 1st floor of Wisma Merdeka; *sushi, sashimi, teppanyaki* and other Japanese dishes. Around M$40. Cheaper Japanese cuisine sold at **Nishiki**, in Jln Gaya; where a set lunch costs around M$15. For moderately-priced, robust Korean food, try **Korea House** in Bandaran Berjaya.

ENTERTAINMENT

There isn't a great deal going on at night, apart from live groups in the Tanjung Aru Resort and the popular disco-cum-karaoke lounges where you can dance, sing and drink until the early hours. Every Sunday night, the Tanjung Aru Resort's **Malam Kampung** gives you the chance to see a cultural show with colorful local dances; call the hotel to book as they're often sold out. For lighter entertainment, the current favorites are:
Tiffiny's, Block A, No.9, Jalan Karamunsing. One of the livelier discos with karaoke lounge.
Bourgoisie, 1st fl, Jln Gaya (near Nationwide Express). Small, crowded and very popular disco.
Rocky's Fun Pub/Cafe, 1st fl, Lot 52, Jalan Gaya (just up from Tong Hing Supermarket). Open for lunch and again at 4.30 pm for drinks, food (hamburgers, fried chicken and seafood, sandwiches etc.), fun and music, with disco getting into full swing after 10.30 pm.
Sedco Square, Kampung Air, is a popular spot for relaxing and people-watching over a drink as well as for eating. When the sun goes down, stalls and restaurants around the square offer seafood, satay, noodles and excellent *woh teh* (Chinese fried dumplings). A bit noisy and the girls employed by the breweries work hard at persuading you to have another beer. Perfectly safe for unaccompanied girls.

SHOPPING

Basketware is one of the best buys in Sabah, ranging from finely woven miniature hats and gaily colored Bajau foodcovers, to Kadazan backpacks and strong Rungus reedwork. The bamboo tube musical instrument, *sompoton*, is another light and attractive souvenir.

Pink, cream and grey **pearls** grown at the Semporna pearl farm can be found in some jewellery and souvenir shops. Modern **beadwork** by the Rungus is inexpensive and cheerful; more costly are the woven fabrics produced by the Rungus and Bajau. Unlike Sarawak, it is very difficult to locate genuine antiques in Sabah. Local **pottery** is popular with many visitors; it is possible to arrange shipping of the large jars used to make rice wine, and which echo the style of ancient Chinese ceramic jars.

Souvenir shops are found on the ground floors of Wisma Sabah, Wisma Merdeka, Centrepoint, and in the Sabah Tourism Promotion Corporation in Jln Gaya. The gift shop at Kinabalu Park is another good outlet. The Filipino market has a wide range of inexpensive **handicrafts from the Philippines**, including a few baskets from Sarawak and Indonesian *batiks*.

Typical goods from Peninsular Malaysia, including *batik* and **pewterware** can also be bought in KK though naturally for a higher price.

Best places for **books** on Borneo are the Sabah Museum gift shop, Borneo Craft (ground floor of Wisma Merdeka) and the giftshop at Kinabalu Park. For novels and more general books, try Times Bookshop, next to Yaohan department store, 2nd floor, Centrepoint.

HEALTH

The best place in Sabah with the most sophisticated equipment and highly trained doctors is Sabah Medical Centre, Likas, 10-15 minutes north of downtown KK. Tel: (088) 424333.

MISCELLANEOUS

To stock up on **food** and drinks for a picnic, or for snacks to take to the islands or Kinabalu Park, try Tong Hing, in Gaya Street. They have a wide range of Western foodstuffs, including cheese and fresh milk; their bakery offers breads, pastries, sandwiches and local favorites. Open from 8 am to 9.30 pm daily.

Licensed **money changers**, who generally offer a better rate than the banks, can be found on the ground floor of the Wisma Merdeka shopping complex, and the ground floor of Centrepoint shopping complex.

SABAH PARKS

Sabah Parks, Jln Tun Fuad Stephens. Tel: (088) 211652. Fax: (088) 221001. Postal Address: P.O.Box 10626, 88806 Kota Kinabalu, Sabah,

Malaysia. They maintain a range of comfortable, moderately priced accommodation at **Kinabalu Park**, the islands of **Pulau Manukan** and **Pulau Mamutik** in the Tunku Abdul Rahman Park, and **Pulau Tiga** south of KK. All accommodation must be booked and paid for in advance. Book well ahead, by mail or fax, to ensure accommodation at Kinabalu Park during July and August, and December, as well as public holidays.

Accommodation at **Pulau Selingan** ("Turtle Island") must be booked via the Sandakan office, tel: (089) 273453; if you're going with a tour operator, obviously they will handle the booking.

Pulau Manukan, Tunku Abdul Rahman Park. 20 chalets, some located near the beach, others on a hillside. M$140 per chalet weekdays and Sunday, M$200 Saturday night and eve of public holidays. Each chalet has 2 twin-bed rooms sleeping a total of 4. Fridge and facilities for making hot drinks but no kitchen. Manukan has a restaurant (open 7.30 am-9 pm), swimming pool (M$1), squash court (M$10 per hour).

Pulau Mamutik, Tunku Abdul Rahman Park. Two-storey resthouse on beach. M$110 per night, M$160 Saturday and public holidays. 3 rooms sleeping 8 persons, cooking facilities, fridge, bathroom.

Gayana Resort, Malohom Bay, Gaya Island. Privately owned accommodation next to boundary of Tunku Abdul Rahman Park. 4 D rooms, AC, attached bath, $150; 22-bed dormitory with fan, shared bathroom, M$40 S. Restaurant, sporting facilities including scuba diving, fishing, canoeing, glass-bottom boat. M$15 return transfer by boat from jetty in front of Hyatt. As this is outside Sabah Park's territory, book at **Borneo Expeditions** (see Tour Operators).

If you are staying overnight in Sabah Parks' accommodation, request when booking transport on the Koktas boat (M$10 per person one way,) or use a private operator.

Boats to Tunku Abdul Rahman Park

Boats for private hire leave from the waterfront outside the Hyatt Hotel. Don't worry about finding them; the boat boys chase any likely tourist in the vicinity. Prices are negotiable but are around M$20 per person to Police Beach, M$10 to Pulau Sapi, Manukan and Mamutik, and M$12 to Sulug; if you are alone or only two, a minimum of $50 for the boat is usually charged. Make sure there are lifejackets on board before departing; if not, the boat is probably unregistered so don't risk taking it. Do not pay until your return trip. Regular weekend services are offered in a larger boat by Coral Island Cruises; tel: (088) 223490.

Glass-bottom Boat

An ideal way to view life on the coral reefs around Pulau Manukan and Sapi is to take a ride in a glass-bottom boat. This can be booked with the Park Ranger while you are on either of these islands but to be sure reserve in advance from Sabah Parks' downtown office before leaving KK. M$8 per person.

TOURIST INFORMATION

Sabah Tourism Promotion Corporation. 51 Jln Gaya, tel: (088) 218620/212121. Also at airport. Open 8 am-4.15 pm weekdays, half-day Saturday. For information and brochures on tours, accommodation, transport, special events. Very helpful and friendly.

SABAH STATE MUSEUM

Jln Kebajikan, off Jln Penampang. Open 10 am-6 pm Mon-Thurs; 9 am-6 pm Sat, Sun, Public Holidays; closed Friday. Admission free.

TOUR OPERATORS

Tour operators based in Kota Kinabalu offer tours for all of Sabah, linking up with specialists in Sandakan for their east coast tours. Prices vary depending upon the number of people in a group. The more imaginative tour operators can arrange for trekking or longhouse vis-

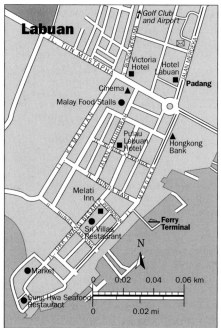

its, and will usually tailor a trip to suit special needs if advised in advance. Tour operators include:

Api Tours, ground fl. Wisma Sabah. Tel: (088) 223848/218658. Fax: (088) 221230. Friendly company with a good range of tours throughout Sabah. They also handle airline bookings for onward travel.

Borneo Eco Tours, 3rd floor, Lot 6, Block J, Sadong Jaya.Tel: (088) 234009. Fax: (088) 233688. Specializing in tours focussing upon Sabah's natural environment, they also offer tours to Brunei and several destinations in Sarawak, a special bird-watching tour, and trekking in the Crocker Range.

Borneo Expeditions, Unit 306, 3rd floor, Wisma Sabah. Tel: (088) 222721. Fax: (088) 222720. Sabah's white-water rafting specialists who also conduct a good range of 1 or 2-day trekking tours. Booking agent for Gayana Resort on Pulau Gaya, tel: (088) 223034.

Borneo's Memories, 1st fl, No. 1 Lorong Ewan (near Tong Hing Supermarket), Kota Kinabalu. Tel: (088) 221586. Fax: (088) 233562. Small company with imaginative range of tours, specializing in trekking and wildlife exploration on west coast.

Coral Island Cruises, ground fl. Wisma Sabah. Tel: (088) 223490 Fax: (088) 223404. Regular weekend boat to Pulau Manukan. Fully equipped small cruise ship makes scuba diving and fishing trips by arrangement to Pulau Sipadan, Pulau Tiga and Layang Layang Reef, about 18 hours from KK.

Discovery Tours, ground fl. Wisma Sabah. Tel: (088) 53787/57735 Fax: (088) 221600. Largest tour operator offering standard tours to all major destinations.

Wildlife Expeditions, 331B, 3rd fl, Wisma Sabah. Tel & fax: (088) 260000. "The" wildlife specialists on the east coast, also offering tours of Kinabalu Park.

SCUBA DIVING

Diver training courses are available in Kota Kinabalu, and divers with evidence of certification can enjoy diving the waters around the islands of the Tunku Abdul Rahman Park. The ultimate diving spot in Sabah is Pulau Sipadan (see p.176 for diving packages).

Borneo Divers & Seasports, 4th floor, Wisma Sabah. Tel: (088) 222226. Fax: (088) 221550. Largest and most professional operator in Sabah, offering Padi Open Water Dive Course from M$650-M$900. Single dives in KK including tanks and belt cost M$65, night dives M$100. They also maintain a lodge at Pulau Sipadan, and an office in Labuan, where diver training and wreck diving are available. **Borneo Sea Adventures**, 1st fl, 8A Karamunsing Warehouse, Kota Kinabalu. Tel: (088) 55390. Fax: (088) 221106. Diver training with the Scuba Schools International certification; also dives around Kota Kinabalu; they maintain Sipadan Dive Centre on Pulau Sipadan. Charges for a single dive in KK M$60, night dive M$80. Three-day Open Water Dive Course M$650.

FERRY TO LABUAN

The cheapest way to travel between Kota Kinabalu and Brunei, and then on the Sarawak, is to take the ferry to Labuan. This departs from the jetty in front of the Hyatt Hotel at 8 am and 1.30 pm daily; M$28 per person; around 2 1/2 hours traveling time. Board the ferry at least 15 minutes in advance to be sure of a seat. (See pp. 162 and 171 for travel from Labuan to Brunei and Sarawak.)

GETTING AROUND SABAH

As the trip by road from Kota Kinabalu to Sandakan on the east coast takes 6-8 hours, **air** travel is recommended for visitors with limited time. Several MAS flights per day link Kota Kinabalu with Sandakan, Tawau and Lahad Datu, with 2 flights weekly to Kudat. **Sabah Air** (tel: 088 56733) offer spectacular helicopter sightseeing tours, as well as the ultimate transportation between Tawau and Pulau Sipadan.

Minibuses leave KK for all major towns in West Sabah, as well as traveling to Tambunan, Keningau and Tenom in the Interior, and even across to Sandakan on the east coast, an 8-hour trip. Minibuses normally start around 7 am, leaving when they are full. They are well maintained, reasonably comfortable and inexpensive, with fares ranging from M$5 to Beaufort, M$8 to Kinabalu Park to a maximum of M$35 to Sandakan.

Long-distance ("outstation") **taxis,** which can be chartered or shared with 3 other passengers, are moderately priced (e.g. M$25 per person for the 4-hour trip to Tenom).

You need not worry that you will be asked to pay more than the standard price for regular transport in Sabah, although if you charter a taxi or mini-bus, you are expected to bargain.

Car Hire prices range from M$130 per day for a self-driven sedan, with more luxurious models and 4WD vehicles costing from M$240. Major hotels can arrange car hire, or contact: **E & C Rent-a-Car**, ground floor, Wisma Sabah. Tel: (088) 57679 **Kinabalu Rent-a-Car**, Hyatt Hotel and Tanjung Aru Resort. Tel: (088) 232602.

KINABALU PARK

Visitors intending to stay at Kinabalu Park must book and pay for accommodation in advance (in cash) at Sabah Parks office in KK (see p.168 for address). There is an entrance fee of M$2 for day visitors to the Park, both at Headquarters and at Poring Hot Springs. If staying overnight, tell the guard and the fee will be waived. The canopy walkway at Poring costs M$2 per person between 10.30 am and 4 pm; 4 pm-10 pm M$30 for up to 3 persons; all other times, M$60 for up to 3. M$5 is charged for those who take their camera along.

Accommodation

Accommodation in Kinabalu Park is available at **Park Headquarters** (1,500 m), at **Panar Laban** and vicinity (3,350 m), and at **Poring Hot Springs** (600 m). Prices are higher on Saturday nights and public holidays (except at Panar Laban and at the hostels) and are indicated in brackets.

At **Park Headquarters**, 2 **hostels** (Old and New) hold 46 and 52 respectively, in 8-bed dormitories. Shared bathrooms (cold water) and kitchen with basic utensils and gas. M$10 and M$15 per bed respectively, students M$3 and M$4. **Twin-bed cabins** with bathroom and hot water M$50 (M$80).

The **Annexe** of the Administration Building has 4 twin-bed Basement Rooms with attached bathroom (hot water) for the same price as the twin-bed cabins. In the same building, the 2-storey Annex Suites sleeping 4 and with 2 bathrooms cost M$100 (M$150).

There is a range of **chalets** with bathroom (hot water), kitchen and fireplace. These include the Duplex Chalets, sleeping 6, M$150 (M$200); Kinabalu Lodge, sleeping 8, M$270 (M$360); and the luxurious Nepenthes Villas, sleeping 4, M$180 (M$250).

The most comfortable accommodation for climbers is the **Laban Rata Resthouse**, which sleeps 54 in heated dormitory rooms. Shared bathrooms with hot water (provided you're not last up the mountain). Restaurant with reasonable range of food at moderate prices, considering the location. M$25 per person.

The nearby **Gunting Lagadan Hostel** has dormitory accommodation, electricity, cooking facilities (though you can eat at the Resthouse restaurant) and shared bathroom with very cold water. M$4 per adult, M$1 student. **Waras Hut** and **Panar Laban Hut** both have dormitory accommodation for 12, electricity, cooking facilities and toilet. M$4 adult, M$1 student. **Sayat**

Sayat Hut, about 1 hr further up the mountain from Panar Laban, is spartan; no electricity, but cooking facilities. M$4 adult, M$1 students.

Poring Hot Springs has 2 hostels, M$8 per person, M$2 for students. The **Old Hostel** has dormitory rooms for 24, kitchen, sitting room and shared bathrooms; **New Hostel,** rooms for 4 and 6 persons, total 42 beds. There are two attractive cabins with bedrooms, balcony, kitchen, bathroom and sitting room; the **Old Cabin** sleeps 6 in 3 bedrooms, M$70 (M$100), while the **New Cabin** sleeps 4 in 2 bedrooms, M$60 (M$80). A **camping ground** with a very basic kitchen and bathroom (bring your own tent) costs M$1 per adult, M$0.50 for students. A **restaurant** was due to open end-1992; very basic foodstuffs sold at store opposite entrance to Poring; best to buy in KK or Ranau if you want to do your own catering.

Climbing Expenses

A climbing permit costs M$10 (M$2 students). A compulsory guide costs M$25 per day for up to 3 persons; M$28 for 4-6; M$30 for 7-8. You can team up with other climbers if you want to reduce expenses. Porters (carrying up to 10 kg) cost M$25 per day. A ride to Power Station, where the climb starts, costs M$10 per person on a shared basis.

Getting There

Unless you have a lot of luggage, don't bother taking the big Ranau bus that leaves KK at 8 am daily (M$8) and stops on the main road about 50 m from Kinabalu Park entrance. **Minibuses** departing from near the Padang (not far from the Ranau bus depot) are faster and leave from early morning until at least mid-afternoon, whenever there are enough passengers on board. Minibuses take about 1 3/4 hours and cost M$8; the driver will take you right into the Park Headquarters.

For your return to KK, wait by the main road in front of the Park for a mini-bus from Ranau.

Although Koktas (the Parks' staff co-operative) is supposed to provide transport between Headquarters and Poring Hot Springs, it rarely seems to be available. Take a minibus from in front of the Park to Ranau (M$3), then charter another from there to Poring (there's no regular public transport). After bargaining, you should get it for about M$5 per person one way. If staying overnight, you can arrange with the driver to collect you to return to Ranau.

What to Bring

As temperatures can drop below freezing, warm clothing is essential; bring an anorak and sweater; tracksuit pants and shorts; hat; light raincoat or poncho; a torch (flashlight); comfortable walking or jogging shoes; at least 2 pairs of socks; gloves for gripping the often icy ropes on the steep granite faces; towel; headache tablets and adhesive strips in case of blisters.

KUNDASANG

Located about 5 km from Kinabalu Park Headquarters, this offers alternative accommodation for visitors. There are a couple of inexpensive lodging houses and the **Hotel Perkasa,** Kundasang Tel: (088) 80316. 74 rooms. M$100-M$120. Dramatic hilltop location with view of Kinabalu's summit; full room facilities, restaurant, bar and tennis.

SOUTH

PULAU TIGA

The comfortable 3-bedroom resthouse with bathroom and kitchen sleeps six. M$30 per person. A fishing boat can be hired from the river in front of Kuala Penyu town; it should cost approximately M$120 for the return trip. Expect to pay at least another M$30 if you want to visit the other islands near Tiga on the way there or back. Book accommodation in advance at Sabah Parks in Kota Kinabalu.

BEAUFORT

If you are arriving by minibus and plan on riding the railcar, ask your driver to let you off at the station. The **railcar** through the Padas Gorge to Tenom leaves at 8.40 am and 3.40 pm Monday-Saturday, 4.05 pm Sunday. Price: M$8.25 one way. As the railcar has very limited seating and is popular (it's much faster than the train to Tenom), ensure a seat by phoning Beaufort station (tel: 087 211518) at least a day in advance. Collect your ticket 45 minutes before departure. While waiting for the train, you can eat at **Christopher's Corner Parking** (Western food and clean toilets) or **Chung Mei** (for noodles or dim sum at breakfast). Both are located in the old shophouses immediately opposite the station.

Minibuses returning to KK leave a block away near the market, but invariably pass the station looking for passengers.

LABUAN

Air-conditioned express ferries leave Labuan daily for **Kota Kinabalu** at 8.30 am and 1 pm, costing M$28 economy and taking about 2 1/2 hours. Vehicular ferries (M$5 per person) take about 1 hour (1/2 hour and M$8 for the express) to Menumbok in Sabah, which is about 2 1/2 hours by minibus from Kota Kinabalu; departures at 8 am and 1 pm daily. Express boats to **Brunei**, costing M$22 and taking 1 1/2 hours, leave Labuan at 8 am, 12.15 pm and 2 pm daily; Labuan-**Lawas**, 1 pm, 2 1/2 hrs, M$20; Labuan-**Limbang**, 12.45 pm, 2 hrs, M$20.

Food and Accommodation

Although it offers a number of upmarket places to stay, Labuan is distinguished by having disproportionately high prices for dirty, dubious "inns". If you have to choose, try the **Melati Inn**, M$35 (S) and M$45 (D) for a room with AC and shared bathroom, M$48 for own bathroom. Best deal in town is $45 (S), $50 (D), M$50/M$60 (Suite) for a comfortable room with attached bathroom, AC, TV in the tranquil surroundings of the **Labuan Golf Club**, about M$5 by taxi from the ferry terminal and M$3 from the airport. Try to book in advance as there are only 4 rooms plus 2 suites. Tel: (087) 412711; Fax: (087) 416260. P.O.Box 276, 87008 Labuan, Malaysia.

The 4-star **Hotel Labuan** charges M$143 for a standard room. Tel: (087) 412502; Fax: (087) 415355. Better value found at the **Victoria Hotel**, just 2-3 minutes away. Rooms with AC, phone, TV, private bathroom cost M$65 S M$87 D. Tel: (087) 412411; Fax: (087) 412550.

Best place in Labuan to eat is the waterfront **Labuan Beach Restaurant**, Jln Tanjung Batu (opposite Sri Sabah), tel: (087) 415611. Enjoy sea breezes with either lunch or dinner on the wide verandah of a colonial style house. Western and local food for M$8-20, live music at night.

There are several coffee shops serving both Chinese and Malay food along **Jalan Merdeka**, near the ferry terminal. Good southern Indian food sold at **Jln OKK Awang Besar**. More stalls behind the New Lido Cinema in **Jln Muhibbah**. Excellent seafood available evenings at **Sung Hwa**, on the first floor of a rather scruffy building opposite the market; chilli crab, prawns, baked crayfish, barbecued stingray all at moderate prices. About M$8 per person.

NORTH

KOTA BELUD

Arguably the most delicious *roti canai* (flaky fried pancakes) to be found in Sabah — crisp, light, not greasy and served with a thick, richly spiced gravy — can be found in the **Bismillah Restaurant** facing the old market in the center of town. If you have to stay in Kota Belud for any reason, nicest and cheapest spot is the **government resthouse**, on a hillock on Jalan Ranau Bypass, a little beyond the *tamu* ground. M$12 per person, book first at the District Office, tel: (088) 97621.

KUDAT

The old part of town consists of a main street running down to the port, with a row of warehouses nearby and a branch of the Standard Chartered Bank. The Chinese-run warehouse selling outboard engines and general marine goods (opposite the bank) will change Philippine *pesos* (which the bank won't accept) into *ringgit*.

The large modern market building is a couple of minutes' walk away, and next to that is a group of newer buildings known locally as the Sedco shophouses. The area, reached via Jalan Melor, is quiet at night and has a range of Chinese and Muslim eating shops, plus two hotels at either end.

Best bet is the clean and friendly 18-room **Hotel Kinabalu** (tel: 088 62493), where prices range from M$36 for a single room with A/C, TV, phone and attached bathroom to M$48 for a standard double room; a deluxe twin-bed room with a view of the sea costs M$60. Offering the same facilities but a little more pricey, the **Hotel Greenland** (tel 088 62211) has 16 rooms ranging from M$39 S, M$56 D to M$126 D for a suite.

KOTA MARUDU

You'll find the usual cluster of Chinese and Muslim coffee shops selling food in the New Town of Kota Marudu, where the main market day, Sunday, attracts vendors from far and wide. There's a **government resthouse** (M$12 per person, book at the District Office, tel: (088) 661416, but the best place is the new 30-room **Marudu Inn** (tel: 088 661200) which costs M$80 per room, single or double occupancy, with A/C, TV, phone, and private bathroom.

— *Wendy Hutton*

Interior & East Sabah

INTERIOR

SUNSURON PASS

Gunong Emas Hotel and Restaurant, Km 52 KK/Tambunan Rd. Tel: (088) 248993 to book the quaint Borneo Treetop Cabins, each a double room with bathroom built around living trees on very steep hillside. M$60 per cabin. Some delicious food in the restaurant, particularly the *woh teh* Chinese dumplings and braised Sabah mushrooms. Also a small private zoo next to the restaurant.

TAMBUNAN

The **government resthouse**, located on a hillock above the village center, is one of the nicest in Sabah. Book in advance (087) 77331 or go to District Office (Pejabat Daerah) nearby. M$12 per person, A/C, attached bathroom.

Best place to eat, or buy food to take away for a picnic, is **Restoran Tambunan**, next to Sabah Bank. Try the local *sambal tuhau*, a condiment made with a ginger-like root, together with rice and Chinese food.

TENOM

The tourist-standard **Hotel Perkasa**, tel: (087) 735811, with full room facilities plus restaurant and bar, is located high on a hilltop above the town. M$65. Right in the main street, next to the BP station, is the moderately priced and adequate **Tenom Hotel**, only M$27 for a double room with A/C and attached bathroom. Nicest of all is the tiny resthouse at the **Agricultural Research Station**, Lagud Sebrang, in a peaceful location on a hill overlooking Tenom Valley. It's 20 km from town and you need to have your own transport to get there, and must bring or cook your own food in the resthouse kitchen. The usual M$12 per person; book in advance. Tel: (087) 735661, and collect key at head office of Research Station.

A favorite evening eating spot with many locals is the **YNL Entertainment Centre**, just across the Padas River on the road to Sapong. Excellent steamed *tilapia*, a freshwater fish. Good *dim sum* available for breakfast in several of the **coffee shops** along Tenom's main street, as well as long, deepfried Chinese savoury doughnuts (*yu tiow*).

It is possible to take the **railcar** from Tenom to Beaufort (6.40 am and 4 pm Monday - Saturday, 4.05 pm Sunday); M$8.25 per person. From Beaufort to KK, take a mini-bus (M$5) or share-taxi. An alternative is to go from Tenom to Keningau by **mini-bus**, then take another minibus to Kota Kinabalu, or to travel the entire distance Tenom-KK by air-conditioned **taxi** (M$25 per person on a share basis).

BATU PUNGGUL RESORT

The Korperasi Pembangunan Desa (KPD) offers a range of accommodation at the **Batu Punggul Resort** and arranges transport from Sapulut by motorised canoe. Bookings must be made in advance at KPD, Inanam (corner Jln Tuaran and Jln Kelombong), tel: (088) 428910, ext. 240.

To reach Batu Punggul independently (usually more expensive and more hassle), take a minibus from Kota Kinabalu to Keningau (about 1 1/2 hours) then transfer to a minibus travelling via Nabawan to Sapulut (around 3 hours). Leave KK no later than 7 am to be sure of finding a minibus in Keningau, and to arrive in Sapulut early enough to reach Batu Punggul (2-5 hours, depending on river level) before dark.

The Batu Punggul Resort resthouse offers a double master bedroom with attached bathroom for M$60, and 3 twin-bedrooms with shared bathroom M$30 D. Sleeping in the open hall of the traditional Murut longhouse, with mattress, pillow and bed linen provided, costs M$6 per person. Simple rooms with sleeping space for 4 cost M$32 per room. There is also a camping ground (often damp), for M$2 per day; tents available for hire at very modest fee. Students enjoy 50% reduction on all accommodation. (New cabins due to open late 1992.)

Meals available at the canteen, while cooking utensils and firewood are available for those who wish to cater for themselves; barbecue areas; cultural performances and the essential accompaniment of rice wine (*tapai*) can be arranged (M$15 per entertainer).

Boat transport from Sapulut to Batu Punggul return (maximum 6 persons) M$250 per boat. Guides cost M$15 per day for jungle trekking; M$20 to explore the caves; M$30 for the climb up Batu Punggul.

SANDAKAN

ACCOMMODATION

Ramada Renaissance Hotel, Km 1 Jln Utara. Tel: (089) 213299. Fax: (089) 271271. 120 rooms and suites. From M$270 S; M$300 D +15%. A surprisingly luxurious hotel built on the site of the old Governor's residence on a lushly forested hill. Complete 5-star room facilities, restaurants, business center, tennis, squash, gymn, landscaped swimming pool and golf arranged at Sandakan Golf Club.

Moderate (M$100-M$199)

Hotel Hsiang Garden, Hsiang Garden, Mile 1 1/2 Leila Rd. Tel: (089) 43191. Fax: (089) 43413. 45 rooms. M$110 S, M$140 D. Despite its unprepossessing location at the back of a complex of shophouses, this offers good value for money; full room facilities, restaurant with corner serving Japanese food, bar.

Hotel City View, Jln Tiga, Block 23, Lot 1. Tel: (089) 271122. Fax: (089) 273115. 29 rooms. From M$104.65 S, M$127.08 D. Full room facilities, restaurant. Clean and comfortable, right in the middle of town.

Inexpensive (under M$100)

Hotel Paris, 45 Jln Tiga. Tel: (089) 218488. 20 rooms. M$25 S, M$30 D without AC; M$38 S, M$48 D with AC. Central location.

Hung Wing Hotel, Jln Tiga. Tel: (089) 218855. 30 rooms. Doubles only from M33.60 non AC; M$40.70-M$54.60 AC. Popular budget hotel in center of town.

"Uncle Tan", Mile 17 1/2, Labuk Road, Sandakan. Fax: (089) 273863. Max. 15 guests. M$20 per person for accommodation and all meals. Simple, friendly home-stay in semi-rural area 5 km from Sepilok; bicycle hire M$3 a day. Most visitors go on to stay at Uncle Tan's "Jungle Camp." All long-distance buses pass Uncle Tan's; from Sandakan town, take any bus from the central station going beyond Mile (Batu) 18.

DINING

Trig Hill, Bukit Bendera Road has several restaurants with dining courtyards high on a hilltop overlooking Sandakan Bay; all specialize in seafood. Evenings only. Many locals claim the **Golden Palace** is the best place to eat; good steamboat (food cooked in type of fondue) as well as all types of seafood. M$15-M$18.

Pasir Putih, about 5 minutes by taxi from downtown, is a popular waterfront collection of restaurants specializing in seafood. M$15-M$18.

Supreme Garden Vegetarian Restaurant, Block 30, ground fl, Bandar Ramai Ramai, Leila Road. Tel: (089) 213292. In same road as Equatorial Restaurant (known to all taxi drivers); specializes in Chinese vegetarian cuisine. Delicious sizzling beancurd, seaweed soup and the full gamut of mock meat dishes, including "vegetar-

ian frog". M$10-M$12.

For a change, try **Korean Restaurant**, Hsiang Garden Estate, Mile 1 1/2, Leila Road. Tel: (089) 43891. Good range of robustly flavored traditional favorites at very reasonable prices. M$8-M$10.

Another possibility is the **Japanese Corner**, Regent Garden, Hotel Hsiang Garden, Mile 1 1/2 Leila Rd. Tel: (089) 43413. Small section of main restaurant set aside for *teppanyaki, shabu shabu* and *sukiyaki*. M$25.

Fast food local style is available at **Fairwood Restaurant**, Jln Tiga almost opp. Kentucky Fried Chicken). Popular and inexpensive place; open 7.30 am-10 pm. M$3-M$5.

Sandakan's oldest restaurant is the unpretentious **Kedai Kopi Sin Cheong Loong** in Jln Tiga opposite Hock Hua Bank; highly regarded chicken rice (*nasi ayam*) and steamed fish (*ikan kukus*) available for lunch only.

TOUR OPERATORS

Although all major tour operators based in Kota Kinabalu can arrange for a tour through Sandakan companies, you may find it preferable and less expensive to deal directly with the specialists. These include:

Api Tours, ground fl, C1, Block 50 (next to Shop & Save), Jln Leila, Sandakan. Tel: (089) 21998. Particularly helpful manager, Patricia Ng, can arrange tours to all major places of interest in and around Sandakan.

S.I. Tours, Lot 3B, 3rd fl, Yeng Yo Hong Bldg, Jln Leila, Sandakan (go through Shop & Save and take lift). Tel: (089) 213502 or 213503. Fax: (089) 271513/273987. Tours to all places of interest to the nature lover. They maintain a very comfortable riverside lodge on the Kinabatangan River at Sukau, just 5 minutes from an area renowned for proboscis monkeys and a magnificent range of birds.

Wildlife Expeditions, ground fl, Ramada Renaissance Hotel, Km 1, Jalan Utara, Sandakan. Downtown office next to Sabah Parks on 9th fl, Wisma Khoo Siak Chiew. Tel: (089) 273093, 214299 (ext. 8063). Fax: (089) 214570. Longest established tour company in Sandakan with fully professional services covering Turtle Islands, Sepilok Orang-utan Sanctuary, Gomantong Caves and the Kinabatangan River, where they maintain a lodge. If you have a particular interest in birds and wildlife, ask for their specialist guide, Ced Prudente. (They also have an office in KK; see details p. 169.)

"Uncle Tan", Mile 17 1/2 Labuk Road, Sandakan. Postal Address: WDT 197, 90009 Sandakan. Fax: (089) 272863. Although not a conventional tour operator, "Uncle" Tan (Tan Su Im) offers in-depth visits to his "jungle camp" on the Kinabatangan River, remote river safaris, visits to Turtle Islands Park, and to nearby Libaran Island, where there is a community of Cagayan islanders, originally from the Philippines. Visitors who don't mind a certain amount of roughing it agree that Uncle Tan lives up to his claim to show visitors "the real Sabah" at unbelievably low prices.

PULAU SELINGAN (TURTLE ISLANDS PARK)

Sabah Parks maintains three chalets, holding a maximum of 20, M$30 per person. Book in advance at East Coast Parks, P.O. Box 768, Sandakan, or go to Regional Office East Coast Parks, 9th fl, Wisma Khoo Saik Chew, Jln Buli Sim Sim. Tel: (089) 273453.

For transport to Selingan, contact any of Sandakan's tour operators or ask Sabah Parks to arrange it for you; M$100 per person for a return trip.

SEPILOK ORANG-UTAN SANCTUARY

Located 25 km from Sandakan town. Take taxi (M$15) or Sepilok bus leaving from central bus station downtown. Morning opening 9 am. Entrance: M$10 (M$1 Malaysians). Cameras free; video cameras M$10. Feeding time 10 am at Platform A; 10.30 am Platform B; video show 11 am. Afternoon opening 2 pm; feeding time 2.30 pm; video show 3 pm.

KINABATANGAN RIVER

It is recommended to use a tour operator to visit this region, owing to the lack of public transport and places to stay (see Tour Operators p.174).

TAWAU

ACCOMMODATION

Belmont Marco Polo Hotel, Jln Clinic, Tawau. Tel: (089) 777988. Fax: (089) 763739. 150 rooms and suites. From M$110 S; M$120 D + 15%. Comfortable, well maintained 4-star hotel popular with businessmen. Coffee shop with local and Western dishes, Chinese restaurant, bar, facilities for use of pool and tennis court at Tawau Yacht Club.
Hotel Emas, Jalan Utara.Tel: (089) 762000. Fax: (089) 763569. 100 fully serviced rooms and suites, health club, disco and karaoke center, games center and restaurant, plus business services. Prices start at M$54 S; M$61 D + 15%.
Loong Hotel, Jln Wing Lok (next to Dewan

Masyarakat). Tel: (089) 765308. M$35 S, AC, TV, attached toilet. Very clean and quiet.

DINING

Several of the **open-air food stalls** facing Jln Sabindo Lima offer a wide selection of Tawau's excellent seafood every evening. Look for the larger Chinese-operated stalls where you can select the basic ingredients and have them cooked to order. Ask for Tawau's raw fish speciality. M$12-M$18. There are also stalls selling Malay food.
The Mint, 1st fl, Block 38, Fajar Complex. Tel: (089) 761429. Opposite St Patrick's and next to the longer established Blue Mountain, this is an amazing find, unique in Sabah: a non-smoking, tastefully decorated restaurant with particularly friendly owners and a menu of delicate Malay-influenced Chinese (Nonya) dishes. Everything is good but don't miss the fried fish with sour mango and the delicious *gula Malacca* dessert. M$15-M$18.
Kedai Kopi Ban Hing, Jln Dunlop (nr corner Jln Habib Hussin). Small, clean and simple, with several good Indonesian dishes, including the *gado gado* salad. M$3.

MISCELLANEOUS

Minibuses to all east coast destinations leave from station off Jln Dunlop. It is possible to take a Landcruiser (8 hours, M$50, departure around 9 am) on a timber road via Sapulut, then a rough public road to Keningau where frequent minibuses leave for Kota Kinabalu.
Transport to Kalimantan
MAS and Bouraq have six flights per week, M$180 for 20-minute trip to Tarakan. Book at Merdeka Travel, Jln Sabindo Lima (opposite food stalls). Tel: (089) 771927; ask for Udin. Ferry service on *M.V.Muhibbah* via Nunukan to Tarakan operated by Sasaran Tinggi, TB 120, 1st fl, Jln Chester. Tel: (089) 778669. Ferry leaves from jetty in front of Shell station in Jln Dunlop. Change money at Wee Kung Ong Trading, 4 Jln Dunlop, near jetty.
Indonesian Consulate, Wisma Indonesia, Jln Apas, Tawau.

SEMPORNA

Semporna Ocean Tourism Centre, P.O.Box 6, Jln Kastam, Semporna 91307. Tel: (089) 781088. Located off the Semporna jetty, this complex includes the **Dragon Inn** and Pearl City Seafood Restaurant. Accommodation in attractively designed wooden chalets built on stilts over the sea ranges from M$68.25-M$157.50 D; 14 twin-bed rooms, 1 family room, 5 double-bed rooms and 4 VIP rooms.

Pearl City Restaurant offers live lobsters, grouper and crabs from nets in sea, plus a wide range of other seafood. Expect M$25 per person, twice as much if lobster is ordered. Fishing boats can be hired via the Ocean Tourism Centre to visit Pulau Gaya and Sibuan; about M$150-M$200 per day.

PULAU SIPADAN

Three dive companies offer packages to Sipadan which include return airfare from Kota Kinabalu (except for Pulau Sipadan Resort), all land and sea transport, food, accommodation and unlimited diving. (Non-divers enjoy a reduction of 20-30% in price, except at Borneo Divers.) A spectacular way to reach Sipadan is to take a Sabah Air helicopter from Tawau; ask your dive company or phone Sabah Air, (088) 51326.

Borneo Divers, 4th fl, Wisma Sabah, Jln Haji Saman, Kota Kinabalu.Tel: (088) 222226; Fax: (088) 221550. The first and the most professional operator on Sipadan, they offer dive packages from US$600 for 3 days/2 nights, extensions US$100 per day.

Pulau Sipadan Resort, 484 Block P, Bandar Sabindo, Tawau. P.O.Box 290, Tawau 91007. Tel: (089) 765200; Fax: (089) 763575. The only operator based in Tawau. Airport transfers and round trip from Kota Kinabalu M$325. 3 day/2 night package ex Tawau M$1,125; 4 day/3 night M$1,250; 5 day/4 night M$1,400.

Sipadan Dive Centre, 10th fl, A1004 Wisma Merdeka, Jln Tun Razak, Kota Kinabalu. Tel: (088)240584. Fax: (088) 240415. Newest operator to erect chalets on Sipadan, furthest from the jetty. 4 day/3 night package from M$1,455. Reputed to serve the best food on the island.

LAHAD DATU

ACCOMMODATION

Hotel Jagokota, Jln Kg Panji. Tel: (089) 82000. 60 rooms with full facilities. From M$50 S, M$75 D. Newest hotel in town, less than 5 minutes from center. Nothing fancy, but best of a mediocre lot.

Hotel Ocean, 1st fl, Jln Cempaka. Tel: (089) 81700. 19 rooms with AC, attached bathrooms. M$38 S, M$46 D, M$2 extra for TV. In middle of main street, clean, good value.

Mido Hotel, Lahad Datu. Tel: (089) 81800. 61 rooms. M$90-M$180. In center of town; full room facilities. The main businessmen's hotel.

Silam Resthouse, Pacific Hardwoods, Km 14, Lahad Datu/Semporna Road. Tel: (089) 83022, ask for Personnel. 6 rooms with attached bathroom. M$60 D, M$110 D. Company-owned hilltop resthouse; the most atmospheric place on the east coast, with billiard table, piano, bar, sitting room and wonderful views. All meals prepared by a family who've worked there since 1963! You'll be lucky to find a room, but well worth trying. M$15 by taxi from Lahad Datu.

DINING

On either side of the Lahad Datu Innoprise Office in Hap Seng Building, you'll find an Indian Muslim restaurant with tasty curries, and a Chinese coffee shop/restaurant with the usual noodle dishes.

DANUM VALLEY

Bookings for accommodation and transport, leaving Lahad Datu every Monday, Wednesday and Friday, should be made in advance through Innoprise Corporation, P.O. Box 11623, 88817 Kota Kinabalu, Sabah, Malaysia, Tel: (088) 243245, or through the Regional Office of Innoprise at Lahad Datu, tel: (089) 81092. Address: 2nd floor, Hap Seng Building, main road Lahad Datu town.

Comfortable resthouse, with 7 twin-bedrooms with attached bathroom and fan (M$75 per day full board); hostel with 15 twin-bed cubicles and shared bathroom (M$30 per person). Hostel guests may use the dining room or prepare their own food in the well-equipped kitchen. Reduced rates are available for Malaysians and undergraduate students ($M35 full board in rest house, M$10 hostel).

Transport to the Field Centre, 85 km from Lahad Datu, M$30 one way; Mon, Wed, Fri only. MAS has daily flights to Lahad Datu from Kota Kinabalu and Sandakan. Forest guides cost M$20 for a half-day (M$15 Malaysians and students); M$30 for a full day (M$30 and M$15 respectively). The international-standard Borneo Rainforest Lodge is due to open late 1993, in another location within the Danum Valley Conservation Area.

— Wendy Hutton

Southwest Sarawak

KUCHING

Kuching, the capital of Sarawak, lies in the far southwest of this huge state (Malaysia's largest). Sibu, and other settlements along the Rajang River, as well as Bintulu, on the coast, are normally reached via Kuching.

GETTING THERE

Kuching can be reached by **air** from Singapore, Brunei, Pontianak (West Kalimantan) and Kuala Lumpur and Johor Baru in Peninsular Malaysia, and by **road** from Pontianak. There is a public bus from the airport to Kuching center; taxi fare should be M$12. Airline offices are:
Malaysian Airlines System (MAS), Song Thian Cheok Road. Tel: (082) 246622
Singapore Airlines, Wisma Bukit Mata Kuching (same building as Standard Chartered Bank). Tel: (082) 240266
Royal Brunei Airlines, Kuching Hilton, Tel: (082) 241082

GETTING AROUND

Kuching is served by large buses as well as taxis. Kuching **taxis** are technically hire cars, transporting passengers on an unmetered per-mile basis. Unfortunately only the driver knows how many miles he's done. Further confusion could be added by the fact that kilometers are the official measure of distance these days, and given on all the "mile" posts. State your destination and agree on a price before taking off. Although the fare from Kuching airport to town should be M$12, cabbies are happy to try for more if they think they can get it.

Kuching town **buses** are white (or grey) and blue, routes numbered but not named on each vehicle. Route diagrams are displayed at a few key bus stops. The Post Office verandah bus stop serves over a dozen uptown bus routes; go to the one outside the vegetable market in Gambier Road for cross-town buses. Catch the grey-and-blue No. 17 for the express boat jetty (for Sibu, Sarikei and coastal destinations) at the Post Office.

Kuching is in the throes of drastic beautification at the time of writing (late 1992); today's **bus stations** may or may not still be in the same place in 1993. At present, the white-and-colourful buses for Damai, Camp Permai and Santubong leave from Khoo Hoon Yeang Street. The green-and-yellow STC buses leave for upcountry from the end of Dockyard Lane or Java Lane, the red-and-yellow ones for Bau in front of Naina Mohammed, a chemists's shop in Mosque Road. Sarawak Transport Company (STC) bus No. 6 serves Semongok Wildlife Centre, Benuk Longhouse and Giam rapids. STC bus No. 9A and 9B serves Gayu Longhouse, Kg Abang and Kg Pedawan. 9B branches off to Annah Rais Longhouse (Rayang). It is possible to get off 9A and walk to Annah, but beware of 9C which veers off in a different direction. Buses for Mongkos (Mentu Tapu Longhouse) and Tebedu (Indonesian border) leave from Serian, not Kuching. Bus routes may change; when in doubt ring the STC's downtown bus station: tel (082) 242967.

Cars can be hired from Mahana Rent-a-Car, including four-wheel drive; Tel: (082) 411370, (082) 488288, fax: (082) 417781

Hornbill Skyways (charter **helicopter**) Kuching Tel: (082) 455737 Miri Tel: (085) 37355)

MISCELLANEOUS

Indonesian Consulate, 1A Jln Pisang. Tel: (082) 241734.
The Manager of Standard Chartered Bank is **Honorary British Consul** in Sarawak. Tel: (082) 252233.
National Parks and Wildlife Dept, tel: (082) 442180, ext 201.
Kuching General Hospital, tel: (082) 257555
Normah Medical Centre (private hospital) Tel: (082) 440055, 937 Jln Tun Datuk Patinnggi (across the bridge).

TOURIST INFORMATION

The **Sarawak Tourist Information Centre** in Main Bazaar is in a pale pink, beautifully restored *godown* (warehouse) formerly owned by Sarawak Steamship Company. All the latest information on bus routes, maps, hotel rates, booking accomodation in National Parks, getting permits etc. Open during office hours; tel: (082) 248088/410944/410942. The STA information booth at the airport is open from 8 am to 9 or 10 pm (open if international flights come in late) 365 days a year, including public holidays. Tel: (082) 240620. Don't be put off by the dark glass which makes the place look uninhabited, just push the door open and go in.

ACCOMMODATION

The hospitality industry in Kuching started at No. 8 Main Bazaar, office of a coastal shipping line; people waiting for the turn of the tide were offered accomodation upstairs. No. 8 is no longer in business, but the town's main hotels are still clustered around and within easy walking distance of the waterfront.

Luxury (over M$100)

Holiday Inn Kuching, Jalan Tunku Abdul Rahman. Tel:(082) 423111; fax: (082) 426169. 320 rooms, single M$167-213 S, M$202-248 D. The first tourist-standard international hotel in Kuching, this is built right on the river. Full room facilities, restaurants, swimming pool.

Kuching Hilton, Jalan Tunku Abdul Rahman. Tel: (082) 248200, fax: (082) 428 984. 322 rooms, M$95-218 S, M$218-241 D. Everything one would expect of a Hilton, plus a great view over the river towards the Istana and Fort Margherita.

Riverside Majestic, Jalan Tunku Abdul Rahman. Tel: (082) 247777; fax: (082) 425858. 250 rooms. M$210-230 S, M$240-260 D. Newest and most luxurious hotel in town, in ideal position close to both the river and town.

Moderate (M$50-$99)

Aurora Hotel, Jalan McDougall. Tel: (088) 24028. 184 rooms, M$95-120 S, M$115-140 D. Once "the" hotel in Kuching, and conveniently close to the Sarawak Museum, the old Aurora recently underwent a facelift. Full room facilities.

Telang Usan Hotel, Ban Hock Road. Tel: (082) 415588; fax: (082) 425316. 66 rooms, M$75-120 S, M$85-120 D. Fairly new and within walking distance of downtown.

Longhouse Hotel, 101 Jalan Abell. Tel: (082) 419333, fax: (082) 421563. 50 rooms, M$65-76 S, M$78-90 D. One of the older establishments.

Borneo Hotel, 30 C-F Jalan Tabuan. Tel: (082) 244122; fax: (082) 254848. 44 rooms. M$70 S, M$80-90 D. Older hotel tastefully renovated in 1991; within easy distance of river and Old Town.

Inexpensive and Budget (under M$50)

City Inn, 275-276 Abell Road, Tel: (082) 414866. 27 rooms, M$49 S, M$66 D. The "small man's Holiday Inn", with all facilities; handy to the bigger hotels.

Green Mountain, 1 Green Hill. Tel: (082) 246952. 19 rooms, M$25 S, M$35 D. One of the more upmarket "el cheapos" with AC and hot water.

Orchid Inn, 2 Jalan Green Hill. Tel: (082) 411417; fax: (082) 241 635.15 rooms, M$35-40 S, M$40-45 D.

Kuching Hotel, 6 Temple Street. Tel: (082) 247512. 10 rooms, M$30 S, M$40 D.

Anglican Resthouse, McDougall Road (inside St Thomas Cathedral compound). Tel: (082) 240188. 5 rooms and two flats, M$18 S, M$20 D, M$35 flat. Shared fridge, showers and toilets for rooms. The flats are spacious with own kitchen, bathroom and view of river.

DINING

Food in Kuching is no problem — you can spend either M$120 on lunch, or only M$2.50. The international hotels have good dining rooms, steak houses and Chinese restaurants. Dress code for their coffee houses is fairly relaxed so the *nasi goreng* and *mee*-weary traveler can indulge in a steak without needing special sartorial effects. Some recommended restaurants include:

Lok Thian in Pending Road (tel: 082-331310) is well known among local gourmets and "the" place to have huge celebratory dinners. The **Golden Dragon** in Central Road (tel: 082 425236) serves an excellent yam basket. "Eleven-fingers Goh" at **Ik Hng** tel: (082 257 676) in the compound of the Public Swimming Pool at Padungan dishes up good Teochew fare — and Mr Goh really does have eleven fingers! Within walking distance of the Old Town there are innumerable coffee shops which serve noodle dishes, rice flour and meat dumplings, slabs of toast stuck together with a generous dollop of coconut cream jam (called *roti kahwin*, "married bread"), coffee or tea freshly brewed by the cup as it is ordered. Most serve *nasi campur* ("mixed rice") at lunchtime, a plate of rice with some meat, a vegetable and a bowl of soup for M$2-3.

A few favorite coffee shops include **Tiger Garden** in Temple Street, which is the haunt of Green Hill denizens. Being near a cinema, it is open until 10 or 11 pm. **Fook Hoi** opposite the Post Office is famous for pork dumplings and *pau* (steamed buns) until late morning, and substantial home-style cooking until nightfall.

Opposite the Chinese temple in Carpenter Street (a few doors from the Post Office, on the other side) there's a "**Chinese food center.**" Right beside the Post Office, the **Islamic Restaurant** serves *halal* food including very tasty unleavened breads with curry sauce. Order *roti*, or *roti telor* if you like an egg incorporated in the savoury pancake.

Another good place for all Indian foods is **Thompson Corner** on Nanas/Palm Road. No.6 town bus will take you here, just tell the driver where you want to get off. (A budget hotel, Thompson Inn, is next door.)

Indian and Malay food is served in **Satok**

Road. Behind the Holiday Inn there's a popular **seafood center**. The local **Pizza Hut** is on the same block, as is the excellent Indonesian Restaurant **Seri Minangkabau**. The shopping center adjoining Holiday Inn conceals **Kentucky Fried Chicken** in the basement, and **Coffee Garden** where you can slurp delicious *won ton* (Chinese ravioli) soup for M$3 a bowl.

The **Permata food stalls** behind Standard Chartered Bank are well patronized after dark and within easy walking distance of most hotels. Local snacks, meals and drinks as well as pizza, spaghetti and one steak stall.

SHOPPING

Sarawak Plaza, the biggest shopping mall in town, is about to be closed down; most of the shops are expected to re-locate at the Riverside Majestic. **Main Bazaar/Gambier Road** are good places for strolling and shopping, especially for cheap clothing and textiles.

The best **bookshops** are in the Holiday Inn and Hilton hotels; in the Hilton, the bookshop also sells handicrafts. For **handicrafts**, try the Sarakraf shop in the Sarawak Tourist Association building for basketware, textiles, ironwork, carving, beadwork, postcards etc.

There are a number of shops, especially along Main Bazaar, selling **handicrafts and antiques**; it's often difficult to tell genuine antiques from copies. Try Sarawak House, 67 Main Bazzar. Sarawak Batik Art Shop has a good stock of *pua-kumbu* (Iban textiles), while Mr Pang also sells his own *batik* paintings. Arts of Asia, 68 Main Bazaar, has Sarawak and general Asian artwork.

Don't miss the **Sunday Market** sprawled along Satok road. From Saturday (not Sunday) afternoon, sellers spread out their wares and by evening, the market with dozens of foodstalls is in full swing. Everything from live poultry to herbal medicines, music tapes to potted orchids. Keep a close grip on your bag.

NIGHTLIFE

From exorbitant to sleazy, Kuching's got it all. The latest are Karaoke lounges where patrons can roar their hearts and each others' ear drums out to taped backing music. **Aquarius** nightclub in Holiday Inn has a good reputation for noise and fun, live bands and singers. **Peppers** in the Hilton Hotel is decorated "Beatles Era," somewhat more sophisticated than Aquarius.

BOAT CRUISE

M.V.*Equatorial*, moored immediately downstream from Holiday Inn Kuching, does sunset cruises from 5.30-8 pm daily, unless the boat is privately booked, or the weather is bad. Tel: (082) 247763, ask for Pauline. (Note: Sarawak River at Kuching is tidal; its natural flow is from the Fort to Holiday Inn.)

TOUR OPERATORS

This is but a small selection of those available in Kuching. Many operators specializing in trips to Gunung Mulu are based in Miri (see p. 186). Shop around, ask Sarawak Tourist Association for information, consult hotel staff, compare prices. One rule of thumb is that a very cheap offer may mean very cheap service too.

Agas Pan-Asia Travel, 2nd Floor Sarawak Plaza. Tel: (082) 428969, fax: (082) 419754. They specialize in longhouses and general tours for the upmarket, comfort-loving tourist.

Borneo Adventure, 55 Main Bazaar. Tel: (082) 245175; fax: (082 422262; Miri office Tel: (085) 414936; fax: (085) 414379. Longhouses and general tours, specialized in nature tours and upland hikes.

CPH Travel Agencies (formerly STA), 70 Padungan Road.Tel: (082) 243 708; fax: (082) 424587; Sarawak Plaza. Tel: (082) 418290. Sarawak's oldest tour operator.

Ibanika Expedition, 411A 4th Floor, Wisma Saberkas. Tel: (082) 424022; fax: (082) 424021. Longhouse and general tours; can provide guides speaking French, German and Japanese.

Interworld Travel, 85 Jln Rambutan. Tel: (082) 252344; fax: (082) 424515. They maintain resthouses near longhouses.

Singai Travel Service, 108 Jln Chan Chin Ann. Tel: (082) 420918; fax: (082) 258320. They offer longhouse and general tours, special interest (nostalgia, business or *very* leisurely).

LEAVING KUCHING

Visitors heading for Sibu (on the Rajang River) or Miri (near Niah Caves, Lambir Hills National Park and Gunung Mulu National Park) can either fly or get there by express boat or boat plus bus. **Express boats** operated by two companies leave for **Sibu** daily. Times change, depending upon the seasons and the tide. Telephone Ekspres Bahagia, (082) 421948, Lai Lai Ekspres (082) 418363) or check the daily paper for schedules. M$38 1st class; M$32 economy. Take the grey and blue No.17 bus from the Post Office (M60 cents) to the express boat jetty.

DAMAI BEACH

Buses operated by Petra Jaya Transport leave from the open market near Electra House for

Damai at 7.30 am, 8.45 am. 10.10 am, 1.30 pm, 4.45 pm and 6 pm. Fare M$2.50. Take Bus 2B.
Holiday Inn Damai Beach Tel: (082)411777; fax: (088)428911. 202 rooms, M$195-265 S, M$218-288 D. Sister to Kuching's Holiday Inn, this is a full resort hotel with a range of recreational facilities, located on a beach near the mouth of the Santubong River and within easy reach of the Damai Cultural Village.
Damai Cultural Village, open 9 am-5.30 pm daily. Stage shows 11.30 am and 4.30 pm. Entry fee of M$45 (child M$25) includes small souvenirs, an information booklet and the show.

BAKO NATIONAL PARK

Book in advance at Tourist Information office if staying overnight. Take bus operated by Petra Jaya Transport leaving from the open market near Electra House at 6.30 am, 7.40 am, 9 am and on the hour, every hour after that until 4 pm. Fare is M$1.90 one way; return ticket (valid 3 days) is M$3. The boat, which leaves from Bako bazaar where the bus arrives, costs M$25 per person one way.

SIBU LAUT

Sibu Laut, located west of Santubong Bay, offers seaside accommodation at **Santin Resort**, Sibu Laut. Tel: (082) 210766. 74 rooms/chalets, M$50 S, chalet M160.

LUNDU

Cheng Hak Boarding House, 1094 Lundu Bazaar. Tel: (088) 735018. 15 (basic!) rooms M$5 S, M$9 D.
Lundu Gading Hotel, 174 Lundu Bazaar. Tel: (082) 735299. 11 rooms, M$48-58 S & D.

PANDAN BEACH

Pandan Beach Bungalows (very basic), contact William Lau Soon Seng Tel: (082) 735134.

SEMATAN BEACH

Lai Sematan Bungalow, Sematan Beach. Tel: (082) 711133. 10 basic units at M$60-100.

LUBOK ANTU

"**L.A.Hilton**", upstairs in a shophouse in Lubok Antu, very basic; ask for Towkay Ang's shop.

SRI AMAN

Hoover Hotel, 139 Club Road. Tel: (085) 321985. 48 rooms, M$39 S, M$59 D.
Alishan Hotel, 120 Council Road. Tel: (085) 322578. 18 rooms, M$42 S, M$45 D.
Champion Inn, 1248 Main Bazaar. Tel: (085)

320140. 12 rooms. Pr iced from M$28 S, M$30 D.

SIBU

Getting There

Sibu is connected by **air** with daily flights to Kuching, Bintulu and Miri; a loop flight on Sundays and Thursdays travels Sibu-Kapit-Belaga-Kapit-Sibu. There are also several daily **express boats** from Kuching; check the newspaper for latest departure times.

Traveling On

Express boats leave on the hour daily for **Kapit** from around 5.45 am until 3.45 pm; M$15; time around 2-3 hours, depending on the current. (It's faster going downstream back to Sibu.) All express boats up the Rajang stop at Kanowit and Song. The earliest express boat, *Kuda Mas*, leaves Sibu at 5.45 am, stopping at **Kanowit**, **Song**, **Kapit** and **Belaga**, continuing up to **Long Murum** and **Long Linah**. Another express leaves for **Belaga** at 9 am, except when the river level is too low. **Note**: as schedules are subject to change, check at the jetty on arrival in Sibu.

Airconditioned **buses** (M$18) depart for **Bintulu** at 6.15 am, 9 am, 12.15 pm and 2 pm daily. Trip takes about 4 hours. **Note:** The 6.15 am bus connects with the bus departing Bintulu at 12.15 pm for **Batu Niah**.

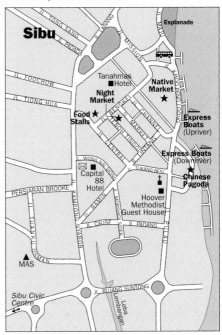

The bus to **Miri** (M$35) leaves at 6.45 am daily and takes 7 1/2 hours. If possible, buy tickets in advance from Syarikat Bas Express next to the Esplanade on the river. Be warned, buses depart on time or even early.

An unofficial mini-bus service operates from Sibu jetty to Miri, stopping at **Batu Niah** en route, enabling you to travel by morning express boat from Kuching to Sibu, then on to Niah without having to stop for the night in Sibu. Stand near the jetty or Chinese pagoda and someone should approach you; price is negotiable but around M$40 to Batu Niah.

Accommodation

Sibu is a busy town with accommodation ranging from very cheap basic rooms around Jln Tukang Besi up to an international standard hotel, with quite a few in the moderate price range. Most convenient of these is **Hotel Capitol 88**, in Jln Wong Nai Siong near the Post Office. AC, TV, bathroom for M$35 S, M$40 D. Best value is the conveniently located **Methodist Hoover Guest House**, next to the Methodist Church in Island Road (Jln Pulau). Five basic but clean twin-bed rooms with fan and attached bathroom for M$10 per person. Popular so try to book in advance tel: (084) 332491. If arriving at night, walk around to the back of building to find the caretaker in separate quarters. Top of the range is the 4-star **Tanahmas Hotel**, Jln Kampung Nyabor. Rooms start at M$140 S, M$160 D, plus 15%.

Dining

Sibu is famous for its Foochow noodles, sold in almost every coffee shop. The night market is an excellent place for all kinds of sweet and savory snacks, roasted fish, barbecued pork and chicken. Good Malay food at the Muslim *Gerai* (foodstalls) between the Tanahmas Hotel and Sibu Municpal Council.

RAJANG RIVER

It is surprisingly easy and relatively inexpensive to get to the main towns on the river. Fast express boats operate along the Rajang from Sibu up to Kapit all year round, stopping en route at Kanowit and Song; older boats stop at longhouses and timber camps along the way. When the river is high, a daily service operates to Belaga and beyond as far as Long Linah, half way along the Balui River. Tributaries close to the main centers of Kapit and Song have regular daily services. More remote longhouses are accessible within a day or two from there.

There are always freelance **guides** operating in these small towns — don't worry about finding them, generally they find you. Ask around in your hotel or possibly the local government office (Pejabat Daerah). Most guides ask at least M$150 or more for a 1-night stay in a longhouse and you can bring your own food.

VISITING A LONGHOUSE

Remember to take along some small gifts and food to help pay for your keep. It is advisable to bring plenty of canned food which you should give to your hostess. Popular items are Ma Ling canned pork, salted fish, sardines in tomato sauce, coffee, Milo, and Chinese (or other) whiskey. Sweets are a firm favorite.

TAKING A LONGBOAT

The price of hiring a longboat increases proportionately to the distance from the main towns and is always expensive. It is better to first find out if there is an express boat following your route, or at least part of it, which could save hundreds of dollars. Take the express boat as far as possible and then hire a longboat and boatmen from the last longhouse.

As a general rule of thumb prices are as follows: longboat hire M$20 per day; driver M$25-30 per day; front-man (look-out) M$20 per day. Outboard engine M$10 per hp; eg 30hp = M$30. Fuel varies between M$6.50-$10 per gallon depending on distance upriver. Reckon on at least 5 gallons per day.

SONG

A small river town halfway between Sibu and Kapit, Song is quite charming with even fewer tourists than Kapit and Belaga. The one hotel in town, the **Capital**, 8, New Bazaar has A/C rooms M$35, fan rooms M$18. Prices are negotiable. Song has a very obliging **guide**, Richard Kho. Tel: (084) 777228.

Close to Song, the **Katibas River** has many Iban longhouses along its banks. A longboat taxi runs every morning, leaving Song around 10 am to go 2 hours up the Katibas. Look for Sepang from Rumah Dagon Nanga Makup, who operates the ferry service; his boat is tied up at the Esso fuel barge each morning. There is also a rusty old *tongkang* which goes further upriver, departing around 11 am.

KAPIT

ACCOMMODATION

Hotels are plentiful in Kapit but quite expensive for those on a tight budget. Most offer comfortable, clean airconditioned rooms with carpet and bath for around M$40, although during quiet times, rates are negotiable. All hotels are in the center of the small town.

Expensive (over M$ 40)

The biggest and most expensive hotel in Kapit is the **Hotel Meligai**. Lot 3 Jln Airport. P.O. Box 139, Kapit 96807. Tel: (084) 796611; Fax: (084) 76817. Overlooking the town, with restaurant, bar and karaoke, AC, phone, TV, hot water from M$45-70.

New Rejang Hotel 104 Jln Teo Chow Beng, Kapit. Tel: (084) 796600; fax: (084) 796341. AC, hot water and TV; M$40-45 (negotiable).

Greenland Hotel, Lot 463-464 Jln Teo Chow Beng, Kapit.Tel: (084) 796388; fax: (084) 706708. Perhaps the best rooms can be found here, with AC, carpet, bath, hot water, TV. M$45-55 depending on the floor (higher floors are cheaper).

Well Inn No. 40 (back portion) Jln Court, Kapit. Tel: (084) 796009. TV, in-house video, and hot water from M$25 (fan, M$38 (AC).

Ark Hill Inn Lot 451, Shop Lot No 10, Jln Airport, Kapit. Tel: (084) 796168; fax: (084) 796341 offers "economical and well organised hotel in Kapit, "Heart of Borneo" Sarawak." 21 AC rooms from M$25-45.

Moderate and budget (under M$40)

Rejang Hotel 28 Jln Temenggong Jugah, New Bazaar, Kapit. Tel: (084) 796709; fax: (084) 796341. The most popular amongst budget

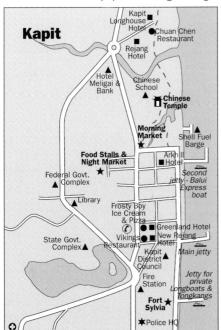

travelers. Large cleanish rooms cost M$15-18 S/D (fan) and M$25-28 S/D (AC). The top floor has bargain rooms for M$10.

The historic **Longhouse Hotel** overlooks the river with similar facilities. From M$20 (fan) and M$30 (AC). Tel: (084)796415.

DINING

The **Ar Kau Restaurant** between the Longhouse Hotel and the Fully Inn is clean, busy and sells food as good as you can eat in Singapore. The varied menu includes steamed fish, wild boar, venison, jungle vegetables, seafood, and Chinese dishes at reasonable prices. The rather dingy **night market** has several stalls selling Iban food. Others sell Malay food and the traveler's staple, *mee* and *nasi goreng* (fried noodles and rice).

Progress has come to Kapit in the form of two 'modern' eateries where you can enjoy fast food in air-conditioned comfort. Behind the New Rejang Inn, the **Vikings Restaurant** sells a passable facsimile of Kentucky Fried Chicken and hamburgers — both extremely agreeable after days in the jungle. Next door, beneath the Greenland Hotel, **Frosty Boy** sells ice cream and sweet pizzas in a clinically clean air-conditioned restaurant.

MISCELLANEOUS

Outside the Telecommunications Building are **phones** where you can call anywhere in Malaysia and Singapore. Try Ling Kee Leng at 5 Kapit Bazaar to **change money** and bargain for a good rate. Alternatively, try one of the three banks.

SHOPPING

There are few handicrafts for sale in Kapit as they are all sent down to Kuching or Sibu. Lai Lai Handicraft and Antiques at 31 Jln Teo Chow Beng, Kapit, is the only shop; it is worthwhile looking at their selection of woven *pua-kumbu* textiles, masks, wood carvings and beads and other antiques.

PERMITS AND INFORMATION

For travel beyond Kapit, **permits** are issued at Pejabat Am on the first floor of the State Government Complex in Kapit. After completing forms, take them to the Police Headquarters then back to the Resident's Office. The free permits are valid for 5 to 10 days for travel to Belaga or up the Baleh River. Permits for travel beyond Belaga are obtainable in Belaga. Staff in the issuing offices seem to be the only ones interested in permits and many travelers don't bother. The office on the top floor of the State complex gives **information** and you could enquire there about guides. Excellent detailed maps of Sarawak are available for sale at reasonable prices.

TOUR GUIDES

Several local guides operate in Kapit and you'll probably meet at least one of them as they hunt for customers. It could be worth asking at the Information Centre in the State Government Complex. Most self-styled guides will ask around M$150 for a one-night visit to a longhouse but price is subject to negotiation. The most organised tour guide is Tan Teck Chuan (Ah Chuan) who can tailor a trip to suit your needs. Find him at 11 Jln Tan Sit Leong, Kapit. Tel: (084) 796352; fax: (084) 796655.

If you want to strike out on your own without a guide, head to the ferry wharf and check departure times for the Baleh River (where there are several interesting longhouses). The express boat leaves several times a day, the first at 7 am. In addition, smaller speedboats powered by two 200 hp outboard engines head up and down the Baleh River to the timber camps. If the first longhouse you stop at is unsuccessful, there is still time to take the boat and try another longhouse further upriver. Alternately, try the Shell jetty where the longboats tie up and ask around for a longhouse which welcomes visitors.

Traveling on

The daily express to Belaga leaves Kapit at 9 am, except when the river is too low. Cost is M$20. During the dry season, express boats are unable to pass the dangerous Pelagus Rapids. It is possible to find a friendly *tongkang* (Chinese trading boat) or logging boat to to Belaga, for around M$50; alternatively, fly, or take the Bintulu-Belaga overland route.

BELAGA

The last town on the Rajang River, Belaga is a small administrative outpost with lots of government offices. If journeying further upriver, this is the last place to stock up on supplies and cigarettes and the last place to enjoy air-conditioned rooms.

Getting there and out

The Belaga express boat leaves **Sibu** wharf at 5.30 am; from **Kapit**, at 9 am. To get to Belaga from Bintulu, see "Overland Bintulu-Belaga." (p.181.) MAS operates a twice-weekly flight from Sibu via Kapit to Belaga on Thursdays and Sundays. Express boats leave Belaga at 6 am

sharp to travel downriver to Kapit and Sibu.

Accommodation

All of Belaga's hotels offer similar accommodation. Chinese-run, they are found on the 1st floor of shophouses in the main bazaar. **Hotel Belaga** has rooms from M$15, M$25 AC. **Bee Lian Hotel** has rooms for around M$25. **Lee Sian Ling Hotel** offer similar accommodation for around M$25 for a room with AC and shower. The cheapest hotel is the **Huan Lilah Lodging** House with basic fan-cooled rooms for M$15 per night.

Miscellaneous

See Mr Nyura Keti at the SAO Office in Belaga Resident's Office (Pejabat Daerah) for permits to go further upriver. If you want a guide, try to contact John Balarik of Rumah Kabal, Belaga; ask at Pejabat Daerah.

BINTULU

This is a convenient staging point between the Rajang and Niah Caves, even if not a tourist destination *per se*. It is possible to travel by express boat to **Tubau** (M$14) and then on to Belaga; boats leave several times daily, starting at 7 am. For **tourist information**, contact Similajau Adventure Tours in Plaza Hotel.

Air-conditioned **buses** leave for **Miri**, via Batu Niah, at 7.30 am, 10.30 am, 12 noon and 1.30 pm daily; M$18; 3 hours. Book in advance if possible at Syarikat Bus Suria.

Very basic **accommodation** available in a couple of dormitory-style Rumah Tumpanggan (lodging houses) facing the river; M$15 for tiny cubicle and shared bathroom. Not recommended for women traveling alone. The comfortable **My House Inn**, Jln Masjid, is opposite the bus station. AC, TV, phone, bathroom. M$40 S, M$45 D. Tel: (086) 336399. Of a similar standard but tucked away near the airport is **Hotel Salehah**, New Commerical Centre, Jln Abang Galau, tel: (086) 332122. M$36 D. The 4-star **Plaza Hotel** offers rooms from M$140 S, M$170 D. Tel: (086) 335111, fax: (086) 332742.

A range of tasty, inexpensive **food** available on the upper floor of the **Central Market**, complete with river view. Above average Malay food is sold at **Ama Restaurant**, in Jln Masjid. A coffee shop near the Council Negeri Monument in Lebuh Raya Abang Galau sets up tables on the pavement around 6.30 pm, and offers good barbecued **seafood**. Savory snacks, cakes and fresh fruit sold at the **night market**. The **Plaza Hotel** offers a range of Western food, including

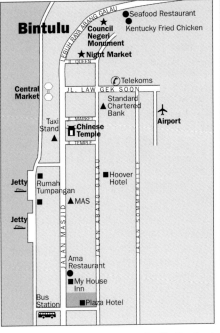

Bintulu

- Seafood Restaurant
- Kentucky Fried Chicken
- ★ Council Negeri Monument
- ★ Night Market
- Telekoms
- ▲ Standard Chartered Bank
- ✈ Airport
- ■ Chinese Temple
- Central Market
- Taxi Stand ▲
- Jetty — ■ Rumah Tumpangan
- ▲ MAS
- Jetty —
- ■ Hoover Hotel
- Ama Restaurant ●
- ■ My House Inn
- Bus Station
- ■ Plaza Hotel

good pepper steaks smothered with the best Sarawak black pepper.

OVERLAND BINTULU-BELAGA

Bintulu-Belaga is becoming an increasingly popular way to get to or from the Rajang. Starting from Bintulu appears to be more direct, and one is less at the mercy of expensive guides. Variations of this journey are numerous, and giving exact information is difficult. Some logging camps are strict about not allowing passengers in dangerous logging trucks; others don't mind. There are no fixed schedules beyond Tubau, so be prepared to be flexible.

We took the express boat from Bintulu to Tubau and stayed overnight in Tubau. Next morning we took a longboat "taxi service" (M$3 per person) to "Centre Camp", from where we had a lift in a Landrover to Long Metik, a logging camp 20 km upstream from Belaga on the Balui River; this costs around M$20-30 per person. From there it is relatively easy to take the express boat or a longboat down to Belaga. It is also possible to travel overland from Tubau to close to Belaga, then hike the remaining 3 hours or so. Ask around at Tubau for the latest information.

OVERLAND BELAGA-BINTULU

From Belaga, go by express boat to Long Metik. A guide to take you there and sort out your travel arrangements to Tubau (worthwhile if you don't speak Malay) should cost around M$60.

From Long Metik, the Balui-Tubau Transport Company will take you to Tubau for around M$50 per person. Others have walked several kilometers from Belaga to "Centre Camp" then hitched a ride to Tubau, or followed the Belaga River from Belaga by longboat and foot as far as the logging camp, to take transport to Tubau. From Tubau take the expressboat to Bintulu for M$14.

TUBAU

Stay overnight at **Angelina Inn** in the main bazaar for M$10 per person. Alternatively it is possible to stay at a nearby longhouse. Next to Angelina Inn is an open-fronted restaurant serving delicious fresh vegetable dishes, wild boar, venison and fresh fish, as well as the ubiquitous *mee goreng* and *nasi goreng*. Cold beers and soft drinks are also available.

On the rivers near Tubau are **longhouses** seldom visited by tourists, although local guides will still ask M$150 to visit and stay overnight. The Jalalong River has several Penan settlements, the Kemena River is generally Iban, while Tubau River is settled by the Kenyah and Kayan.

If you're looking for a **guide,** try to find a Kayan man, Inglebert Lasah, who is often around Tubau bazaar. For M$200, he will take you to a longhouse to stay, stopping at a few other longhouses en route for a visit.

— *Jill Gocher/Wendy Hutton/Heidi Munan*

Northeast Sarawak

MIRI

Getting There and Away

Miri is connected by frequent **flights** with Kota Kinabalu, Labuan, Bintulu, Sibu, Kuching and Bandar Sri Begawan (Brunei). There are also departures for Marudi, Gunung Mulu National Park, Lawas, Long Lellang, Mukah and Bario. Miri to Bario flights leave daily; M$70. Miri to Long Lellang every Wed. and Sat., M$46.

Buses connect Miri with Brunei, Bintulu (p.183) and Sibu (p. 180).

Buses to Kuala Belait in **Brunei** cost M$11.50 and depart at 7 am, 9 am, 10.30 am, 1 pm and 3.30 pm. Book at Miri Belait Transport company at the bus station. A much quicker and more comfortable way to Bandar Seri Begawan in Brunei is the **door-to-door van service** run by Nee Tien Poh, tel: (085)33898; departing Miri 11 am and 3 pm; M$20.

Buses to **Batu Niah**, via **Lambir Hills**, depart at 7 am, 10.30 am, 12 noon, 2 pm and 3 pm. Tickets from Syarikat Bas Suria. Buses leave frequently for the 45-minute trip to **Kuala Baram** (M$2.10), where the express boats depart for Marudi at 8.10 am, 9 am, 10 am, 11.30 am, 12.30 pm, 1.30 pm and 3 pm. Kuala Baram to Marudi takes about 2 hours and costs M$15.

An air-conditioned bus to **Sibu** leaves daily, M$35 for the 7 1/2-hour trip. Buses to **Bintulu** (air-conditioned) depart 4 times daily; M$18 for a 4-hour trip.

Accommodation

Miri's reputation as an expensive town extends to its accommodation, where even the bottom-line accommodation is not really cheap. Top hotel right in town is the 4-star **Park Hotel**, Jln Raja, Tel: (085) 414555, fax: (085) 414488, with rooms from M$115 S, M$130 D. Two new resort hotels along Taman Selera beach are due to open end 1992/beginning 1993.

Several hotels in the medium-price category are found near Jalan Eu Seng and Jalan Nahkoda Gampar, in the newer area of town. **Cosy Inn**, tel: (085) 415522, is very clean and comfortable, M$72.26 S, M$80.70 D. Less expensive is the **Today Inn**, tel: (085) 414000, at M$56.70 S, M$61.20 D.

Old stalwart **Tai Tung**, near the river,

charges M$8 for a dormitory bed complete with woven sleeping mat; non-AC room is M$27 S; AC room is M$38 S, M$45 D, all with shared bathroom. There are several basic lodging houses in the lane between China and High Streets. Best value in Miri is the **Mulu Inn**, right opposite the bus station and Wisma Pelita Tunku shopping centre, tel: (085) 410611; rooms with AC, TV, phone, bathroom cost M$37 S, M$47 D. The Mulu Inn Branch, near the river, is not the same standard, although prices are the same.

Dining

Interesting and inexpensive Malay food found at the **food stalls** at the end of China Street, just behind the temple. Better at night when its cooler. Delicious Kuching *laksa* (spicy noodle soup) or Chinese porridge for breakfast at the **coffee shop** on the corner of China Street, directly under the Mulu Inn. If you're near MAS, try the ready-cooked Chinese dishes sold at **Ming Chang Fast Food**, in Halaman Kabor. For moderately priced and very good seafood, try **Tanjong Seaview Restaurant**, near Taman Selera Beach. The stalls selling local food at Taman Selera are particularly pleasant at night. Milkshakes and Western fastfood available on the ground floor of **Wisma Pelita Tunku**.

Shopping

Miri offers the best range of goods outside of Kuching. The multi-storey Wisma Pelita Tunku

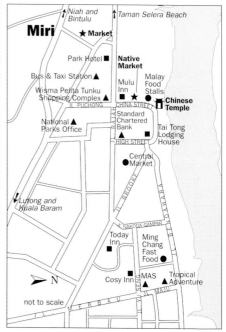

has a wide range of shops, including fast food outlets, a supermarket, two bookshops (the better although slightly more expensive Book Centre is on the 1st floor), and a shop selling a limited range of souvenirs and handicrafts (Kong Hong Enterprise, 1st floor). If you're going to Marudi, wait to buy basketware there; cheaper and a wider selection.

Tour operators

If you have time, the best policy is to shop around in Miri to find the best price and possibly save a substantial sum. Among the many operators offering tours are:
Borneo Adventure is a reliable and well organized Kuching-based company with branch office in Miri. They do Mulu, Headhunters' Trail and Bario Highlands treks. 9th fl, Wisma Pelita Tuanku, (next to main bus station) Miri. Tel: (085) 414935.
Borneo Overland Services offer reasonably priced service but best to book ahead. 37 Jalan Brooke, Miri. P.O. Box 1509, 98008 Miri. Tel: (085) 30255; Fax: (085) 416424.
Tropical Adventure was the first operator to start taking tourists to Mulu; thoroughly professional. They also arrange treks in the Bario Highlands, do the Headhunters' Trail as well as tours in Kalimantan. Lot 228, 1st Floor, Jalan Maju (near MAS office), Beautiful Jade Centre, P.O. Box 1433, 98007 Miri. Tel: (085) 419337; fax: (085) 414503.
Transworld Travel Services. 2.04, 2nd Floor, Wisma Pelita Tunku (next to main bus station), Miri. Tel: (085) 422277/422278/38989; fax: (085) 415277.

National Parks Office

For information and accommodation bookings for the National Parks and permits to visit Gunung Mulu, go to the quaint old office of the National Parks and Wildlife Office, Forestry Department. Tel: (085) 36637. Ask for their informative and well-produced brochures. The office is tucked away in the low-rise complex opposite Wisma Pelita Tunku (see map).

LAMBIR HILLS NATIONAL PARK

Located just 24 km and about 30 minutes from Miri, Lambir Hills can be reached by taxi (M$25 one way) or bus (M$2.40). Take any of the buses to Bakong, Bekenu, Niah or Bintulu run by Syarikat Bus Suria, departing from the terminus in front of the multi-storey Wisma Pelita Tunku; all pass by the entrance to the Park and will stop on request. First bus leaves Miri 6.30 am, last at 4.30 pm.
National Parks and Wildlife maintain a can-

teen near the entrance to the Park, and have four two-bedroom chalets at M$20 per room. There is also a resthouse sleeping 3; M$40 per night. Unfortunately, the chalets are located near the highway, and too close together for privacy, so don't come here expecting a jungle hideaway.

MARUDI

Express boats going both up and downriver start leaving at first light. Times and destinations are clearly displayed on the notice board in front of each boat. Leave your bag on a seat (no valuables inside) to reserve it well in advance, and be on board 15 minutes before departure.

Most romantic place to stay in Miri is the old colonial **Government Resthouse**, overlooking the river and about 10 minutes walk upriver from the jetty. Book at the Pejabat Daerah in Fort Hose, then walk another 5 minutes. Only 4 rooms, M$40 each; no food available. Best hotel in town is the **Alisan**, just off the main square; AC, TV, phone, bathroom, M$40 S, M$45 D; non AC rooms M$20 S, M$28 D. The **Hotel Zola** opposite charges similar rates.

Ready-cooked Chinese dishes and noodles cooked to order can be found at the **Yong Siang Coffee** Shop, immediately in front of the jetty. Malay and other food at the stalls by the market in the square; a bit hot at midday, though.

NIAH NATIONAL PARK

Getting there

Buses to Batu Niah leave daily from Miri, Bintulu and Sibu. From Batu Niah, you can reach the Park either by footpath alongside the Sungei Niah (45 minutes and free), by longboat (10 minutes, M$10 per boat) or taxi (15 minutes, M$10 per taxi).

From Miri, a taxi costs around M$60 or M$15 per person on a shared basis. Asking price often starts around M$100, so be firm. From Bintulu, a taxi costs M$100 per taxi or M$25 per person on shared basis.

Leaving

Buses to **Bintulu** depart Batu Niah at 6 am, 7 am, 12 noon and 3 pm (2 1/2 hours). The 6 am bus connects with the 9 am Bintulu-Sibu bus. Bus to **Miri** departs Batu Niah at 6.45 am, 7.45 am, 10.45 am, and 1 pm.

Miscellaneous

Permits are free and easily obtainable at the Park Office. It is no longer necessary to obtain special permission to visit the Painted Cave. A guide is optional and not really necessary. Information at Park HQ is in the form of an exhibition center, explaining the flora and fauna as well as birds' nest ecology. Pick up a brochure on Niah in Miri if possible, as they may not always be available at Niah.

Accommodation

Cheap and cheerful lodging is available at the **Park Hostel** at Pangkalan Lubang. M$3 per person gives you a sheet and blanket, cooking utensils and bunk bed in one of three 12-bed dormitories. The large comfortable verandah overlooking the river is a pleasant place to meet with fellow guests.

In 1994, a new **2-star hostel** is expected to open with upgraded facilities, although similar prices will be charge for dormitory accommodation.

Across the river within Niah National Park are 4 relatively new 2-bedroom **chalets**, completely self-contained and costing M$20 per standard double room, M$30 deluxe room (double these prices for the entire chalet).

Bookings for accommodation within the Park can be made in Miri at National Parks and Wildlife Office, Foresty Department. Tel: (085) 36637. Keep your receipt for presentation at the Park. If you are not arriving during school holidays, you can take your chance and just arrive at the Park.

Alternative accommodation is available in Batu Niah village at the clean and comfortable **Niah Cave Air-Cond Hotel**. Rooms overlook river and cost M$15 S; M$25 D; M$30 triple.

What to Bring

A strong torch (flashlight) is indispensable. Bring a water bottle to last until you make it back to the Chinese provision shop opposite the Park Office. A plastic poncho (M$6 in Batu Niah) is good for sudden showers. Jogging shoes with a good grip and mosquito repellent are necessary; t-shirts and shorts or cotton trousers are fine. Buy provisions in Batu Niah; the morning market sells fresh vegetables, fruit and meat. Just outside the Park is a provision shop selling basic necessities. Batu Niah village has several restaurants and coffee shops. The best is perhaps at the Niah Caves Hotel, with river prawns, wild boar, fish, soups and the usual fried rice.

GUNUNG MULU NATIONAL PARK

A new regulation requires all non-Malaysian visitors to Mulu to employ the services of a tour company, resulting in a bunch of deliriously happy tour operators and many disgruntled independent travelers who would much prefer a less rushed and regimented visit. It's possible that this regulation may change, so before booking a trip to Mulu, check the Miri office of National Parks and Wildlife, tel: (085) 36637 for current regulations.

Ironically, it is cheaper and certainly far less troublesome to travel with a small group and guide than try to go independently. All visitors should be aware that whichever way you go to Mulu, you must be prepared to spend money — traveling in the Mulu can be expensive.

Permits

With the current regulations, all non-Malaysian visitors must take a guided tour. In addition to this, visitors must have three permits: one from the National Parks and Wildlife Office, one from the Resident's Office and a Police clearance. A tour company can take care of all these formalities. It seems to be possible to obtain your permit on arriving at Park Headquarters, if you fly from Miri.

Getting There

Getting to Mulu, 100 km from the coast, is an adventure in itself although a journey that once took days can now be accomplished in 35 minutes with the new MAS flight, direct from Miri. Alternatively, spend a day or more and do the upriver trip by express boat and longboat, and get the feeling of what Sarawak was like when river travel was the sole form of transport.

By Air: At present there are two daily flights to Mulu from Miri. Some time in 1993, there should be extra flights, direct from Kota Kinabalu and Brunei. Book with MAS or at the airport. Cost is M$69 one way, approximately the same price, or cheaper, than going by boat.

There are also several daily 15-minute flights between Miri and Marudi, costing $29 one way. From Marudi, you can take the boat upriver.

By Boat: A tour agency can arrange the trip and will either pick you up in Miri, meet you at Kuala Baram, Marudi or at the Park itself. If you want to travel on your own, take a taxi (M$16) or bus (M$2.50) from Miri to Kuala Baram, the mouth of the Baram River (30 minutes). Express boats upriver depart from here, the first boat leaving for Marudi at 7 am and the last at 2.45 pm. The journey to Marudi takes around 2 1/2 hours and costs M$12.

From Marudi, express boats depart to various points upriver. To get to Mulu, look for the express to Long Panai/Kuala Apoh (depending on the water level.) The one daily boat leaves around 12 noon and costs M$12.

When the water level is high, the express boat goes to Long Terawan, otherwise, on arriving at Long Panai, find the longboat going to Long Terawan, costing M$10. From Long Terawan, a boat leaves for Mulu at 3.30 pm daily, costing around M$35 per person or M$150 per boat for less than 5 persons. The trip to the Park takes 2 1/2 hours; the boat will drop guests in front of the the various lodges at Long Pala or at National Park HQ if so desired.

Although sounding complicated, it is a well trodden route with people journeying every day. The longboat waits for the connecting vessel from downriver.

Returning to Miri

The longboat leaves the Park at 5.30 am enabling passengers to catch a connecting express down to Marudi.

Accommodation

Most tour operators have their own lodges on the Melinau River at Long Pala, just outside the park boundaries. Casual visitors can stay for around M$10 per night if they're not fully booked.

The **National Park Headquarters** have several grades of accommodation starting at M$5 per night for a dormitory bed. The main hotel block has six beds to a room for M$60 per room whether one or six occupants. Top of the line are the newer two-roomed air-conditioned chalets, each with 2 beds, for M$150 per chalet.

The **Melinau Canteen** (opposite park HQ) offers beds at M$5 per night. Meals cost extra.

The Japanese owned **Gunung Mulu Royal Resort**, due to open late 1992, will bring 5-star accommodation to the wilderness, with 150 rooms and a forthcoming golf course.

Eating

Dining is not a major experience in Mulu just yet. Those on a tour package generally take meals at the lodge they are staying in. Servings are hearty if lacking in exotic appeal. There is a canteen at Park HQ, and across the river, the Melinau Canteen serves simple, reasonably priced meals.

What to Bring

For a trip to Headquarters area only, you need comfortable walking shoes, shorts, sunhat, swimsuit, a warm jacket or sweatshirt for early morning river trips, poncho/rain sheet for sudden showers, plus moquito repellent. To go on the tougher treks to Mt. Mulu, the Pinnacles or on the Headhunters' Trail to Limbang there are a few other essentials required to make the trip more enjoyable: strong torch (flashlight), sleeping bag, water bottle, sleeping mat. A simple first aid kit should include antiseptic, calomine lotion for leech and insect bites, plasters and sunscreen. Bring a hat or cap, change of clothes, sensible footwear—either jogging or walking shoes with a strong tread. Shorts are much better than long trousers because you get very hot walking and its easier to see any leeches that may attach themselves to your leg.

Cavers can get specialist equipment at the park, but should bring strong footwear and long shirts and pants.

When traveling independently, buy food in Miri or Marudi. Some food is available from the Melinau Canteen opposite Park HQ in Mulu.

Guides

No matter whether you arrive in the Mulu with or without a tour operator, you must be accompanied by an official park guide before entering the National Park. The guides' function is twofold: to help preserve the flora and fauna by ensuring visitors observe regulations, and to answer any questions about the Park. On a tour, guide fees are included in the overall price but others will have to pay the set charges.

Guide to show caves: M$20 per cave
Adventure Caving for Sarawak Chamber + two others: M$80
Adventure Caving for two caves excluding Sarawak Chamber: M$60
To Mulu Summit (4 days/3 nights): M$110, extra days (per day): M$20, night allowance: M$10
Pinnacles (3 days/2 nights): M$80, extra days (per day): M$20, night allowance: M$10
Porters charge M$15 per day or M$25 for 1 day and 1 night.

Getting Around

Within the Park, longboats are available for hire. From the airport to Park HQ the longboat "taxi" charges M$5, while to the lodges at Long Pala, it's M$10 per person.

Money and Communications

There is no bank or post office within the park. Money should be changed in Miri or Marudi. There are currently no telephones within the park, although emergency calls can possibly be made from one of the private lodges who have their own radio phone, or from the new resort.

Don't forget to reconfirm flights before leaving for Mulu.

LIMBANG

There are daily flights between Limbang and Miri (M$45) and Lawas (M$25). Frequent speedboats to Brunei until 5 pm (M$15). A new government resthouse on river about 1 km out of town costs M$10 per person. There are a number of sleazy hotels; best of a bad lot is **Borneo Hotel**, Main Bazaar, M$20 S, M$28 D with fan, M$38 AC. If you want something clean and comfortable try **National Inn**, Jln Buangsiol, AC rooms from M$73 S; **City Inn**, Jln Buangsiol, M$55 S, M$65 D, AC. **Centrepoint**, Jln Buangsiol, from M$50 S. Stalls above new market offer good range of **food** and river view. Numerous coffee shops which close at 6 pm. Best in evenings is **Maggie Cafe** in Jln Buangsiol which has tables outside by river and sells beautiful seafood. **Buses** to Nanga Medamit leave hourly until 3.30 pm.

LAWAS

Flights from Lawas to Bario (M$129) every Monday and Sunday. Lawas to Ba Kelalan (M$46) daily. Lawas to Long Semado Tues. and Sat. (M$40). Lawas to Kota Kinabalu, Mon. and Thurs (M$47). Lawas to Labuan, Thursday (M$31). Lawas to Limbang, daily (M$25). **Bus** Lawas to Kota Kinabalu 2 pm, M$20. **Landcruiser** to Ba Kalelan, 5 hours, M$35. Ask on Jln Lawas Damit, close to bus station. Best deal for hotels is clean, old-style Chinese hotel, **Hup Guan**, above a billiard room in Jln Liau Siew Ann. Rooms with fan from M$15-$30. Among the many clean, basic hotels above shops is **Million Hotel**, M$40 S, M$45 D, with AC, Jln Muhibbah. **Mee Sing Restaurant and Cakehouse** is good for basic Chinese food; **Malay food stalls** near ferry.

BARIO HIGHLANDS

What to bring

See p.188 "What to Bring" for advice on basic items needed for trekking. If you need them, bring cigarettes and alcohol as they will not be available. Take gifts (the further from town, the more appreciated): coffee, tea, sugar, tinned food, sarongs; for the Penan, add rice.

Porters/guides

While a few people around Bario speak a little English, the lingua-franca is Malay. Learn a few words and bring a dictionary, or, better still an English-speaking guide, easily available through a travel agency in Miri, possible but more diffi-cult in Bario. Guides charge M$40 per day, as do porters. Count on about 20 kg per porter, in either your knapsack or an elongated bag which will fit into their traditional, expandable back-packs. Remember that unless you do a round-trip, you have to pay for the time it takes your guide/porters to return home. One day is enough for them from Ba Kelalan to Bario.

Eating/Sleeping

In Bario and Ba Kelalan there is simple accom-modation, M$25 per night, plus M$8 for meals. Outside of these towns you either sleep in a longhouse or a single-family unit. You will usual-ly (but not always) be provided with a sleeping mat and pillow. The meals are rice-based with a vegetable or two (if available) plus some kind of meat (monkey, porcupine, boar, deer or some-thing out of a tin). It is usual to give your host M$10 for a place to sleep and M$5 per meal. These costs are for single travelers; its less per person for two or more, according to the num-bers.

Transportation

By air, from Miri and Lawas. By road, Lawas to Ba Kelalan. (See Miri and Lawas for details.)

Weather

The only general consensus is that it rains in November and December with little precipita-tion in February, March and April. For the other months, your guess is as good as anyone's.

Trail conditions

The Bario-Ba Kelalan trail is in good shape, with the first and last stages (mostly) in motorcy-clable shape. In the jungle, hand-rails along log or bamboo bridges comfort the faint-hearted. Long stretches of mud have embedded logs to balance upon. (Watch out: the mud can be deceptively deep!) Everything is slippery when wet; a walking stick (*tongkat*) helps lots.

Leeches (locally called *lematak*)

No one, except perhaps the strangest of per-verts, likes leeches. Before putting on socks, rub your feet and ankles with one or more of the following: salt, soap, raw tobacco, insect repellent. But if you wade across any water, whatever was applied will wash off. Wear leech socks or high-top jungle boots, tightly laced with pants tucked in at the top. This should keep the swarms down to manageable numbers.

Brunei Practicalities

ENTRY FORMALITIES

A valid passport is required of all visitors. Visas are waived for visits up to 30 days for British nationals, Malaysians and Singaporeans. Visas are waived for visits up to 14 days for nationals of Belgium, Canada, France, Germany, Indonesia, Japan, Luxembourg, South Korea, Sweden, Switzerland, Thailand, the Netherlands, the Philippines, and the Republic of Maldives. Nationals of all other countries must obtain a visa through Brunei embassies or consultates before entering Brunei. Visas can be processed in 1-3 days at the Brunei High Commision in Singapore. There are no Brunei consular offices in either Sabah or Sarawak.

The sale of liquor is banned in Brunei Darussalam. However, non-Muslims over 17 years of age may each bring in 2 litres of liquor and 12 cans of beer for personal consumption. The alcohol brought in must be declared upon arrival on a special customs form.

GETTING THERE AND OUT

Most visitors arrive by **air.** Five airlines service Brunei Darussalam including MAS (Tel: 02-224141), Philippine Airlines (02-244075), Royal Brunei Airlines (02-242222), Singapore Airlines (02-227253) and Thai Airways International (02-242991). The airport tax is B$5 for passengers traveling to Malaysia and Singapore and B$12 for all other destinations.

Boats depart Bandar from near the Customs Building on the river front for the Malaysian towns of Labuan (B$25 for First Class one-way fare; B$20 for economy), Limbang (B$10), and Lawas (B$25). Passenger traffic to Labuan is particularly heavy during holidays, Fridays and Sundays. The *Ratu Samudra* departs Bandar daily for Labuan at 8 am (check in at 7.15 am or earlier for immigration formalities) and makes the return trip from Labuan at 2 pm. The *Mutiara Laut* accommodates additional passengers Friday through Sunday with a second trip departing at 9 am and returning at 3 pm. Ticketing office personnel (Suite 201-203, Giok Tee Bldg, Jln MacArthur, BSB 2686; Fax 02-243058) suggest booking weekend seats 2 months in advance and purchasing tickets 2 weeks in advance, tel: (02) 243057, (02) 24305.

Boats to Limbang and Lawas leave and arrive with greater frequency but it would be best to start your journey early in the day.

Buses from the towns of Miri and Limbang stop at Brunei's border but finding connections to Bandar late in the day is a risky proposition due to arbitrary cancellation of scheduled runs. The fare to Miri from Kuala Belait is B$9.50

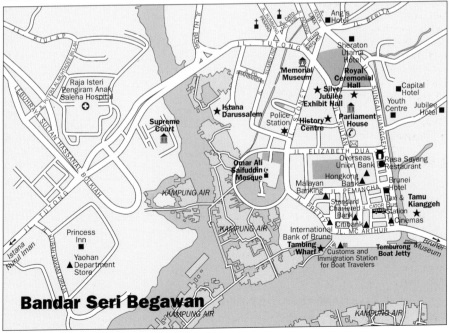

Bandar Seri Begawan

with buses departing at 7.30 am, 9.30 am, 11 am, 1.30 pm and 3.30 pm. When traveling by bus, start early and be prepared for long waits.

There is also a daily door-to-door **van service** between Miri and Bandar operated by Nee Tien Poh, BSB tel: (02) 222945, Miri tel: (085) 33898. Mr Nee charges B$20 per person (well worth it for the convenience); his vans leaves BSB at 5 am and depart Miri at 11 am and 3 pm.

LOCAL TRANSPORTATION

The **bus terminal** is on the street level of the multi-storey carpark on Jln Cator. Existing bus service is infrequent and unreliable. No daily schedules are posted but the upcoming departure time for each route/destination is displayed prominently behind the windshield. Rather old vehicles transport passengers to and from the airport; from Bandar to other towns such as Tutong, Seria, and Kuala Belait; and within Bandar.

Taxis do not cruise the streets of Bandar but are summoned by telephone (02) 222214 or (02) 226853 until 8 pm or hired in front of some hotels or the multi-storey carpark on Jln Cator. Taxis have meters and charge B$3 for the first km and 20 cents for each 200 m up to 20 km; thereafter, 10 cents for each 200 m. Add a surcharge of B$5 for trips to and from the airport, a surcharge of B$25 for outstation trips. Each minute of waiting will cost 20 cents. There is a 50% surcharge between 9 pm-6 am. A taxi summoned by telephone costs an additional B$3. It costs about B$8 to go from Jln Cator to the Brunei Museum, about B$16 to the airport.

The cheapest **car rental** is about B$100 per day. A surcharge of B$40 per day is levied for cars driven into Malaysia.

Residents of the Water Village rely on **water taxis** to get to different points in BSB. Fares depend on the distance travelled (B50 cents-$2); tourists can count on paying several times the normal rate. State your destination and settle the price at the start of the trip.

Boats with covered cabins leave for **Temburong** from the Jln Residency jetty between 7 am and 5 pm, either on the hour or when the boat is full. The one-way fare is B$7.

ACCOMMODATION

(All luxury and moderate class rooms have air-conditioning (AC), bathroom, TV, video and phone.)

Luxury (Over B$200)

Sheraton Utama Hotel. Jln Bendahari, Tel: (02) 244272, Fax: (02) 221579. 156 rooms. The premier hotel in Bandar, just a few minutes' walk from town center. Restaurant, coffee shop, business center, shops, pool, valet service, B$230-400.

Moderate (B$100-$200)

Brunei Hotel. Jln Pemancha, Tel (02) 242373, Fax: (02) 226196. 73 rooms. In town center. Restaurant. will provide guests with transport to shopping complexes and airport. B$160-400.

Riverview Inn. Jln Gadong, Tel: (02) 221900, Fax: (02)221905. 126 rooms. 3 km from town centre. Restaurant, coffee house, pastry shop, food center, business center, shopping arcade. B$150-550.

Ang's Hotel. Jln Tasek Lama, Tel: (02) 243553, Fax. (02) 227302. 84 rooms. A few minutes' walk from town center. Restaurant, poolside cafe, garden pool. Will provide guests with transport to shopping complexes. B$138-168.

Princess Inn. Jln Tutong, Tel: (02) 241128, Fax: (02) 241138. 117 rooms. 3.5 km from town center, located in Seri Complex. Restaurant, free transport to town. B$110-154.

Jubilee Hotel. Jln Kg Kianggeh, Tel: (02) 228070, Fax: (02) 228080. 42 rooms. A few minutes' walk from town center. Restaurant, coffee House, business center. Transport provided to shopping centers. B$100-450.

Hotel Capital. No.7, Simpang 2, Kg. Berangan, Tel: (02) 223561, Fax: (02) 228789. 50 rooms. Located near Youth Centre, short distance from town center. B$70-138.

Budget (Under B$70)

Bradoo Inn Guest House. 6B Simpang 130, Jln Sungai Akar, Jln Muara. Tel: (02) 333112, 336723. Fax: (02) 220812. 10 rooms. A new establishment only 5 minutes from airport but far from town center. AC and bathroom. B$45-70.

Youth Centre. Jln Kianggeh, opposite Royal Ceremonial Hall. Tel: (02) 222900, 229423. 24 beds for women (6 to a room) and 20 beds for men (4 to a room) available on first come, first served basis; neat attire will help secure a bed. No AC, communal bathroom. Flat fee of B$10 per night for up to 3 nights, B$3 for each additional night. No age limit.

DINING

Restaurants and coffee shops serving standard Chinese and Indian Muslim food can be found along **Jalan Sultan**, the main drag of BSB. Vendors in the *tamu* (open-air market beside the Kiangggeh River) sell inexpensive take-away food (B$1-5) for breakfast and dinner. After eating places have closed in the town center (9 pm), a variety of fried noodles, rice and meat and vegetable dishes, as well as barbecued fish and chicken can still be purchased at these stalls.

Bumiputra Commercial and Trade Centre, 7th floor (opp. multi-storey car park). Numerous food stalls offer freshly cooked home-style Malay food and a view of the capital during lunch time. Three dishes (choose from a large variety of meat, fish or vegetable preparations) served with rice, and soup cost about B$4. Cold and hot drinks as well as canned sodas are available; open from 7 am to about 6 pm.

G K Restaurant, Spg 92, Jalan Gadong, 5.5 km from town center. This is the place for fresh seafood because diners select the ingredients for their dinner from aquarium tanks. Ask the friendly waitresses for recommendations.

Rasa Sayang Restaurant, top floor, Bangunan Guru-Guru Melayu, Jalan Kianggeh. Besides the standard Chinese menu, this restaurant offers Nonya dishes, a fusion of Chinese and local cuisines. When ordering, ask the waitresses for recommendations. Major credit cards accepted.

Stadium Restaurant, Hassanal Bolkiah National Stadium, 7 km from town center. A sumptuous buffet of Chinese vegetarian food is served at lunch (B$12) and dinner (B$14) on the first and fifteenth day of the lunar month (call 02-244858 to check dates).

Tenaga Restaurant, 1st Floor, Bangunan Hasbullah, Jalan Gadong, 5 km from town centre. Service is slow in this North Indian Muslim restaurant because dishes selected are cooked to order. The wait is worth it. Sauces are thickened with ground cashew and yoghurt and breads come fresh from the *tandoori* oven. Individual dishes range in price from B$7-10; a fixed price vegetarian lunch is B$4.50, with meats B$6.50.

SHOPPING

Most of what is consumed in Brunei is imported. Locally crafted items such as baskets and mats can be bought at the *tamu*, but be aware that some of the items on sale may have originated in neighboring Malaysia or the Philippines. The Arts and Handicraft Centre offers locally made items. Packages of uncooked *keropok* (made from shrimp, fish or cuttlefish) are bulky but light and will give friends at home a taste of Brunei. What looks like a plastic chip magically expands when fried in hot oil to become a crispy, light wafer that melts in the mouth.

BANKS AND MONEY CHANGING

Singapore currency is accepted at par with the Bruneian currency for all transactions. Money changers at the departure point for boats to Malaysian towns give better rates than banks for conversion between Malaysian and Bruneian currency. The rate of exchange for the Brunei dollar in late 1992 was US$1=B$1.60. Banks are located in the town center and open from 9 am-3 pm weekdays, from 9 am-11 am on Saturdays.

WHAT TO WEAR

Loosely fitted but modest summer clothing will be appropriate for walking around town. Light weight slacks are preferable to shorts. Either a sunhat or folding unbrella will provide protection against the scorching sun. If planning a nature walk, bring a bottle of mineral water. Always carry a supply of toilet paper; most public facilities supply only water.

MEDICAL CARE

Visitors need only pay a small fee for treatment at the Emergency Room of the government medical facility (4 km from town center), Raja Isteri Pengiran Anak Saleha Hospital. The Hart Medical Clinic, a private practice, is located more conveniently in town center (47 Jln Sultan, 02-225531).

BUSINESS HOURS

Government offices are opened from 7.45 am-12 noon, and from 1.45 pm-4.30 pm. During Ramadan, the fasting month, working hours are from 8 am-2 pm without a break. Government offices are closed on Fridays and Sundays. Private businesses are usually open from 8 am-5 pm Monday through Friday, and on Saturday morning. Shops open by 9 am and all the large department stores and supermarkets are opened seven days a week.

TRAVELING TO INDONESIA

Visas can be obtained from the Indonesian Embassy, Spg 528, Lot 4498, Kg Sungai Hanching Baru, Jln Muara, Tel: (02) 330180. Open 8.30 am-12.30 pm Monday-Thursday and Saturday. Allow 4 working days.

— *M.M.Ng*

Travel Advisory

This information is valid for the Malaysian states of Sabah and Sarawak only. As Brunei is a separate country with its own regulations, relevant information is given in Brunei Practicalities (p.187).

Sabah and Sarawak, despite being full of challenge and excitment, are remarkably easy for the traveler. English is widely understood, the people are particularly friendly, there are timetables (much of the time) and transport leaves on schedule (most of the time). You won't be asked to make "unofficial" payments to expedite permits, nor are you likely to encounter beggars. Even the jungles are benign and were described by one scientist who has worked in all continents as "the most user-friendly forests in the world."

When to Visit

There is no clearly defined season for a visit, although the rainy season can limit your enjoyment somewhat, especially in Sarawak. Sabah's east coast is affected by the stronger winds and more frequent rain of the northeast monsoon, especially December through February. The west coast is generally dry at this time, with the rains of the southwest monsoon starting in May and peaking July to September.

Sarawak's rainfall is greater than that of Sabah, especially in the southwest of the state. Although it can rain any time of year, the heaviest rainfall is during the months of December to February.

Immigration and Visas

Sabah and Sarawak each maintain control over immigration into their states, so even if you have entered Peninsular Malaysia, you must go through immigration again on arrival in Sabah and Sarawak. The same applies when you are traveling between Sabah and Sarawak. To enter both of these states, your passport must be valid for at least 6 months.

Commonwealth citizens (except India and Sri Lanka), British protected persons or citizens of the Republic of Ireland, Switzerland, Netherlands, San Marino and Lichtenstein do not need a visa to enter Malaysia.

Citizens of Austria, Belgium, Denmark, Finland, France, Germany, Iceland, Japan,

South Korea, Luxembourg, Norway, Sweden, Tunisia, Italy and USA do not require a visa for a visit not exceeding three months.

Citizens of ASEAN countries do not need a visa for a visit not exceeding one month.

Citizens of Aghanistan, Iran, Iraq, Libya, Syria and South Yemen do not need a visa for a visit not exceeding two weeks, while a one-week visa-free stay is granted to citizens of Albania, Bulgaria, Czechoslovakia, Hungary, Poland, Romania, Russia and Yugoslavia.

Citizens of North Korea, Cuba, Vietnam, People's Republic of China are allowed to enter Malaysia subject to visa approval, while citizens of Israel and South Africa are not allowed to enter Malaysia.

Airport Tax

A tax of M$5 is levied for all flights within Sabah and Sarawak, and to Peninsular Malaysia. To all other destinations, including Brunei, the tax is M$20.

Customs

There is no-duty free allowance for visitors arriving from Peninsular Malaysia and Singapore, or traveling between Sabah and Sarawak. Visitors arriving from other destinations may bring in 250g of tobacco or cigars or 200 cigarettes, plus a one-quart bottle of liquor.

Pornography, weapons and walkie-talkies are prohibited, while possession of narcotics and other illegal drugs carries the death penalty. Firearms are subject to licensing.

Drugs

The usage of any type of narcotic drug whatsoever is illegal and punishable by death. Malaysia is extremely strict at enforcing the penalties for drug abuse, and foreigners are not exempt. Be warned.

Getting There

Both Kota Kinabalu in Sabah and Kuching in Sarawak are linked by air with Peninsular Malaysia, Brunei and Singapore, as well as having flights to other countries in the region. There are no regular passenger ships into either Sabah or Sarawak, although local **ferry** services link Brunei via Labuan with Kota Kinabalu. Brunei is also linked by fast **boats** with Limbang and Lawas, both in Sarawak. Tawau, on the east coast of Sabah, is linked by both ferry and air with Tarakan in Indonesian Borneo (Kalimantan).

The national airline, MAS, operates daily flights from Kota Kinabalu and Kuching to Peninsular Malaysia (Kuala Lumpur and Johor

Baru) and also to Singapore and Brunei. These flights are heavily booked at holiday times so try to book well in advance.

International flights to **Kota Kinabalu**, Sabah, are operated by MAS, Singapore Airlines, Cathay Pacific, Philippine Airlines, Thai Airways International and Royal Brunei Airlines, linking it with Singapore, Bangkok, Hong Kong, Seoul, Kaoshung, Taipei, Tokyo, Manila and Brunei. There are also several weekly flights from Tawau on Sabah's east coast to Tarakan, Kalimantan.

Kuching in Sarawak has daily MAS flights to Kuala Lumpur and to Singapore, as well as 2 flights a week on Singapore Airlines to Singapore, and 3 per week to Brunei. Kuching is connected with Pontianak (Kalimantan), with flights run by MAS. It is also possible to travel by bus between Kuching and Pontianak.

Traveling About

Frequent **flights** link major towns within both Sabah and Sarawak, cuting down traveling time dramatically in areas where the terrain is particularly challenging or roads non-existent.

Taxis, although expensive by Malaysian standards, are available within the towns of Sabah and Sarawak. Most taxis are equipped with meters, although often the driver prefers to negotiate the fare in advance. For details of fares and telephone numbers, see Practicalities.

Taxis plying between various towns up to about 4 hours away can be found in both Sabah and Sarawak. Called **outstation taxis**, they can be either shared or chartered.

A network of **minibuses** operates between the villages and towns of Sabah, leaving from a bus terminus whenever enough passengers have boarded. These are generally fast, clean, inexpensive and relatively comfortable. They will drop you off wherever requested along the route, and even make a small diversion to take you to your destination. These are usually also available for private charter.

Because of the more challenging nature of the roads in Sarawak, buses or **express boats** rather than minibuses are used for long-distance transportation. Be warned that most express boats and ferries in Sarawak and plying between Brunei, Labuan and Kota Kinabalu play wrestling videos with the volume full blast; bring earplugs for self-protection.

Hire cars are available on the production of a valid driving licence from your country of origin. Driving is on the left-hand side of the road. One quaint but somewhat puzzling method of giving an address exists in Sabah and Sarawak,

where locals are apt to tell you a particular place is located at a certain milestone, e.g at 26 miles (*batu*) from Miri. Malaysia has used the metric system for around 15 years, and signposts are all in kilometers, yet old habits die hard. You can work out the conversion (1 mile = 1.6 km). Since road conditions vary enormously (in some places, from bad to worse), always ask the time it takes to reach a destination rather than the distance.

Accommodation

International standard hotels are available in both Kota Kinabalu and Kuching, as well as in some of the other major towns. Smaller hotels usually offer rooms with air-conditioning, TV, telephone and private bathroom.

Outside of these areas, accommodation is usually rather basic but not as inexpensive as one might expect, particularly in Sabah. Family-run hotels or "home stays" are virtually non-existent, and the less expensive hotels are usually located on the upper floors of a typical Chinese shop in the center of town.

The national parks systems in both states offers good accommodation at reasonable rates within major parks, while resthouses run by the state governments also offer accommodation. Government officers have priority in the latter, so it's often hard to get in; the resthouses offer excellent value in Sabah, but are usually much more expensive in Sarawak.

In remote areas, you will always find the locals happy to give you somewhere to sleep for the night, even if it is only a mat on the floor.

Currency

The Malaysian currency is the *ringgit* or dollar, which is divided into 100 *sen* (cents). There is no restriction on the amount of local currency you are permitted to bring into or take out of the country.

The rate of exchange fluctuates, but at the end of 1992, the rates were: US$1-M$2.54; GBP 1-M$4.52; A$1-M$1.86; S$1-M$1.54.

Official money changers offer the best rate of exchange, and a quicker service than banks. The least favorable rate is offered by hotels. Change money in either Kuching or Kota Kinabalu before traveling further afield to ensure the best rate of exchange and to avoid embarassment in areas where there are no foreign exchange facilities.

Credit cards are accepted at major hotels in the bigger towns of Sabah and Sarawak, as well as a few restaurants. Elsewhere, cash is preferred.

Prices

Prices within this guide are quoted in Malaysian *ringgit* (dollars), except for Brunei where the Brunei dollar (worth about 40% more than the *ringgit*) is used. The Malaysian currency is generally quite stable in relationship to other major currencies. Prices were valid as of late 1992.

Tipping

Hotels classified by the government as "tourist class" impose a 10% service charge and 5% government tax; this 15% tax is also added to restaurant bills within the hotel.

Elsewhere, service charge is not imposed. Although a tip is sometimes left in more expensive restaurants, this is not obligatory. Elsewhere in Sabah and Sarawak, tips are not expected and may, if offered, even be refused. This is still a place where a simple smile and a "thank you" (*terima kasih*) when paying the bill is sufficient recompense for services rendered. Taxi drivers do not expect to be tipped.

Health

The standards of health and hygiene in Sabah and Sarawak are, as in Peninsular Malaysia, generally good. You can eat and drink virtually anywhere, and ice is safe.

Some people get diarrhea from an abrupt change in diet, such as eating very spicy food or a lot more fruit than usual; it can also come from contaminated food. A tried and tested local remedy for "traveler's tummy" that can be purchased in most pharmacies as well as Chinese stores even in remote regions is the Chinese herbal compound, Po Chai Pills. Take two glass phials of these tiny pills initially, then one each two or three hours until the problem clears up. Drink plenty of water with salt and sugar added to avoid dehydration until you've recovered. If you are traveling in remote areas, you may want to take malaria prophylactics to avoid catching this disease, which may still be found in several isolated areas.

A good mosquito repellent is strongly recommended. You can buy either a stick or gel (preferable to aerosols) in supermarkets or pharmacies in Kota Kinabalu and Kuching. Mosquito coils, a spiral of incense that keeps mosquitoes at bay, will ensure a good night's sleep in areas where these pesky insects are a problem. Forget mosquito nets — they're too hot.

Carry a good antiseptic or antibiotic cream in case of any scratches; wounds can quickly turn septic in humid conditions.

Another essential item for your medical kit is a good sun protection cream. Time and again, visitors reveling in the tropical sun finish up getting painfully burned, especially when on or near the water. Don't toast yourself for hours around a pool, on the beach or on the top of a Sarawak express boat. You'll regret it later. A sunhat (buy one locally) is remarkably effective at keeping you cool and helping prevent sunburn.

Private medical clinics, as well as government hospitals and polyclinics offer a surprisingly good standard of medical care, even in many remote locations.

Climate

Sabah and Sarawak enjoy a tropical climate with mean temperatures ranging between 22°C and 32°C in lowland areas, with high relative humidity. During the rainy season, the maximum temperature is generally lower. In hilly regions, especially around the Bario Highlands in Sarawak and the Murut region of southwest Sabah, it can be quite chilly at night. Mount Kinabalu, like mountains anywhere, can be just plain cold, with the temperature near the summit dropping to zero or below on occasion.

Sabah has more defined seasons than Sarawak. The northeast monsoon blows from December through March, with the east coast experiencing frequent showers and strong winds, while the west coast is generally sunny and dry. The tables turn from May, when the west coast experiences rainfall, especially from July to September. Showers are often heavy, but generally shortlived.

Sarawak, particularly around Kuching, has a less defined dry season and rain can fall throughout the year. You can be sure, however, that you'll need your umbrella from December through February. Heavy rain causes river levels to rise dramatically, especially in the Rajang and Baram, slowing most upriver travel considerably (except for the superpowered express boats) and making certain rapids hair-raising, to say the least.

Clothing

Pack clothing in natural fabrics only; the combination of synthetics and high humidity is too uncomfortable to be contemplated, especially when it comes to underwear.

Loose, comfortable cotton clothing such as bermuda shorts and shirts or t-shirts is ideal; long cotton trousers are good for the evenings and traveling in remote areas where local sensibilities may be disturbed by shorts, especially when worn by women. Leave your denim jeans at home; they'll be too hot.

Although dress standards are considerably less conservative than in Peninsular Malaysia, women will avoid unwelcome attention by not wearing excessively tight clothing, plunging necklines or mini-skirts.

If you plan on climbing Mount Kinabalu, be sure to pack an anorak and track suit. A sweatshirt is a good idea for early morning travel anywhere in the region; air-conditioned buses and express boats can be surprisingly cool before the sun gets into full swing.

Festivals

Both Sabah and Sarawak celebrate almost all the major festivals of Peninsular Malaysia. Indigenous festivals are an excellent opportunity for the visitor to see traditional costumes, dances, sports and other activities, and to enjoy the food and beverages of the various peoples of Borneo.

Throughout the month of May, Sabah's Kadazan/Dusun community celebrates the Harvest Festival (Pesta Kaamatan), with small local celebrations taking place at villages and towns along the West coast and in the Interior, near Tambunan and Keningau. Ritual thanks to the rice spirit are conducted by priestesses, then the fun begins. The State-level Harvest Festival is held in Kota Kinabalu on 30th and 31st of May annually, at the grounds of the Kadazan Dusun Cultural Association in Penampang. The festivities culminate in the choice of the Harvest Festival Queen.

In conjunction with the Harvest Festival celebrations, the Sabah Fest, held for one week from around 15th May, includes displays of traditional handicrafts in shopping centres and hotels, performances of dance and music at the Sabah Museum and selected venues, a cultural pageant and several sporting events.

The last Sunday in July is the occasion for the Pesta Rumbia or Sago Festival in Sabah's Kuala Penyuh area, about two hours south of Kota Kinabalu. Traditional sports, demonstrations of sago making and ample opportunities to try the culinary possibilities of the versatile sago palm.

A traditional rafting festival is held during October near Kampung Kiulu, about an hour from Kota Kinabalu, with visitors invited to take part on a variety of original craft down the rapids.

Sarawak's Dyak communities celebrate their harvest festival with the Gawai Dyak, held at state level in Kuching on 1st June. An offering ceremony (miring) is made to the rice spirit, followed by various dances, including the Iban war dance (ngajat). Blowpipe demonstrations and cock-fighting can also be witnessed at this time.

As in Sabah, other celebrations take place in smaller centers around Sarawak; check with local tourism authorities for information on locations and dates, which change annually, and for news on any other festivals which may be taking place during your visit.

Etiquette

The peoples of Malaysian Borneo are remarkable warm and friendly, quietly curious but never intrusive. With so many different ethnic groups and religions, the people of Sabah and Sarawak have developed an easy tolerance for the ways of others. Provided you behave with normal consideration and courtesy, you are unlikely to offend, and even if you do unwittingly commit a breach of local etiquette, you will probably not even be made aware of this.

Sharing is very much a part of local life, and you may find you're spontaneously invited to join in if you happen to arrive during mealtime. You may even find someone at the same coffee shop table offering to share food with you. Use your own judgement to decide whether this is just a courtesy or a sincere invitation.

A few pointers worth remembering. Remove your shoes before entering any home. As Muslims (who make up between 20-30% of the population in both states) consider it impolite to give or receive anything with the left hand, try to avoid using this at all times. Still with the hands, it's considered rude to point at anyone or anything with your forefinger; try using your whole hand instead.

Photography

Color print film is widely available in Sabah and Sarawak, although you may find it cheaper to purchase this in the capital before going further afield. Color transparency film (slides) is harder to locate outside of Kota Kinabalu and Kuching, especially faster rated film.

Processing of color prints is available in all towns in the region, although transparencies (except for Kodachrome, which has to be sent overseas) can be processed only in Kuching, Miri, Kota Kinabalu and Sandakan. Local processing of both print and transparency is generally of a good standard, and relatively inexpensive compared with most Western countries.

Heat and humidity are a constant challenge to the photographer. Try to store your camera equipment and films in a zip-lock plastic bag with silica gel to absorb moisture (uncooked rice is a suitable standby), and never leave it in direct sunlight.

The best time of day for color photography is before 10 am or after 4 pm, when the side lighting and color density generally make for a more interesting picture. The harsh flat light of mid-day should be avoided if possible.

Most people in Sabah and Sarawak are happy to have their photographs taken, although women —like women the world over — like to look their best and might be upset if you want to photograph them looking hot and disheveled up to their knees in mud in a padi field. It's polite to ask before you start snapping a way; a gesture with your camera and a smile should be enough.

Tour Operators

Sabah and Sarawak have developed independently with virtually no contact between the states until after the founding of Malaysia. Partly for this reason, and also because there is no road transport between Sabah and Sarawak (except for a road that stops in Lawas), most tour companies operate only in the state where they are based. Although major operators have links with a tour company in the neighboring state, if you're planning to visit both Sabah and Sarawak, you'll be better off if you deal with the experts in each of the two states. (See Practicalities for details.)

Time

Sabah and Sarawak are, like the rest of Malaysia, 8 hours ahead of GMT (Universal Time).

Business Hours

Most offices and shops open for business around 8.30-9 am, although small businesses and markets start operating considerably earlier. Offices close around 5 pm, while supermarkets and departments stores generally remain open until around 9 pm.

Banks operate from 10 am-3 pm Monday through Friday, and from 9.30-11.30 am on Saturday.

Government offices open at 8am from Monday through Saturday. They close for lunch from 12.45 am-2pm Monday to Thursday, and from 11.30 am until 2 pm on Friday. Closing time is 4.30 pm Monday through Friday, and 12.45 pm on Saturday.

Post offices are open from 8 am-5 pm.

Telecommunications

Public phone boxes, many of them using a phonecard, are found in most towns in Sabah and Sarawak. International calls may be made from hotels and from Telekoms offices in major towns. Outside the main post offices you can generally find at least one phone box where you can used a phone card for overseas calls (International Direct Dialing).

Language

The national language of Malaysia, Bahasa Malaysia, is in official use in Sabah and Sarawak. Based on Malay, the language is very similar to Bahasa Indonesia. The many different ethnic groups in Malaysian Borneo speak literally dozens of languages and sub-dialects, but generally communicate between each other in Bahasa Malaysia. English is widely spoken in the towns, especially in Sarawak, but once you're out in more remote areas, a few words

good morning/ good day	selamat pagi/ selamat siang
good afternoon/ evening	selamat petang
good night	selamat malam
thank you	terima kasih
goodbye (to someone leaving)	selamat jalan
goodbye (to someone staying)	selamat tinggal
yes	ia
no	tidak
good/not good	baik/tidak baik
how much?	berapa?
expensive/cheap	mahal/murah
good, I'll take it	baik, saya mengambil
this/that	ini/itu
where?	di-mana?
what?	apa?
left/right	kiri/kanan
stop here	berhenti sini
go fast	cepat/lekas
go slowly	pelan-pelan
food	makanan
drink	minuman
room	bilek
bathroom	bilek mandi
toilet	tandas
what time	jam berapa?
one o'clock	pukul (or jam) satu
two	dua
three	tiga
four	empat
five	lima
six	enam
seven	tujuh
eight	lapan
nine	sembilan
ten	sapuloh
my name is John	nama saya John
I am from Australia	saya dari Australia

Further Reading

The following is a cross section of relevant literature. As only a few bookshops in Sabah and Sarawak carry good books, try to buy in advance; airport bookshops at Changi (Singapore) are a good source.

Arts and Crafts

Chin, Lucas and Mashman, V. (ed). *Sarawak Cultural Legacy: A Living Tradition*. Kuching, 1991. A series of features on many different aspects of Sarawak's rich traditions and material cultures, covering everything from beads to Iban blankets, traditional architecture to Melanau shamans.

Munan, Heidi. *Sarawak Crafts: Methods, Materials and Motifs*. Singapore 1989. An excellent introduction to the subject, available in an affordable series, Images of Asia, published by Oxford University Press.

Sellato, Bernard. *Hornbill and Dragon*. Jakarta, 1989. Lavish illustrations and an authoratative text on Borneo arts by a French anthropologist who has spent 20 years in the region. A must for any coffee table.

Peoples and Customs

Evans, Ivor. *Among Primitive Peoples in Borneo*, Singapore 1990. This reprint of a work originally published in 1922 is perhaps the most interesting of the books written by Evans, arguably the best writer on British North Borneo in the first part of this century.

Freeman, J.D. *Report on the Iban*. London, 1970. One of the earliest anthropological studies much quoted by other scholars. He did his studies among the Baleh Iban in the 1950s, where the Iban were still traditional.

Kedit, P.M. *Modernisation Among the Iban of Sarawak*. Kuala Lumpur, 1980. A study of contemporary Iban by the head of the Sarawak museum's ethnology department.

Hose, Charles & McDougall, William. *The Pagan Tribes of Borneo*. London, 1966. Hose served the Brooke Raj for 23 years, most of them spent in the Baram River area of Sarawak. This work, first published in 1912, is a classic of Borneo ethnography and is the result of his years of detailed observation.

Hose, Charles. *Natural Man: A Record From Borneo*. Singapore, 1988. Written for a more popular audience than *The Pagan Tribes of Borneo*, this is basically a precis of that more weighty work and is a sympathetic view of the cultures and customs of Sarawak's tribes.

King, Victor T.(ed) *Essays on Borneo Societies*. Oxford, 1978. A collection of very readable anthropological essays on the social organization of several ethnic groups, including the Bajau Laut, Kayan, Kenyah, Melanau, Lun Dayeh and Rungus.

Morrison, Hedda, Wright, Leigh & Wong, K.F. *Vanishing World: The Ibans of Borneo*. New York 1972. One of the most beautiful books of its kind, this includes superb black-and-white photographs by the renowned Hedda Morrison, who lived in Sarawak from 1947-1967, sensitive colour photographs by a Chinese Sarawakian, and an equally satisfying text by an American historian.

Munan, Heidi. *Culture Shock! Borneo*. Singapore 1988. An accurate and often humorous guide to the cultures and customs of "the natives", with advice on how (and how not!) to behave.

Sutlive, Vinson H. *The Iban of Sarawak: Chronicle of a Vanishing World*. Illinois, 1978. A comprehensive and readable reference on Iban society, analysing both traditional and modern lifestyles.

History and Economy

Ave, Jan. & King, Victor. *Borneo: The People of the Weeping Forest*. Leiden, 1986. One of the best introductions available, with a wealth of information on the history, geography, politics, cultures, economic development and other aspects affecting the peoples of Brunei, Kalimantan, Sabah and Sarawak.

Chew, Daniel. *Chinese Pioneers on the Sarawak Frontier*. Singapore, 1990. Interesting glimpses into the lives of early Chinese immigrants to Sarawak, based on many oral interviews as well as scholarly research.

Leong, Cecilia. *Sabah: The First 100 Years*. Kuala Lumpur, 1982. A thorough if not inspired record of one century of Sabah's history, from the creation of British North Borneo in 1881.

Nature and Ecology

Beccari, Odoardo. *Wanderings in the Great Forests of Borneo*, Singapore 1986. A reprint of a classic work by an Italian naturalist, who regarded the 2 1/2 years he spent in Sarawak in the mid-1860s as the happiest in his life.

Cubbitt, Gerald & Payne, Junaidi. *Wild Malaysia*. London, 1990. Magnificently photographed and very well written, this book includes extensive coverage of the natural history of both Sabah and Sarawak.

Francis, Charles M. *Pocket Guide to the Birds of Borneo*. Kuala Lumpur, 1984. A condensation of the classic *Birds of Borneo* by Bertram E. Smythies, this is the perfect book to take on any field trip.

Hanbury-Tenison, Robin. *Mulu, The Rain Forest*. London, 1980. An highly readable account of the scientific expedition to Gunung Mulu carried out by the Royal Geographic Society and the Sarawak government in 1977.

Hose, Charles. *The Field Book of a Jungle-Wallah*. Singapore, 1985. This slender volume's sub-title, *Shore, River and Forest Life in Sarawak*, gives an accurate idea of its contents. Hose's eye for detail, his endless curiosity about natural history as well as people, and his sense of humor make this a fascinating book, even for the non-specialist.

Payne, Junaidi & Andau, Mahedi. *Orangutan: Malaysia's Mascot*. Kuala Lumpur, 1989. Inexpensive, with lots of photographs and a wide ranging and highy readable text, this makes an excellent souvenir of a visit to Sepilok or Semangoh orang-utan sanctuaries.

Payne, Junaidi, Francis, Charles & Phillipps, Karen. *A Field Guide to the Mammals of Borneo*. Sabah, 1985. Excellent illustrations and detailed descriptions to help identify that flash of fur in the forest. No less than 13 pages of bats!

Wallace, Alfred R. *The Malay Archipelago*, Singapore, 1983. Like Spenser St John's book, this is one of the classic works, the result of Wallace's 8 years traveling from the Malay Peninsula to Borneo and across the Indonesian archipelago. Wallace, a naturalist, observed and recorded the flora and fauna as well as the local customs. His sharp eye, easy style and ability to view the locals with a minimum of prejudice still make him one of the greatest travel writers ever to have visited Borneo.

Travel and Bibliography

Barclay, James. *A Stroll Through Borneo*. London, 1980. Barclay, an ardent conservationist, spent 5 months trekking in Sarawak and Kalimantan in the late 1980s having anything but a stroll; the resulting book makes for interesting reading.

Beekman, Daniel. *A Voyage to and from the Island of Borneo*. New York, 1973. A reprint of an 18th-century account by an English captain who visited Banjermasin in what was then Dutch Borneo.

Brooke, Margaret. *My Life in Sarawak*. Singapore, 1987. Margaret de Windt became the second Rajah's wife, mother of the last Rajah and his two brothers. *My Life* is her most successful book about the genteel life in Victorian Sarawak, first published in 1913 and now available in a paperback reprint.

Chalfont, Lord. *By God's Will — A Portrait of the Sultan of Brunei*. London. 1989. Respected diplomat and journalist, Lord Chalfont goes beyond the gossip and cliches to present a balanced look at Brunei and it's current sultan.

Hansen, Eric. *Stranger in the Forest*. London, 1988. Highly personal account by an American who trekked across Sarawak and almost to the coast of Kalimantan and back, mostly with Penan guides, in the early 1980s.

Keith, Agnes. *Land Below the Wind*. Difficult to find as no longer in print, this is a highly entertaining description of life among the colonial British and the natives in Sandakan, then capital of British North Borneo (Sabah) in the late 1930s. Keith, an American, regarded the British with a wryly affectionate and sometimes acerbic eye.

Harrisson, Tom. *World Within, A Borneo Story*. Singapore 1984. Typical of Harrisson's egocentric and highly original style, this is a fascinating account of the remote Kelabit living in the Bario Highlands during WWII, when Harrisson and other Allied forces parachuted behind Japanese lines.

King, Victor T. (ed) *The Best of Borneo Travel*. Singapore 1992. Spanning four centuries of travel writing, with everyone from Pigafetta to Eric Hansen, this anthology has an informative and entertaining introduction by a widely respected authority on Borneo.

MacDonald, Malcolm. *Borneo People*. Singapore 1985. A delightfully warm and interesting account of this distinguished diplomat's travels in Sarawak, especially among the Iban of the Baram and Rajang rivers, in the 1950s.

O'Hanlon, Redmond. *Into the Heart of Borneo*, New York, 1984. The funniest book ever written on Borneo, about a quasi expedition he made up the Rajang and Baleh with the poet and journalist, James Fenton. Information on everything from penis pins to where not to relieve oneself in a river (a whirlpool).

St John, Spenser. *Life in the Forests of the Far East*. Singapore, 1986. One of the best books ever written on Sabah, Sarawak and Brunei, by an idefatigable traveler and fair-minded administrator who lived in the region for 13 years in the middle of the 19th century. His descriptions of the peoples he encountered, and of his countless trips ranging from the headhunters' route along the Limbang River to the ascent of Mount Kinabalu with Hugh Low still make fascinating reading.

Index

Bold indicates an article on the subject. Italics denote photographs or illustrations.

Maps

When It Comes To Service At
The Sheraton Utama Hotel

WE LEAVE EVERYONE ELSE BEHIND!

Not only does the Sheraton Utama have a history of over 10 years experience in providing service excellence to their many guests but they still have a brand new hotel.

All of the hotels 154 guest rooms and suites have recently been completely refurbished and in the process they have taken into account the needs of the most discerning travellers.

Rooms for non-smokers, special rooms for our Sheraton Club International members and a fitness centre with modern equipment are all part of the new look.

SHERATON UTAMA HOTEL - BRAND NEW
BUT OVER A DECADE OF EXPERIENCE!

Sheraton Utama
H O T E L

P. O. BOX 2203,
BANDAR SERI BEGAWAN 1922,
NEGARA BRUNEI DARUSSALAM,
TELEPHONE: (02) 244272,
TELEFAX: 271579 SHER BRUNEI, TELEX: (809) BU 2306.

ITT Sheraton.

GRA • BALI • BANDUNG • BANGKOK • BANGALORE • BEIJING • BOMBAY • BRUNEI • DHAKA • GUILIN • HONG KONG •
AMPUNG • MADRAS • MANILA • NEW DELHI • SEOUL • SHANGHAI • SINGAPORE • TAIPEI • TOKYO BAY • TIANJIN • XIAN
OR RESERVATIONS IN: SINGAPORE 65-7326000 • MALAYSIA 800-1-001 (Toll free) • HONG KONG 852-7393535 • INDONESIA
62-21-586918 • THAILAND 66-2-2363535

We take you places others don't.

At Sabah Air, we believe in venturing into areas where others don't go. Take for instance the Maliau 7-stepped waterfalls, deep in the Tawau jungle, to the heights of Mt. Kinabalu, the highest mountain in South East Asia.

We fly to any part of the country, from major and rural towns to the Island of Sipadan, a haven for amateur and professional divers.

With our fleet of helicopters and fixed wing aircraft, Sabah Air is without doubt your most flexible air tour operator.

See Sabah by Air, Fly Sabah Air

PENERBANGAN SABAH SDN BHD
(Sabah Air Pte. Ltd.)

KOTA KINABALU
Sabah Air Bldg, Old Airport Road. Locked bag 113, 88999 Kota Kinabalu, Sabah, Malaysia.
Tel: 088-56733, Reservation/Ops: 51326 Telex: MA 80073 SABTER Fax: 088-235195

SANDAKAN
Sabah Air hangar, Sandakan Airport. Locked bag 56, 90009 Sandakan, Sabah, Malaysia.
Tel: 089-660527, 660545, 667505

TAWAU
Tawau Airport, Locked bag 15, 91009 Tawau, Sabah, Malaysia. Tel: 089-774005